My Last Chance to Be a Boy

My Last Chance to Be a Boy

Theodore Roosevelt's
South American Expedition
of 1913–1914

Joseph R. Ornig

With a Foreword by Tweed Roosevelt

Louisiana State University Press
Baton Rouge

Louisiana Paperback Edition, 1998
07 06 05 04 03 02 01 00 99 98   5 4 3 2 1

Library of Congress Cataloging-in-Publication Data
Ornig, Joseph R.
    My last chance to be a boy : Theodore Roosevelt's South American
  expedition of 1913–1914 / Joseph R. Ornig ; with a foreword by Tweed
  Roosevelt.
        p.   cm.
    Includes bibliographical references (p.   –   ) and index.
    ISBN 0-8071-2271-8 (paper)
    1. Roosevelt-Rondon Scientific Expedition (1913–1914)   2. Brazil—
  Description and travel.   3. Zoology—Brazil.   4. Roosevelt River (Brazil)
  5. Roosevelt, Theodore, 1858–1919—Journeys—Brazil.   I. Title.
  F2515.O76   1998
  918.104'5—dc21   97-51138
                                                                        CIP

For My Mother

"I am an old man now, and
I did have a murderous
trip down South, but it was
mighty interesting."

T. R. to Jack Willis,
September 1914

It was madness to go to
South America and it cost him
his life, but what he accomplished
there is a tale of painful and
inspiring heroism which is not
nearly so well known as it deserves
to be.

Edward Wagenknecht
The Seven Worlds of Theodore Roosevelt

Contents

Acknowledgments

The author would like to thank the following publishers and sources for permission to quote excerpts from their works:

American Museum of Natural History, Department of Ornithology, for the River of Doubt Diary of George K. Cherrie and the letters of George K. Cherrie, Leo E. Miller, Henry Fairfield Osborn, and Frank M. Chapman. Reprinted by permission.

Ave Maria Press, "Mind in Action (The Life of John Augustine Zahm)," by Father Patrick J. Carroll, published serially in *The Ave Maria* from January 5 through July 20, 1946. Reprinted by permission.

Devin-Adair Publishers, Inc., Old Greenwich, CT, *Theodore Roosevelt's America: Selections from the Writings of the Oyster Bay Naturalist*, edited by Farida A. Wiley, New York, 1955. Permission to reprint granted by publisher.

Farrar, Straus & Giroux, Inc., and *The Emporia Gazette* (Estate of William Allen White) for permission to quote from "Theodore Roosevelt," by William Allen White, in *Theodore Roosevelt: A Profile*, edited by Morton Keller, Hill & Wang, New York, 1967.

Harcourt Brace & Company, *Theodore Roosevelt: A Biography*, copyright 1931 by Henry F. Pringle and renewed 1959 by K. D. Massel and R. M. Pringle, reprinted by permission of the publisher.

HarperCollins Publishers, *Theodore Roosevelt the Naturalist*, Paul Russell Cutright (Harper & Brothers, New York, 1956). Reprinted by permission.

Harvard University, The Houghton Library, the Theodore Roosevelt Collection, for permission to quote from the letters of Theodore Roosevelt and Edith K. Roosevelt; from Theodore Roosevelt's 1913 Excelsior Diary; and from Major James Ancil Shipton's 1913 Diary.

Harvard University Press, *The Letters of Theodore Roosevelt*, edited by Elting E. Morison, Cambridge, MA: Harvard University Press, copyright 1951, 1952, 1954 by the President and Fellows of Harvard College, copyright 1979, 1980, 1982 by Elting E. Morison. Reprinted by permission of the publishers.

Houghton Mifflin Company, New York, *Released for Publication*, by Oscar King Davis, Boston and New York, 1925; and *Theodore Roosevelt: An Intimate Biography*, by William Roscoe Thayer, Boston and New York, 1919. Reprinted by permission of the publishers.

International Creative Management, *T. R. & Will: A Friendship That Split the Republican Party*, by William Manners (Harcourt Brace & World, New York, 1969). Reprinted by permission.

Macmillan Publishing Company, New York, *A Book-Lover's Holiday in the Open*, by Theodore Roosevelt (Charles Scribner's Sons, New York, 1916); *Departing Glory: Theodore Roosevelt as ex-President*, by Joseph L. Gardner (Charles Scribner's Sons, New York, 1973); *Impressions of Great Naturalists*, by Henry Fairfield Osborn (Charles Scribner's Sons, New York, 1924); *My Brother, Theodore Roosevelt*, by Corinne Roosevelt Robinson (Charles Scribner's Sons, New York, 1921); *Selections from the Correspondence of Theodore Roosevelt and Henry Cabot Lodge, 1884–1918*, vol. II, edited by Henry Cabot Lodge (Charles Scribner's Sons, New York, 1925); *The Happy Hunting Grounds*, by Kermit Roosevelt (Charles Scribner's Sons, New York, 1920); *The Roosevelt Family of Sagamore Hill*, by Hermann Hagedorn (Macmillan Publishing Company, New York, 1954); *The Works of Theodore Roosevelt*, National Edition, vol. I, *Ranch Life and the Hunting Trail*, by Theodore Roosevelt (Charles Scribner's Sons, New York, 1925); *Through the Brazilian Wilderness*, by Theodore Roosevelt (Charles Scribner's Sons, New York, 1914); reprinted by permission of the publisher.

Sylvia Jukes Morris, for permission to quote from *Edith Kermit Roosevelt: Portrait of a First Lady* (Coward, McCann & Geoghegan, New York, 1980).

Penguin USA, Inc., *Autobiography of a Bird Lover*, by Frank M. Chapman (D. Appleton Century Co., New York, 1935), and *Through South America's Southland*, by John Augustine Zahm (D. Appleton & Co., New York, 1916), reprinted by permission of the publisher.

Princeton University, Manuscripts Division, Department of Rare Books and Special Collections, for the letters of Theodore Roosevelt (1914, Scribner's Archives). Printed with permission of the University.

Province Archives Center, Indiana Province, Congregation of Holy

Cross, Notre Dame, Indiana, for the letters of Father John Augustine Zahm, C.S.C. Reprinted by permission.

Putnam Publishing Group, *Dark Trails: Adventures of a Naturalist,* by George K. Cherrie (G. P. Putnam's Sons, New York, 1930). Reprinted by permission of the publisher.

Random House, Inc., *A Sentimental Safari,* by Kermit Roosevelt, Jr. (Alfred A. Knopf, New York, 1963). Reprinted with permission of the publisher.

Royal Geographical Society, "A Journey Through Central Brazil," by Theodore Roosevelt, *The Geographical Journal,* February 1915. Reprinted with permission of the Royal Society.

Russell & Volkening, Inc., literary agents, New York, *The Seven Worlds of Theodore Roosevelt,* by Edward Wagenknecht (Longmans, Green Company, New York, 1958). Reprinted by permission.

The Archives of the University of Notre Dame, for permission to reprint the letters of Father John Augustine Zahm, C.S.C. (Albert Francis Zahm Papers, UNDA).

The Explorers Club, New York, for permission to quote from *Theodore Roosevelt: Memorial Meeting at The Explorers Club, March 1, 1919.*

The Natural History Press, "Theodore Roosevelt, Naturalist," by Henry Fairfield Osborn (*Natural History,* September 1919); and *Bankers, Bones, and Beetles,* by Geoffrey Hellman, Garden City, New York, 1968. Reprinted with permission of the publisher.

The New York Times Company, for permission to reprint excerpts of *Times* articles copyrighted 1913, 1914, 1919, and 1929. Reprinted by permission.

Theodore Roosevelt Association, Oyster Bay, Long Island, New York, for permission to quote from Frank M. Chapman's Introduction to *Through the Brazilian Wilderness,* copyright 1928 by the Roosevelt Memorial Association; and from Frank M. Chapman's March 1928 speech before the R.M.A.

University of Notre Dame Press, *Notre Dame's John Zahm: American Catholic Apologist and Educator,* by Ralph E. Weber, copyright 1961. Used by permission of the University of Notre Dame Press, Notre Dame, Indiana.

Foreword

Theodore Roosevelt, my great grandfather, did not view the presidency as an end in itself, but rather as a tool to be used to accomplish an end. Although he is mostly remembered for his political achievements, it was his private life and interests which shaped his convictions as to what was best for the nation. These convictions drove him throughout his political career. Today, most historians believe his greatest contribution as president was his work for conservation. During his tenure in the White House from 1901 to 1909, he designated 150 National Forests, the first 51 Federal Bird Reservations, 5 National Parks, the first 18 National Monuments, the first 4 National Game Preserves, and the first 21 Reclamation Projects. Altogether, in the seven and one-half years he was in office, he provided federal protection for almost 230 million acres, a land area equivalent to that of all the eastern states from Maine to Florida. He succeeded in the face of public apathy and strong congressional opposition because he believed what he was doing was right and he was willing to take great political risks to make it happen.

His conviction came from a lifetime love affair with the outdoors and natural history. His first interest was birds. As a boy, he spent days, and later weeks, in the woods studying their habits. His notes are accurate, professional, and detailed, extraordinary for one so young. He collected specimens initially on Long Island, New York, where his parents rented a summer home. Later, while still in his teens, he collected throughout the Northeast and in Europe, Africa, and Asia during family trips. He mounted more than 200 of his specimens, some of which found their way to the American Museum of Natural History in New York City. Recently one of the museum's ornithologists showed me an example of his efforts, an Atlantic puffin. The curator explained that puffins are hard to prepare because, if the least bit of subcutaneous fat is overlooked, the specimen will eventually disintegrate. Roosevelt's puffin, over a century after it was collected, was still in perfect condition.

As Theodore Roosevelt grew older, his outdoor sorties became more ambitious. While at Harvard College, he made frequent hunting trips to the northern wilderness of Maine, and he camped with his friend Henry Minot in the Adirondacks. After graduation, he spent several weeks hunting in the Midwest with his brother Elliott, but so far he had done nothing really out of the ordinary for a bold boy of his generation and background. It was not until 1883, when Roosevelt was twenty-four, that his adventures reached a new level. In the fall of that year he went to the Dakota Territory to hunt for buffalo. For the next four decades, even during his presidential years, Roosevelt spent on average one month a year sleeping under the stars. Often alone, frequently with no more than a gun, a horse, and a little hardtack, he would ride off for days at a time. Six of these trips originated at his ranch in the Dakota badlands. The first was a seven-week, 1000-mile ride to the Big Horn Mountains in Wyoming. Later it was to the Coeur d'Alenes in Montana, to the Selkirks in British Columbia, and to the Bitter Root Mountains, to Yellowstone, and to Two-Ocean Pass—all in Wyoming. Many other expeditions followed, for example to the Nueces River in Texas, to the canebrakes of Louisiana, to the Rockies in Colorado, and to Yosemite in California. None were outings, all were arduous, but none compared to his last two great adventures—one to Africa and the other to South America. The first was a triumph and the second almost a disaster.

The African safari, undertaken when Roosevelt left the White House in 1909 at the age of fifty, was both a hunting trip and a collecting expedition for the Smithsonian Institution. It was a success in both objectives. Roosevelt and his son Kermit managed to shoot a representative sample of all the large African game animals and the Smithsonian received over 11,000 specimens, ranging from bull elephants to tiny insects, giving it the best collection of African specimens of any museum in the world.

Roosevelt's second great expedition, his voyage of discovery down the River of Doubt, a remote tributary of Brazil's Amazon, was an entirely different story. Although it was the most arduous and dangerous he ever undertook, it was not well planned, and happened almost by accident. It lasted three months, cost six lives—three died supplying the trip and three on the trip—and almost killed Roosevelt. The survivors counted themselves lucky to reach civilization alive. Roosevelt wrote at length about the journey (no one should miss his book *Through the Brazilian Wilderness*), as did five other members of the expedition, including Colonel Candido Mariano da Silva Rondon, the legendary Brazilian explorer.

The primary sources are fascinating, but they tell only part of the story. Substantial details were discreetly left out because so much of what was interesting concerned the personalities—and those involved were by no means always on their best behavior. However, years have passed, and now the whole story can be told, and what a story it is! It involves world-famous figures struggling through the jungle encountering snakes, threatening natives, murder, petty disagreements, major lapses of judgment, heroic rescues, starvation, disease, swarms of biting insects, religious confrontations—all the ingredients of a first-rate adventure, and it's all here in Joseph Ornig's excellent book, *My Last Chance to Be a Boy*. He is a tenacious researcher whose years of dogged digging in newly discovered private sources, from both the United States and Brazil, have paid off.

There is another reason this book is important. For the first time, it records in detail Roosevelt's triumphant speaking tour through South America, which preceded his expedition down the River of Doubt. This tour, much ignored by historians, is significant for several reasons. In recent years it has been fashionable to portray Roosevelt as much hated in South America because of his supposedly belligerent foreign policy towards the region. Ornig demonstrates that, quite to the contrary, Roosevelt was as much admired in South America as elsewhere. Everywhere he went he was welcomed tumultuously. Huge crowds gathered to see him and to hear him speak. Roosevelt, never one to avoid the difficult, chose to talk about a most sensitive subject, the Monroe Doctrine and the Roosevelt Corollary, which many viewed as paternalistic. Apparently he charmed them. "I think," he wrote a friend, "I have been able under pressure to state the Monroe Doctrine in a way . . . so as to make it correspond exactly to the facts and to our national needs." Not an inconsequential task given the nature of the audiences.

For me this book is of special interest. In 1992, along with nineteen colleagues, I retraced my great-grandfather's South American trip down the River of Doubt, now renamed the Rio Roosevelt. Since 1914, only one other group of outsiders has successfully descended the river, an expedition commissioned by the Theodore Roosevelt Association and lead by G. M. Dyott. During our expedition, we found that both nothing had changed and everything had changed.

First the similarities. For most of our trip, what we saw must have been virtually identical to what Roosevelt saw—mile after mile of uncut virgin forest. Where Roosevelt reported being enveloped by sweat bees, we were plagued by the same scourge; where Roosevelt saw an Indian path emerging from the jungle, we saw the same; and, of course, the river was the same—wide and slow in places, fierce and dangerous in others. Our group, like the one that preceded us, was made up of Brazilians, Indians, and Americans. We had language difficulties and cultural misunderstandings, but we learned to respect each other for our skills and knowledge. At times our differences threatened to spin out of control, but, just as with the previous expedition, we overcame them. Reading Joseph Ornig's book has served to put perspective on much of what happened on our trip.

Although the similarities were startling, so were the differences. The members of Roosevelt's expedition did not see a single Indian while they were on the river, but they saw many signs that Indians lived along the way. They came across paths, footbridges, and recently deserted huts. They even heard the Indians calling to each other, and on one occasion an expedition dog was shot full of arrows. We, on the other hand, were accompanied by two Indians from the region and on one memorable occasion spent a day in an Indian village. Even though this tribe, the Cinta Larga, had only been contacted within the last 25 years, they were not unaffected by the modern world. When we first arrived at the village, we found it apparently deserted. This did not surprise us, as the literature is full of deserted Indian villages, the inhabitants fleeing at the first sign of strangers. However, after a short search, we found the missing Indians. They were all huddled in one of the huts, gathered around a generator-driven TV set, watching, if you will believe it, *Star Trek*. It was surreal. There was Captain Kirk, flying in space, battling the Klingons. The whole crew was speaking Portuguese, although as far as the Indians were concerned, it might just as well have been Klingonese. I have often wondered what they could possibly have been thinking as they watched the screen. *The Enterprise* aside, the rest of their existence was in many ways little different from what it had been in Roosevelt's time.

Another major difference between our expedition and Roosevelt's was our equipment. We had high-performance white water rafts, light-weight, nourishing food, modern medicine to protect us from malaria and other tropical diseases, and insect repellent, which, while not entirely effective, was at least partially so. Most importantly, we had an accurate map (prepared by the Brazilian mapmaker who accompanied Roosevelt) and knew exactly how much farther we had to go. Also, we had life vests while Roosevelt's expedition did not. They were lucky indeed that more men were not lost in the rapids—a testament to their skill rather than their foresight.

For all our modern conveniences, our trip was not without difficulties, but we shot over rapids they took days to portage; when we had to portage, we carried only five 500-pound rafts instead of the seven 2500-pound dugout canoes they were saddled with; we ate sufficiently while they starved; and we remained healthy whereas they were constantly sick. They were explorers, while we were merely adventurers, and there is a world of difference. Roosevelt was five years older than I, 65 pounds heavier, and in much worse shape, but he survived and did so with grace and humor. His comrades suffered all kinds of privations and for the most part did so stoically, without complaint. My respect for the achievement of my predecessors grew every day I was on the river.

Amazonian wilderness adventures are not for everyone, but this book is. Roosevelt once said, "I am always willing to pay the piper when I have had a good dance; and every now and then I like to drink the wine of life with brandy in it." On finishing Ornig's book, you will know what Theodore Roosevelt meant.

—Tweed Roosevelt

My Last Chance to Be a Boy

I
The Old Lion Is Dead

The fire had gone out during the night in the old nursery at Sagamore Hill. The simple second-floor room, so warm in the daytime when the winter sun poured through the south-facing windows, was chilly in the predawn January darkness. James Amos kept his sickroom vigil like a faithful servant, sleeping upright in a stiff-backed chair, his grizzled black head nodding over folded hands. Half consciously, he listened for the regular rise and fall of the sick man's breathing from the wide sleigh bed nearby. Edith Roosevelt had tiptoed in at 2:00 A.M. to check on her husband. He appeared to be sleeping comfortably, lying on his side. Reassured, she had gone back to bed without disturbing him, closing the door softly.

Two hours later, at 4:00 A.M., Amos was jolted awake by the harsh sounds of strangled breathing. He called the nurse, who was sleeping in the adjoining room. When they saw that the patient had stopped breathing, they woke Mrs. Roosevelt. She ran to her husband's side and called to him, "Theodore, darling!"[1] but there was no response. Dr. Faller, the family physician, was summoned, but he could not revive the still form lying on the bed. Theodore Roosevelt was dead at the age of sixty. It was January 6, 1919, in the first year of peace since the Great War had ended.

The nation that awoke that gray January morning was stunned to hear newsboys shouting the headlines of special editions that had been rushed to the streets. It seemed incredible that such a vigorous, familiar figure could be gone so suddenly. Few people realized that Roosevelt had been in and out of hospitals during the preceding year. Up to the last hour, he had deceived his physicians, his family, and himself as to

1

how seriously ill he really was.[2] The official cause of death was pulmonary embolism—a blood clot in the lung—brought on by the combined effects of inflammatory rheumatism and recurrent malaria. That he died in bed seemed oddly fitting. On learning the news, the vice president of the United States, Thomas R. Marshall, clamped down on his cigar and remarked, "Death had to take him sleeping, for if Roosevelt had been awake, there would have been a fight."[3]

By noon, flags were lowered in New York City and across the country. More than a thousand telegrams expressing sorrow and disbelief poured into the little telegraph office at Oyster Bay and were carried up to the house in canvas mailbags. One of T. R.'s four sons, Archie, an army captain home on convalescent leave, cabled his older brothers, Ted, Jr., and Kermit—still overseas—with the sad news: "The old lion is dead."[4] Later that day, pilots from a nearby army corps training field began a vigil of their own by circling low over the roof of Sagamore Hill, engines droning in dirgelike monotone. The fliers dropped laurel wreaths on the front lawn in the ancient way of honoring a fallen chieftain.

Life in New York City was briefly suspended on January 8, the day of Roosevelt's funeral. Wagon drivers in Manhattan's slushy streets tied ribbons of black crepe to their horses' manes and draped American flags in the harnesses. At midday, church bells began tolling across the city in which eight generations of Roosevelts had lived and worked. On the decks of warships anchored in the Hudson, blue-clad crews stood at rigid attention while the guns banged out salutes. Just before 2:00 P.M., as Roosevelt's flag-covered coffin was being lowered into the ground, the traction company turned off the power grid for a full minute. Streetcars and subway trains ground to a halt, the lights dimmed, and thousands of ordinary men and women stood with bowed heads for a moment of silence.[5]

Even in death, Roosevelt's hold on the popular imagination remained strong. For days afterward, the newspapers carried reminiscences and tributes from all over the world. The sense of loss ebbed slowly, and people began to contemplate "a world without Roosevelt in it."[6] For more than twenty years, he had dominated the American scene as no public figure had since Lincoln. Who else in his generation could claim to have accomplished so much along so many different lines: two-term president of the United States, governor of New York, Spanish-American War hero, historian and biographer, renowned hunter, naturalist, and explorer? By his own reckoning, written in a letter a month before his death, "Nobody ever packed more varieties of fun and interest in . . . sixty years!"[7]

Had Roosevelt lived, he undoubtedly would have been nominated for president again in 1920 on the Republican ticket. He towered above all other possible candidates and had begun organizing a campaign committee when he died. His chance to serve an unprecedented third term was cut short by a decision he had made seven years earlier. In 1913, still robust at fifty-five, he had led a scientific expedition to South America that culminated in the exploration of an unmapped river deep in the Brazilian jungle. He did so to escape from political pressures at home and to find a new challenge for his restless energy. He also felt his age creeping up on him.

It was to be his last great adventure, one that exacted a fearful price from his body. During a two-month ordeal, malaria, exhaustion, and an infected leg injury combined to ruin his once-magnificent health. His sister, Corinne Roosevelt Robinson, always claimed that "the Brazilian wilderness stole away ten years" from her brother's life. He came back from South America "a man in whom a secret poison still lurked," and which eventually killed him.[8]

His death in 1919, just as World War I was ending, was a tragedy for his family and the nation. At a critical moment in history, the United States was left without his strong leadership and courageous voice. It was an unnecessary sacrifice, but Roosevelt would not have been Roosevelt if he had not gone to South America. "I had to go," he explained to a friend. "It was my last chance to be a boy."[9]

NOTES

1. Morris, *Edith Kermit Roosevelt*, p. 433. **2.** *New York Times*, 1-7-19. **3.** Thayer, *T. R.*, p. 450. **4.** Morris, *Edith Kermit Roosevelt*, p. 434. **5.** *New York Times*, 1-9-19. **6.** White, *Autobiography*, p. 551. **7.** Wagenknecht, *Seven Worlds*, p. 4. **8.** Robinson, *T. R.*, p. 278. **9.** Wagenknecht, *Seven Worlds*, p. 11.

II
We Have Many
Common Interests

In the autumn of 1913, ex-president Theodore Roosevelt was invited by the governments of Brazil, Argentina, and Chile to speak on the political reforms he had championed as a third-party candidate in the 1912 U.S. presidential election. Roosevelt had lost in his effort to make a political comeback, and defeat left him jaded about reentering the public arena so soon. To spend two months on the foreign lecture circuit seemed, as he wrote an English friend, "not much better or less worrying or more interesting than a two months' speaking campaign in my own beloved country." But when it was over, he hoped to come home by a most adventurous route. "I have a funny little Catholic priest, who is a friend of mine, a great Dante scholar, and with a thirst for wandering in the wilderness coming with me. He has for years been anxious to have me go north through the middle of South America." Instead of making the conventional sea voyage back, they were going to see if it was possible to travel the length of the continent, from Buenos Aires some four thousand miles north to the West Indies and home.[1]

The priest who drew up this itinerary was Father John Augustine Zahm, a retired provincial of the Congregation of the Holy Cross, a Catholic order of French origin, which founded Notre Dame University at South Bend, Indiana. Zahm was well known in his day as a theologian, university administrator, and scientific lecturer. In his later years, he took to roaming through the more remote parts of South America on his own and writing travel books. While there, he conceived the idea of organizing a scientific expedition to be led by Theodore Roosevelt.

Zahm's friendship with Roosevelt dated back to 1904, during T. R.'s first term, and was based on a mutual passion for the works of Dante. The bookish president and the erudite priest also liked to exchange ideas about the Bible, history, and science. With so much in common, they soon became, as T. R. said, "cronies."[2] Zahm's ecclesiastical duties frequently brought him to Washington, and he was able to drop in at the White House, sometimes taking groups of seminary students with him to meet the president.

Unlike Roosevelt, who descended from New York City's old Dutch aristocracy, Zahm grew up on a frontier farm in Indiana, the second of fourteen children of an Alsatian immigrant. At his baptism, the infant Zahm stared up so intently at the ceiling that a guest predicted he would become an astronomer.[3] Instead, Zahm chose to study the mystery that lay behind the stars and was ordained a priest in 1875. Serious, scholarly, and ambitious, he rose rapidly through the teaching ranks of Holy Cross and in 1898 gained election as head of the sixty-odd schools, hospitals, and orphanages that comprised the United States province of the order.

As provincial, Zahm's greatest contribution was the transformation of Notre Dame from a sleepy seminary school into one of the great Catholic universities. He dreamed of creating "a community of saints and scholars" operating in a modern environment and sought to achieve it overnight. He brought electric lighting, railroad service, and fully equipped laboratories to the South Bend campus with unheard-of speed and went into debt to do so. Like a gambler, no cost was too great for him. "I want [it] . . . to be equal to any in the U.S.—without exception," he boasted of a new mechanical arts building under construction. "My ideas may seem utopian, but I am thoroughly in earnest & have never been more sanguine of success in anything I have undertaken."[4]

Zahm's free-spending ways eventually brought him into conflicts with higher church officials, who feared he would bankrupt their province. A sympathetic friend compared him to Napoleon: "His plans are so great and expensive and his energy so intense, that each new improvement only opens up a prospect for another and a greater one . . . Father Zahm will never be understood, nor his work appreciated by this generation."[5]

By 1906, Zahm's clashes with his superiors led to his nervous breakdown and removal as provincial. At fifty-five, his ruddy complexion and penetrating clear blue eyes still suggested vigorous health, but his hair had already turned white. He complained to his father general that "for more than a year I have not had a single night's refreshing sleep."[6] Ailing and embittered, Zahm left Notre Dame, never to return. He took his doctor's advice and headed for the Caribbean, doing so in secrecy so that his religious colleagues would not know where he was. He went to the trouble of faking his return address on postcards and letters, and induced homeward-bound travelers to mail them from widely scattered places across the United States. Only his brother, Albert, knew his real whereabouts. Incognito, Zahm reached South America and promptly fell in love with the tropics. There he found a new purpose in life—to retrace the steps of the Spanish conquistadores and to awaken North Americans to the trade and tourism potential of the Southern Hemisphere.

Twice during 1907, Zahm crossed the continent alone, from east to west through Venezuela and Colombia, and then back again across the Andes and down the Amazon. He did so "with an ease," one observer remarked, "which argued the dispensations of a special Providence."[7] The successful outcome of his trips led Zahm to the erroneous conclusion that "travel, even in the least frequented parts of South America, was far from being as difficult as it has long been depicted."[8] The dangers from wild animals and Indians, he believed, had been greatly exaggerated. Throughout his time in South America, he had felt "quite safe as if [he] had been taking a promenade down . . . Fifth Avenue, New York."[9]

Zahm was already planning a third expedition to South America when he returned to the United States at the end of 1907. He wanted to explore regions still unknown to scientists, such as the bird-rich swamplands of upper Paraguay and the trackless forests of the Brazilian Mato Grosso. This time, however, he wanted a companion, someone "who had . . . made nature study a predominant part of his life-work." His choice was Theodore Roosevelt, soon to be retiring as president of the United States, and who was also a preeminent naturalist.[10]

Late in 1908, Zahm paid a call at the White House to propose that when Roosevelt was "free from presidential cares," they travel together to South America.[11] For moral support, Zahm had brought along John Barrett, the director general of the Pan-American Union, an organization devoted to improving U.S.–Latin American relations. Zahm extolled the exploration and scientific potential, and Barrett stressed the diplomatic value that such a goodwill mission would have.

Roosevelt was not interested in going to South America to make speeches, but he was greatly intrigued by Zahm's glowing descriptions of the tropical landscapes and historical sites to be seen. When the subject of hunting came up, the president declared that more than anything else, he wanted a chance someday to kill a jaguar, the king of South American big-game animals.[12] He might have accepted Zahm's offer then and there had it not been for the fact that he was already deep in planning an extended hunting trip to Africa. They agreed to talk about it after Roosevelt's return. Thus, as Zahm wrote, "the project was never abandoned. It was merely deferred."[13]

Politics lay behind Roosevelt's decision to spend the first year of his post-presidential life in Africa. Back in 1904, on the eve of winning a second term in his own right, he had announced he would follow the tradition of his predecessors and not seek a consecutive third term in 1908. He picked a member of his cabinet, William Howard Taft, the secretary of war and a close friend, to succeed him. Once Taft had been safely nominated, Roosevelt felt free to begin planning his retirement, which was to begin with a long hunting trip. He was determined to stay out of the country for at least a year, so that Taft would have a chance to establish himself as president. The British big-game hunter Sir Harry Johnston suggested T. R. try Central and South America as hunting grounds because they were less well known. But Roosevelt worried about looking like "an envoy from this country"[14] if he went there so soon after leaving office. Africa was remote enough. Besides, as T. R. gleefully admitted later, "the lion and the elephant exercised too strong an attraction for me to be able to resist them."[15]

Roosevelt prepared for the African trip with the thoroughness of a general planning a military campaign. He arranged to have the American Museum of Natural History in New York send him weekly batches of books on African game animals. Within a few months of systematic study, he had absorbed an expert's knowledge of the subject. A fellow hunter, Carl Akeley, sent a plaster bust of an elephant's head to the White House so the president could study where to aim the killing shot.[16] Never wanting to be anywhere without books, T. R. devised a portable library numbering some sixty pocket-sized volumes, starting with the Bible and running down the centuries through Homer, Shakespeare, *The Federalist*, and Mark Twain. These were bound in tough pigskin to withstand sweat and dust. To avoid being caught blind in the field, the nearsighted Roosevelt had nine extra pairs of eyeglasses sewn into various parts of his hunting clothing.

As 1908 ended, Roosevelt's joy in escaping the burdens of office burst out in a note to President-elect Taft:

> Ha! Ha! *You* are making up your Cabinet. *I* in a light-hearted way have spent the morning testing the rifles for my African trip. Life has compensations![17]

Three months later, in March 1909, Roosevelt sailed for Africa and a new career as a self-styled "hunter-naturalist." With him was his second son, Kermit, who had needed no encouragement to drop out of his freshman year at Harvard University to be his father's "side-partner" in the biggest safari ever conducted on the Dark Continent. Roosevelt's wife, Edith, had not wanted her middle-aged husband to risk being clawed by lions or bitten by tsetse flies, but knew she could not hold him back. Dreading the long separation, Edith had remained at Sagamore Hill on sailing day. "She was perfectly calm and self-possessed when we left home," Kermit told a family friend at the dock, "but I had the feeling her heart was broken."[18]

The African expedition was sponsored by the Smithsonian Institution of Washington, D.C., which had long wanted to obtain a complete collection of East African wildlife. Altogether, the trip cost $75,000—equivalent to ten times that amount in today's currency. The money came in part from Roosevelt's pocket and from donations by wealthy philanthropists such as Andrew Carnegie. *Scribner's Magazine*, a popular monthly of the day, offered the former president $50,000 to write about his experiences in serial form.

For an entire year, Theodore and Kermit Roosevelt roamed over what is now Kenya, Uganda, and the southern Sudan on a grand-scale hunt, often staying for weeks at a time as guests on the vast farms of British settlers. The hunters were supported by three naturalists, 260 native bearers, and what Roosevelt called "an immense amount of scientific impedimenta"—including four tons of salt to preserve hides.[19]

By March 1910, the two Roosevelts had between them shot over five hundred head of game, from elephants to gazelles, often at ranges as dangerously close as fifty yards, since neither of them was a good marksman. On one occasion, while hunting for hippos in a rowboat manned by natives, the former president wounded one of the huge mammals in a shallow bay covered in water lilies. The enraged beast charged at the small boat with its jaws wide open. "I used my entire magazine in stopping it," T. R. reported to his friend, Massachusetts senator Henry Cabot Lodge, "while Kermit industriously took its photograph during the process."[20]

Kermit's coolness in the face of danger was a source of pride as well as concern for his father. "It is hard to realize that the rather timid boy of four years ago has turned out a perfectly cool and daring fellow," T. R. wrote his eldest son, Ted, Jr. "Indeed he is a little too reckless and keeps my heart in my throat, for I worry about him all the time; he is not a good shot, not even as good as I am, and Heaven knows I am poor enough . . . the day before yesterday he stopped a charging Leopard within six yards of him, after it had mauled one of our porters."[21]

The results of the expedition far exceeded the sponsoring museum's expectations. Roosevelt's naturalists shipped back more than eleven thousand mammals, birds, fishes, insects, and plant specimens. The collection was so enormous that the Smithsonian was able to mount only a fraction of the total. The remainder was given away to other museums when a stingy U.S. Congress refused to raise money for the taxidermy work.

From Africa, Roosevelt proceeded to round out his year abroad by touring Europe in the company of his wife and youngest daughter, Ethel, both of whom had met the male members of the family at Khartoum, where the expedition disbanded. Since leaving the presidency, Roosevelt had adopted the title of colonel, his old rank from the Spanish-American War. As such, he expected to be treated as a private citizen, but Europeans found the glamour of the Rough Rider image too potent to resist. They lionized him as the foremost living American, cheered him on the boulevards, and packed the halls where he spoke. Rushing from one Old World capital to another with his family and suitcases in tow, T. R. recalled his presidential tours in the United States: "The same crowds, the same official receptions . . . the same wearing fatigue and hurry . . ." and never having time to talk to the people he cared to talk to.[22]

In June 1910, Theodore Roosevelt returned to New York to a reception such as no American ex-president had ever received. A battleship and a destroyer flotilla waited to escort his ocean liner into New York Harbor and were trailed by hooting tugs, fireboats, and flag-draped private yachts. A twenty-one-gun salute, an honor normally reserved for heads of state, boomed from the ramparts of Fort Wadsworth. Over the waterfront rose a din of steam whistles and thumping brass bands. A ballad by the poet Wallace Irwin conveys the immense popularity Roosevelt enjoyed at this time:

> Thunder and smoke, how the Patriots woke
>   From Kalamazoo to Nome.
> Your Uncle Sam fell off o' the porch
>   And the Statue of Liberty swallowed her torch
> When Teddy came sailing home.[23]

Hundreds of friends were waiting for him as the Colonel stepped ashore. "I'm so glad to see you!" he kept exclaiming as hand after hand reached out, the "so" sounding like a firecracker going off.[24] The procession up Broadway was even more tumultuous. Tens of thousands of cheering, waving New Yorkers lined the sidewalks and sat in open office windows above the street. Roosevelt stood up in his slow-moving carriage, holding his top hat over his head and bowing, while an honor guard of Rough Rider comrades clip-clopped alongside.

Roosevelt was too astute a politician to believe that such adulation could last for long, however. Within a few months, he predicted, they would be "throwing rotten apples" at him.[25] In the meantime, he was resolved to stay out of politics and devote himself to natural history, his greatest interest. "One thing I want now is privacy," he told reporters when the welcoming ceremonies ended. "I want to close up like a native oyster." He hoped "the representatives of the press" would not seek him out at Sagamore Hill, "because I have nothing to say."[26]

T. R. was soon forced to break that unaccustomed silence. Taft as president had proved to be a weak leader. The Republican Party was badly split between two feuding factions: the conservative Old Guard, led by Taft, and the reform-minded insurgents whom Roosevelt identified with. As the congressional election of 1910 got under way, both camps appealed to T. R. to come out on their side for the sake of the party. Unable to heal the rift between them as he had first hoped, he was forced into the unpleasant task of choosing sides. He backed progressive candidates and actively stumped for them, fully aware, as he wrote Senator Lodge, ". . . that I shall be held responsible for the smashing defeat at the polls which is almost sure to follow."[27]

When the votes were counted, Republicans were soundly beaten across the board. For the first time in sixteen years, the Democrats took control of the House of Representatives. The blame was laid squarely at the Colonel's door. He was called a "megalomaniac," whose meddling had wrecked the Republican Party. Less than five months after his triumphal return from Africa and Europe, newspapers derided T. R. as "a discredited and broken politician."[28]

He had not wanted to get into the fight, the Colonel explained to Ted, Jr., after the election, "but events shaped themselves so that I could not stay out without being a craven and shirking my plain duty." The only good thing he saw coming out of it was "the doing away with the talk of nominating me in 1912."[29]

The year 1911 was one of contentment for the Colonel, beginning in January, when Ted, Jr., announced that his wife was expecting their first child. "Three cheers!" a delighted grandfather-to-be wrote back. "Mother and I are almost as delighted as darling Eleanor and you."[30] A home, wife, and children were what really counted in life, he told his son in a subsequent letter:

> I have heartily enjoyed many things; the Presidency, my success as a soldier, a writer, a big game hunter and explorer; but all of them put together are not for one moment to be weighed in the balance when compared with the joy I have known with your mother and all of you . . . Really, the prospect of grandchildren was all that was lacking to make perfect mother's happiness and mine.[31]

For the first time in years, there was no need to worry about money. The Colonel expected to earn $40,000 in royalties from the sales of his *African Game Trails*, which Charles Scribner's Sons published in a two-volume edition. Contrary to popular belief, Roosevelt was not a wealthy man. He had lost most of his inheritance from his father when the great blizzard of 1888 wiped out his cattle herd and those of other ranchers in the Dakota Badlands. Before becoming president, his meager civil servant's salary had been barely enough for Edith to raise six children and maintain the household and staff at Sagamore. He wrote histories and biographies to supplement his income, but not until he moved into the White House did his books sell well. After leaving office, Roosevelt earned his living as a lecturer and journalist, mainly as contributing editor to *The Outlook*, an influential public affairs magazine, for which he was paid $12,000 a year. This money was "very important for me to have," he wrote Ted, Jr., "as long as the family are being brought up and four of them have to be supported entirely by me."[32]

Free of politics at last, Roosevelt turned his attention to scientific matters and wrote a forty-thousand-word monograph on "Revealing and Concealing Coloration in Birds and Animals." It was meant as a rebuttal to Abbott H. Thayer, an artist and amateur naturalist who had written categorically that animals owed their survival to how well their coloring blended into the background. Roosevelt was angered at what he regarded as the "utter looseness and wildness" of Thayer's theories[33] and brought up one example after another of animals he had observed whose skins and feathers were distinctly "advertising" and therefore had nothing to do with survival. "I am having a lively time at the moment," he informed Ted, Jr., as he put the finishing touches to his article. "None of my political, literary or social friends will ever know that I have written it, but it will attract frenzied dissent and tepid assent among obscure zoological friends here and abroad."[34]

There was more than lukewarm interest on the part of the American Museum of Natural History, which published the Colonel's essay in its *Bulletin* for August 1911. The museum's curator of birds, Frank M. Chapman, was keenly interested in Roosevelt's thesis and came out to Sagamore Hill before the publication date to go over the details. It so happened that Senator Lodge was also visiting that day. Chapman, a shy, thoughtful naturalist whom museum colleagues dubbed "the bird man," sat between the talkative Roosevelt and the bearded, cautious old Lodge, and described the luncheon conversation as "neutral." But as soon as the dishes were cleared, the Colonel called Chapman to come out on the lawn to observe birds in the nearby trees. The two naturalists became so absorbed in their discussion that Lodge was ignored, until Edith appeared on the porch with a gentle reminder, "Theodore, have you forgotten that Henry is waiting for you in the library?"

"By George, I had," the Colonel replied and turned to Chapman. "Excuse me for a moment while I settle the affairs of State and then I'll return to the infinitely more important subject of the protective coloration of animals!"[35]

While Roosevelt had been in Africa, Father Zahm had settled down as chaplain at Holy Cross Academy in Washington, D.C. He lived there in seclusion, surrounded by his notes and reference works, and wrote two books on his South American travels. Besides recounting his own adventures, Zahm exhorted North American businessmen to invest in the tropics and spoke of the economic boom that was sure to follow the opening of the Panama Canal in 1914. He also assured would-be explorers that "there was never any danger even in the wildest and most untravelled parts of the country."[36]

None of Zahm's brethren at Holy Cross had any idea he had been in South America. There was a prankish side to his personality that delighted in withholding information until the right moment. When he was asked, "What volume are you working on now?" Zahm would reply, "It takes years to write an outstanding book," and turn the question back on the intruder.[37] To keep up this elaborate hoax, he chose a pseudonym, Dr. H. J. Mozans—a partial anagram of J. A. Zahm. It was under this authorship that his first book, *Up the Orinoco and down the Magdalena,* was published in 1910. Only his brother and the publisher, D. Appleton & Co., knew Dr. Mozans's real identity.

In the spring of 1911, Zahm renewed his friendship with Theodore Roosevelt by sending him a proof copy of his second work, *Along the Andes and down the Amazon.* "I wish to ask you a great favor," wrote Zahm. Would the Colonel write an introduction for him? As for the pen name of Mozans, Zahm explained, "I do not wish anyone to suspect the author's real name . . . Of course, I know you will say nothing about the matter to anyone."[38]

Roosevelt went along with Zahm's request, even though he complained to another author at the time of being "bedeviled to write introductions for books dealing with worthy objects."[39] Only his regard for the priest and their mutual interest in South America prompted him to find the time to write a generous tribute:

> He is an extraordinarily hardy man, this gentle, quiet traveler . . . he loves rivers and forests, mountains and plains, and broad highways and dim wood trails; and he has a wide and intimate acquaintance with science, with history, and above all, with literature.

It was "a delightful book from every standpoint," Roosevelt concluded, and he considered Dr. Mozans an ambassador of goodwill for having written it.[40] "Is the enclosed all right?" the Colonel wrote back to Zahm. "If not, wire at once and suggest any changes you want. Of course, I shall keep absolutely secret about your identity." Could he use the word "priest" instead of "traveller" for greater interest?

"Nothing could be more flattering," Zahm answered, ". . . but, for the present at least, it will for special reasons be best to use the word 'traveller' . . ." When the book was published, he hoped to see Roosevelt in New York. "We have many common interests to talk about—not the least of which are the wonders and glories of the tropics."[41]

The publication of Zahm's twin volumes created a stir among diplomats and travelers familiar with South America. No one had heard of a Dr. Mozans, and there was talk that he was a fake. "You may be amused to know," the Colonel wrote Zahm in June 1911, "that yesterday a gentleman happened to mention that he doubted if Mozans was a real character, or had ever been down where he stated he had been. I told him that I happened to know who Dr. Mozans was and that he was a very real character, and most certainly had been down on the trip!"[42]

Zahm's light-hearted attitude toward South American exploration drew a sharp rebuke from the other side of the Atlantic. A British army officer, Col. P. M. Fawcett,* who had spent years in the Bolivian and Amazonian rain forests, criticized Zahm for encouraging amateurs to go into the backcountry. Every year, wrote Fawcett, expeditions were "sacrificed to rashness or inexperience." Cutting through virgin jungle was "exacting work"—half a mile a day was considered good progress. He warned of water snakes "of a size incredible by scientists," and of insect-borne disabilities that were "hard to exaggerate." Hostile natives posed the greatest threat of all. It was "inviting people to suicide to tell them that there is no danger from Indians away from trails & rivers . . ." There were regions in South America "into which the explorer can only enter with the almost certainty of catastrophe."[43]

Zahm was not deterred by this advice and continued to confidently plan the details of his great expedition in secret. But as 1912 approached, it seemed increasingly unlikely that Theodore Roosevelt would ever find the time to go with him. It was an election year, and there was growing speculation that T. R. would challenge the incumbent president William Howard Taft for the Republican nomination.

The Colonel did not want to run for president in 1912. He sensed defeat for the Republicans that year, and his instincts told him he would be better off waiting until 1916 to make another try for the White House. But he also recognized that the United States, rapidly becoming urbanized, needed to make fundamental changes in the way it governed itself, or risk social upheaval. As he debated the wisdom of running, there were calls from across the country for him to take a stand. *The New York American* chided his Hamletlike indecision with the blunt headline: "TR: RU or RU not?"[44] A petition signed by seven Republican governors declared that he was the overwhelming favorite among Republicans and the only one who could lead the party to victory. As the pressure mounted, Roosevelt began to see it as his duty to fight Taft for the nomination. By the end of February, he made up his

---

*In 1925, Colonel Fawcett's name was added to the list of famous missing persons when he disappeared while searching for a fabled lost city in the Roncador Mountains of Brazil's Mato Grosso. He and his party are believed to have been killed by Indians.

mind and entered the primaries with a ringing call to battle: "My hat is in the ring and the fight is on!"[45]

The Colonel did not reckon on the resourcefulness of the Taft forces to hold on to power. At the Chicago convention in June 1912, they used parliamentary maneuvers to unseat delegates pledged to him and install their own men, thus clinching the nomination for Taft. Crying "theft" and "steamroller tactics," the Colonel and his disgruntled supporters stamped out of the hall and held their own rump convention at a hotel a few blocks away. They formed a new political organization: the Progressive Party, or, as it came to be more popularly known, the Bull Moose Party, after Roosevelt told a reporter, "I'm feeling like a bull moose!"[46]

He needed that strength in the campaign that followed. Pitted against the Republican Taft and the Democratic candidate Woodrow Wilson, Roosevelt was attempting to do what no presidential candidate had ever achieved: win on a third-party ticket. The planks in his Progressive Party's platform were startlingly radical for the time—among them, women's suffrage, an income tax, and giving the people instead of the state legislatures the right to elect U.S. senators. Most radical of all was the proposal for the recall of unpopular judicial decisions by the electorate, a measure Roosevelt wholeheartedly endorsed. This issue alone alienated him from many conservative Republican regulars who had been his supporters in the past. "The great bulk of my wealthy and educated friends regard me as a dangerous crank," T. R. admitted to an overseas correspondent, "because I am trying to find a remedy for evils which if left unremedied will in the end do away not only with wealth and education, but pretty much all our civilization."[47]

One of Roosevelt's educated friends who did not desert him was Father Zahm, an ardent Progressive. From his quiet study at Holy Cross Academy, the priest offered political advice and sent the Colonel favorable clippings from Catholic newspapers, "little straws that show how the wind is blowing," he wrote encouragingly, and gave the Latin benediction "Prospere Procede et Regna" (Prosper, Proceed, and Rule).[48] Such expressions of loyalty brought a warm response from the embattled T. R.: "Win or lose, Father, there are certain friendships I have tested in this campaign . . . and among these friendships is my friendship with you."[49]

The climax of the 1912 campaign came on October 14, when a deranged ex-saloon keeper shot Roosevelt at point-blank range in the chest. The candidate had just left his brightly lit hotel and was standing up in the rear of his open touring car when the gunman stepped out of the darkness and fired. The impact threw Roosevelt against the seat. He quickly put his hand to his mouth, and when he saw there was no blood, guessed "the chances were twenty to one" that he was not mortally wounded. The bullet's force was blunted when it passed through his thick army greatcoat, metal spectacle case, and folded-over fifty-page speech. The wadded paper deflected the bullet up into the rib cage and away from vital organs, saving his life.

T. R. remained conscious throughout and insisted on being driven to the auditorium where he was scheduled to speak. As they drove, the doctor attached to the campaign pleaded with him to go to a hospital. "No," Roosevelt replied, "this is my big chance, and I am going to make that speech if I die doing it."[50]

When Roosevelt stepped out on the stage, the audience was unaware that someone had tried to kill him. "Friends," he said, holding up his hand to silence their applause. "I shall have to ask you to be as quiet as possible. I do not know whether you fully understand that I have been shot, but it takes more than that to kill a Bull Moose." He pulled the folded speech from inside his coat and showed the hole in it to the shocked spectators. "The bullet is in me now, so that I cannot make a very long speech, but I will try my best."[51]

He spoke for an hour and a half, his voice fading to a whisper before he finally consented to go to the hospital. The doctors found the bullet lodged in the fourth rib, an inch from the right lung, and decided to leave it there, to let the wound heal around it. From his bed, the Colonel dictated a midnight telegram to Edith, reassuring her that he was "in excellent shape" and that the wound was "trivial."[52]

A wave of sympathy welled up for Roosevelt, who suspended his campaign in order to recuperate at Sagamore Hill. Newspaper editorials were unreserved in praising his courage. Even the conservative *New York Times*, no friend of the Progressive Party, had to salute him: "Only the exceptional man, the extraordinary man, can offer to the world such an exhibition of fortitude as Theodore Roosevelt gave, when, suffering a serious hurt . . . he insisted on making his speech . . . It was rash . . . even an act of folly, but it was characteristic, and the judgment of the country will be that it was magnificent."[53]

But it did not change many votes. Roosevelt had the dubious satisfaction of outpolling his rival Taft in the popular vote, but his entry as an independent candidate guaranteed the election of Woodrow Wilson. The Progressive Party won only a handful of congressional seats, for all of Roosevelt's strenuous campaigning. As the results became known, he wrote his British parliamentarian friend, Arthur Lee, that "there is no use disguising the fact that the defeat at the polls is overwhelming. I had expected defeat, but I had expected that we would make a better showing."[54] "We have fought the good fight," he assured a fellow Progressive, "we have kept the faith . . . Probably we have put the ideal a little higher than we can expect the people as a whole to take offhand."[55]

The reaction against Roosevelt for breaking with the party of his father was swift and severe. The telephone rang less often at Sagamore Hill, and the number of visitors and newspaper reporters willing to climb the steeply winding Cove Neck Road to gain his ear and be inspired by him dwindled. Roosevelt took his status as pariah hard. When his personal physician, Dr. Alexander Lambert, dropped in on him unannounced one day, the Colonel gripped his hand and exclaimed with relief, "You cannot imagine how glad I am to see you! I have been unspeakably lonely. You don't know how lonely it is for a man to be rejected by his own kind."[56]

The Colonel's mood of gloomy introspection was lightened by messages of support from those who believed in what he had tried to accomplish by forming a third party. Among these was a curiously prophetic greeting from Father Zahm on the last day of 1912:

> Wishing you every blessing for 1913. You have made history as you probably never did before during the year just closing & you will make more during the years to come.[57]

With a new year came new hope. "Black care rarely sits behind a rider whose pace is fast enough," T. R. had once written to explain his need for constant mental and physical engagement with the world around him.[58] There was work to be done, and in the spring of 1913, he pushed himself to the limit.

To begin with, he had three books to complete by summer, including an autobiography. The hardest thing about writing of his public career, he observed to Senator Lodge, was to keep his temper in check "and not speak of certain people . . . as they richly deserve."[59] The Colonel also resumed his duties as contributing editor to *The Outlook* after a year's absence. Twice a week, he took the train to Manhattan to turn in articles and attend editorial conferences at the magazine's headquarters at 287 Fourth Avenue. When these sessions went on too long to suit him, he was seen to quietly pull a book from his pocket and begin reading while the other editors droned on.[60]

In time, the bitter feelings stirred up in the 1912 campaign faded.

Roosevelt's reputation and popularity had not materially suffered. A poll taken by the *Independent* magazine that spring voted him "America's most useful citizen . . . He has such a hold on the public that he can sway it more powerfully than any man now living." Proof of that were the sackloads of mail arriving each day at his *Outlook* office and the steady stream of visitors spilling out into the corridors and adjoining offices. Roosevelt's British-born private secretary, Frank Harper, found it "physically impossible" to arrange appointments with all the people who wished to see the former president.[61] During a two-week period in February alone, Roosevelt was forced to decline 171 speaking invitations.[62] Nor was there any refuge at Sagamore Hill, thirty miles away on Long Island, where the guest list of politicians, social workers, explorers, authors, and foreign diplomats resembled a hotel register. Edith Roosevelt, mistress of what amounted to a perpetual open house, described her husband at this time as "working like a steam engine." He was "tired and jaded—having far too much to do, and the least interruption upsets him."[63]

Looming over everything was the fate of the Progressive movement. In the aftermath of defeat, the party clung to Roosevelt like a dying man, even as it tore itself apart in the hunt for scapegoats. "At the moment my chief task is to prevent the Progressives from fighting one another," he wrote in exasperation to Kermit soon after the election. Keeping the peace meant writing long, impassioned letters and making speeches in city after city before Bull Moose audiences on the need to build a national organization if they were to count for anything in the future. "I think I shall be able to keep both sides together," he told his son, but it was all "very weary work," and he resented having to do it at his age. ". . . [T]his whole business of leading a new party should be for an ambitious young colonel, and not for a retired major general."[64]

The only way for Roosevelt to escape such overwhelming pressure was to leave the country again for an extended time. An opportunity to do so came at the close of the 1912 campaign. The Historical and Geographical Society of Rio de Janeiro asked him to deliver a series of lectures in the spring and summer of 1913. This had been accompanied by the offer of a hunting trip from the president of Brazil. At the time, Roosevelt had declined, explaining to Kermit that it was too soon after the election "to go on a tour which would look as though I was advertising myself."[65]

The Brazilian invitations were followed in January 1913 by one from Buenos Aires, from the Museo Social, a federation of civic and educational institutions in Argentina that brought men and ideas together. Its president, Dr. Emilio Frers, referred to rumors of a forthcoming Roosevelt visit to South America and stated that no prominent North American had addressed his organization since 1906, when Secretary of State Elihu Root had made an official visit. If the Colonel included Argentina in his itinerary, he could be assured of a warm welcome from the Argentine people, "who have heard so much about you, about your public career and the high ideals you stand for." Dr. Frers then got down to business and proposed an honorarium of $6,000 in U.S. gold dollars, in exchange for a minimum of three speeches "on subjects, the choice of which would be left entirely to your discretion."[66]

At first Roosevelt turned down the Argentine proposal, reluctant to "merely make an ordinary speech or to go on an ordinary trip."[67] But it did open the possibility of seeing Kermit, who had gone down to work for the Brazil Railway Company after graduating from Harvard in June 1912. Kermit had since moved on to become a bridge-building supervisor for the Anglo-Brazilian Iron Company at São Paulo. In April 1913 he wrote his father about a hunting trip he had made on the outskirts of that city. "The forest must be lovely," a wistful Colonel replied, "sometime I must get down to see you, and we'll take a fortnight's outing, and you shall hunt and I'll act as what in the North Woods we used to call 'wangan man' and keep camp!"[68]

As the idea of a South American tour began to form in Roosevelt's mind, it occurred to him that he might at last be able to realize Father Zahm's long-deferred dream of an expedition into the interior. Before informing Zahm of this, though, he wanted to find out if the American Museum of Natural History would be interested in providing several naturalists to accompany him and make a collecting trip out of it as well. He wrote to Frank Chapman and accepted a lunch date at the museum early in June to discuss the matter.

By coincidence, Zahm had made the same request of Chapman only a few days earlier. After having kept the project alive for five years, Zahm had given up hope that Roosevelt would ever make the South American trip. By now sixty-two years old and in uncertain health, Zahm decided he could wait no longer. He outlined his plan to Chapman and asked him to recommend "a first-class ornithologist" who spoke Spanish fluently and who was knowledgeable about South American birds.[69]

Chapman had already discovered, through an editor friend at D. Appleton & Co., that Zahm was the famous Dr. Mozans. With his secret out, Zahm laughingly agreed to drop his disguise. Chapman went on to suggest a naturalist for the expedition: George K. Cherrie, who had collected tropical birds for twenty years and spoke Spanish like a native. Cherrie had just returned from a museum-sponsored trip in the Columbian Andes. Chapman was not sure if Cherrie would want to return to South America so soon but offered to contact him. Zahm mentioned that he was about to go out to Sagamore Hill and tell Roosevelt of his decision. "You may save yourself the trip," Chapman responded, "for Colonel Roosevelt is going to take luncheon with me here tomorrow and I shall be glad to have you join us."[70]

NOTES

1. T. R. to Arthur Hamilton Lee, *Letters*, 7-7-13, #5863, p. 741. 2. T. R., *Brazilian Wild.*, p. 1. 3. Carroll, Patrick J., "Mind in Action," *The Ave Maria* (1-5-46), chapter 1, p. 18. 4. Weber, *Notre Dame's John Zahm*, p. 37. 5. Ibid., p. 153. 6. Carroll, "Mind in Action," *The Ave Maria* (5-4-46), chapter X, p. 559. 7. Chapman, Introduction to T. R.'s *Brazilian Wild.*, p. xii. 8. Zahm, *Up the Orinoco*, p. 427. 9. Ibid., p. 283. 10. Zahm, *South America's Southland*, p. 4. 11. Ibid. 12. Wagenknecht, *Seven Worlds*, p. 20. 13. Zahm, *South America's Southland*, p. 7. 14. T. R. to Henry Hamilton Johnston, 2-15-09, *Letters*, Vol. 6, #5173, p. 1522. 15. T. R., "A Journey through Central Brazil," *The Geographical Journal*, p. 98. 16. T. R. to Carl Ethan Akeley, 2-27-09, *Letters*, Vol. 6, #5193, p. 1539. 17. Pringle, *T. R.*, p. 507. 18. Hagedorn, *Roosevelt Family*, p. 281. 19. T. R. to Andrew Carnegie, 6-1-09, *Letters*, Vol. 7, #5217, p. 13. 20. T. R. to Henry Cabot Lodge, 7-26-09, *Letters*, Vol. 7, #5225, p. 24. 21. T. R. to T. R., Jr., 5-17-09, *Letters*, Vol. 7, #5214, p. 10. 22. T. R. to George Otto Trevelyan, 10-1-11, *Letters*, Vol. 7, #5521, p. 354. 23. Hagedorn, *Roosevelt Family*, p. 285. 24. Ibid. 25. Ibid., p. 295. 26. Pringle, *T. R.*, p. 535. 27. T. R. to Henry Cabot Lodge, 9-15-10, *Letters*, Vol. 7, #5327, p. 218. 28. Hagedorn, *Roosevelt Family*, p. 295. 29. T. R. to T. R., Jr., 11-11-10, *Letters*, Vol. 7, #5347, p. 160. 30. T. R. to T. R., Jr., 1-14-11, *Letters*, Vol. 7, #5382, p. 206. 31. T. R. to T. R., Jr., 1-22-11, *Letters*, Vol. 7, #5391, p. 213. 32. T. R. to T. R., Jr., 8-22-11, *Letters*, Vol. 7, #5509, p. 335. 33. T. R. to Charles Atwood Kofoid, 2-2-11, *Letters*, Vol. 7, #5397, p. 220. 34. T. R. to T. R., Jr., 5-5-11, *Letters*, Vol. 7, #5430, p. 260. 35. Chapman, Frank M., Speech before Theodore Roosevelt Memorial Assoc., March 1928. 36. Zahm, *Along the Andes*, p. 515. 37. Carroll, "Mind in Action," *The Ave Maria* (5-18-46), chapter XI, p. 620. 38. Ibid. (5-4-46), chapter X, pp. 564, 592. 39. T. R. to James Rudolph Garfield, 4-28-11, *Letters*, Vol. 7, #5423, p. 246. 40. Zahm, *Along the Andes* (T. R.'s Introduction), pp. x, xii. 41. Carroll, "Mind in Action," *The Ave Maria*, (5-11-46), chapter X, p. 592. 42. Ibid. 43. P. H. Fawcett to J. A. Zahm, 1-27-13, *JAZP*. 44. Manners, *T. R. & Will*, p. 206. 45. T. R. to Herbert Spencer Hadley, 2-29-13, *Letters*, Vol. 7, #5644, p. 513. 46. Manners, *T. R. & Will*, p. 237. 47. T. R. to Henry Rider Haggard, 6-28-12, *Letters*, Vol. 7, #5726, p. 568. 48. J. A. Zahm to T. R., 6-3-12, *PPS* 49. Carroll, "Mind in Action," *The Ave Maria* (6-8-46), chapter XII, p. 723. 50. Manners, *T. R. & Will*, p. 281. 51. Gardner, *Departing Glory*, p. 274. 52. Hagedorn, *Roosevelt Family*, p. 317. 53. Ibid., p. 319. 54. T. R. to Arthur Hamilton Lee, 11-5-12, *Letters*, Vol. 7, #5775, p. 633. 55. T. R. to James Rudolph Garfield, 11-8-12, *Letters*, Vol. 7, #5777, p. 637. 56. Hagedorn, *Roosevelt Family*, p. 328. 57. J. A. Zahm to T. R., 12-31-12,

PPS. **58.** T. R., *Works, Ranch Life,* Vol. 1, p. 329. **59.** T. R. to Henry Cabot Lodge, 2-27-12, *Letters,* Vol. 7, #5832, p. 710. **60.** Wagenknecht, *Seven Worlds,* p. 11. **61.** Frank Harper to R. W. Lawrence, 6-3-13, *PPS.* **62.** Wagenknecht, *Seven Worlds,* p. 159. **63.** Hagedorn, *Roosevelt Family,* p. 333. **64.** T. R. to Kermit Roosevelt, 12-3-12, *Letters,* Vol. 7, #5796, p. 660. **65.** Ibid. **66.** Dr. Emilio Frers to T. R., 1-28-13, *PPS.* **67.** T. R. to Rómulo Sebastian Naón, 6-16-13, *Letters,* Vol. 7, #5855, p. 731. **68.** Roosevelt, Kermit, *Happy Hunting Grounds,* p. 40. **69.** Zahm, *South America's Southland,* p. 8. **70.** Ibid., p. 9.

III
Just the Right Amount
of Adventure

A little before 1:00 P.M. on Friday, June 6, 1913, Theodore Roosevelt stepped briskly through the open doors of the dining room of the American Museum of Natural History and was surprised to see Father Zahm standing next to Frank Chapman and other guests. With a look of inquiry, T. R. pointed to the priest and asked Chapman, "Do you know who he is?" Then, turning to Zahm, he burst out, "You are the very man I wished to see. I was just about to write you to inform you that I think I shall, at last, be able to take that long-talked-of trip to South America." He referred to the lecture offer from Argentina and said he was on the verge of accepting it.[1]

For Zahm, this news came as "a most agreeable surprise" and "about the last thing I thought likely." At the luncheon, he and Roosevelt agreed to join forces and made tentative plans. Zahm proposed that their expedition ascend the Paraguay River, cross over the great divide formed by the Brazilian Plateau, and then descend the Rio Tapajós to its junction with the Amazon. From there, Zahm wanted to continue on into Venezuela via the Orinoco and its tributaries and end up with a horseback ride across the plains to Caracas, on the Caribbean coast.

Roosevelt had no special itinerary in mind, beyond joking to his lunch partners that he didn't wish to be the "thousandth American to visit Cuzco [Peru]." His main interest was in finding some unspoiled part of South America where the potential for collecting new species of birds and animals was greatest. When Chapman assured him that the Paraguay-Tapajós region was practically untouched by naturalists, T. R.

approved Zahm's route, although he was doubtful if there would be enough time to go north of the Amazon.[2] His one proviso was that they must not set foot on Colombian territory; hatred of Roosevelt still festered there ten years after he had used his presidential powers to help create the Panama Canal Zone out of a former province of Colombia.[3]

Chapman pointed out that although the route Zahm chose had been followed for centuries by traders and natives, it was "far from the beaten track" and led through a region where death by poisoned arrow, drowning in rapids, and infection from disease-carrying insects all were distinct possibilities. T. R. shrugged this off with the same answer he had given the doctors who warned him not to speak at the auditorium in Milwaukee after being shot: "I'm ahead of the game and can afford to take the chance."[4]

Any reservations the Colonel had about speaking in Argentina were removed the following evening when the Argentine minister to the United States, Rómulo S. Naón, spent the night at Sagamore Hill. Suave and dapper, with a pencil-thin mustache, Naón convinced Roosevelt that the Museo Social was acting on behalf of the Argentine people when it had asked him, as a leading spokesman for democratic government, to carry the gospel of the Progressive Party to the new democracies in South America. "When you put the appeal to me in this way," he wrote Naón some days later, "I did not feel at liberty to refuse." Naón evidently knew he had a winning argument, for he had checked on steamship schedules beforehand. "I expect to leave on the 4th of October as you suggested," T. R. concluded, and then added in an enthusiastic postscript that "I would like my speech to be on *World* Democracy; not merely that of the United States."[5]

News of his decision quickly made its way onto the pages of the *New York Times*, which reported on June 13:

T. R. ON PROGRESS MISSION
He Will Preach the New Political Faith in Argentina[6]

Roosevelt soon broadened the diplomatic scope of his lecture tour by adding the other two members of the A B C powers—Brazil and Chile—to the agenda. He informed Brazilian Ambassador da Gama that he would be "passing through Rio" in late October and would "accept with the greatest pleasure" a renewed invitation to address the Historical and Geographical Society—which was promptly made. Not to be outdone by its neighbors on the other side of the Andes, Chile sent formal invitations to speak at the universities of Valparaiso and Santiago, which were also accepted by Roosevelt.[7]

The Colonel now turned his attention to the exploration side of his South American tour. The October 4 sailing date was less than four months away, and he was scheduled to spend the summer in the Arizona desert hunting mountain lions with his two youngest boys, Archie and Quentin. As a result, he left the organizing of the expedition to Father Zahm. Roosevelt asked him to come to Sagamore Hill "without fail" on June 17 and present him with an estimate of how much time the trip would take and "the amount of mischance" they might be exposed to. "I don't in the least mind risk to my life," wrote T. R., "but I want to be sure that I am not doing something for which I will find my physical strength unequal." He instructed Zahm, on his return to Washington, to see the Brazilian ambassador and the Paraguayan minister "and ask if they will give us a little aid, at least to the extent of letters to the officials in the interior."[8]

By June 16, no word had come from Zahm in Washington. The Colonel, in Boston to speak at Bunker Hill Day ceremonies, wired him at Holy Cross Academy:

> Have received no reply about coming tomorrow. Please telegraph. Very important I should see you then.[9]

Not until June 23 did Zahm finally reach Oyster Bay with an overnight bag in his hand and a rough timetable worked out for the trip. If all went according to plan, counting from the October 4 sailing date, he put the expedition in Caracas, Venezuela, by February 1914. All this was based, of course, on the most optimistic notions of time and distance. No one could foretell delays from accidents and transportation break-downs, but Zahm's jaunty attitude toward exploring lulled Roosevelt into a false sense of security. The two middle-aged adventurers bent over a map of South America, and Zahm traced a bony finger along the curving course of the Paraguay River up to a town called Corumbá, where deep-draft steamers had to stop. From here, he said, tapping the spot on the map, they would run light boats to the highest navigable point on the upper Paraguay, then cross the ranges of the Serra dos Parecis Mountains to the headwaters of the Tapajós, and continue their journey down to the Amazon. Zahm was confident the South American governments would provide them ample assistance. He was also investigating a new type of steel-hulled motorboat said to be able to climb rapids, which would make their river trip comparatively easy.

The portage between the headwaters of the Paraguay and Tapajós rivers concerned Roosevelt, since it lay through a virtual blank space on the map. He urged Zahm to get the Brazilian authorities to send some men over the route "to find out just what we have ahead of us." The overland crossing and the numerous rapids on the Tapajós and its tributaries represented "the most difficult and risky part of our journey," he pointed out, "and we ought to take every possible step in advance to provide for them."[10]

Risk seemed far from the Colonel's mind when he wrote Kermit of his developing plans. He promised to spend a week visiting his son in São Paulo between lecture engagements. "I cannot tell you how I am looking forward to seeing you. I hope that mother will come down with me; but it is possible she may not," since he intended coming out through the Brazilian forest. "It won't be anything like our African trip. There will be no hunting and no adventure so that I shall not have the pang I otherwise would about taking it and not taking you along—which of course would never do."[11]

Gradually, the expedition Father Zahm had nursed in his imagination for five years began taking shape. The next day, June 24, Roosevelt had a proposal to make to the American Museum of Natural History. Seated in Frank Chapman's cluttered office, where the acrid odor of dried bird skins mingled with arsenic and other chemicals, he offered to pay for the traveling expenses and food for a museum naturalist and give him every opportunity to collect while in the field. All specimens obtained would become the museum's property, and T. R. would prepare a paper on his observations of South American wildlife.

Chapman spoke of George K. Cherrie as his choice for a naturalist to accompany Roosevelt's expedition. After describing Cherrie's virtues, which included "the test of companionship in the field," Chapman added that "in addition to all these, Colonel, he has six children and is a Bull Mooser." "Fine," T. R. responded. "Tell him we'll hunt Bull Moose in Brazil."[12]

In his report to the museum's president, Henry Fairfield Osborn, the normally reserved Chapman let his enthusiasm spill over: ". . . it would be of the highest importance to secure Colonel Roosevelt's cooperation in South America, a field where we have already made such an excellent start in zoological work." Since 1910, the American Museum had been conducting an intensive investigation of bird and animal distribution on the southern continent. In 1913 alone, five separate expeditions were at work at widely scattered sites, collecting specimens and recording details of habitat, climate, and topography.[13]

Chapman had just returned from one of these field trips, studying bird life on the eastern slopes of the Colombian Andes. He had been assisted by Cherrie, who had gone back to his farm at Newfane, Vermont. Chapman believed Cherrie could be enticed away for a six-month stint with Roosevelt for a salary of $150 per month, plus equipment, and asked Osborn to approve the choice. In the meantime, Chapman dispatched a hasty note to Cherrie: "Please do not make any definite arrangements for South American trips until you hear from me."[14]

The seal of museum approval came down the next day when Osborn, a longtime friend of Roosevelt, wrote him: "I can hardly express to you how much your offer to co-operate with the American Museum pleases, both for your sake and because of the historical association of your Father, in the foundation of the museum."[15]

A generation earlier, in 1869, T. R.'s father, the first Theodore Roosevelt, had been among the founding members of the museum when it opened for business in a disused arsenal building in the middle of Central Park. The senior Roosevelt's plate glass works had supplied the original windows and display cases. T. R.'s own close connection with the museum began at the age of fourteen. In 1872 the fledgling institution recorded the gift of:

> 1 Bat, 12 Mice, 1 Turtle, 1 Skull, Red Squirrel; and
> 4 Bird Eggs from Mr. Theodore Roosevelt, Jr.[16]

In the decades that followed, the museum had benefited greatly from Roosevelt's passionate interest in natural history and his prowess as a hunter. It was one of many museums that received an unexpected windfall from the overflow of hides and skeletons the Colonel brought back from his 1910 African expedition. The articles he contributed to the museum's journal, such as his essay on revealing and concealing coloration among species, distilled a lifetime spent observing animals in the wild. Osborn, a noted paleontologist in his own right, thought enough of Roosevelt's scientific abilities to devote a chapter to him in his *Impressions of Great Naturalists*.

Tempering Osborn's eagerness to see Roosevelt lead an expedition to South America under the museum's banner was worry over how to pay for the naturalist's salary and kit. In 1913 the American Museum was gripped by a severe cash shortage that threatened to set back its worldwide program of exploration. Hoped-for endowments had not materialized, nor had the annual appropriation from a financially strapped New York City government. The museum was forced to borrow $60,000—an enormous sum at the time—to keep its operations going. Salaries had been frozen, and construction halted on a new wing fronting on Central Park. Instead of seeing walls of red Nova Scotia granite rising above their heads, passersby stared down at a gaping fenced-in hole that someday would be the museum's new basement.[17]

Help came from Cleveland H. Dodge, a western copper magnate and museum patron who had provided funds for Roosevelt's African trip. Dodge once again opened up his checkbook and underwrote the $1,500 needed to keep the naturalist in the field for six months.

The prospect for getting substantial assistance from the Brazilian authorities moved closer to reality on July 3, when Roosevelt conferred for three hours in his *Outlook* office with José Alves de Lima, private secretary to the Brazilian foreign minister, Dr. Lauro Müller, who was then making an official visit to the United States. De Lima, owlish-looking with a sleek gray pompadour and rounded glasses, was a publicity-minded diplomat. He regarded Roosevelt as a true friend of Brazil, especially after T. R. as president had raised the American legation at Rio de Janeiro to embassy status. In 1912 de Lima had befriended Kermit Roosevelt on his arrival in Brazil. When Kermit hinted that his father might some-day visit that country, de Lima broke the news prematurely in an article in Rio's leading newspaper and lobbied his government to receive the former president "with full honors and with every possible distinction," even though he was now a private citizen. The invitations from the Rio Historical and Geographical Society had soon followed.[18]

Having succeeded this far, de Lima was primed to smooth out any questions Roosevelt might have about a state visit. When T. R. questioned whether yellow fever, the great curse of the tropics, had been conquered in Brazil, de Lima asked him to read the obituaries in the Rio papers when he got there, to see how thoroughly the disease had been stamped out. T. R. wanted to know what his reception would be like. De Lima flashed a diplomat's smile and answered, "President Roosevelt, we have more interest in your visit to Brazil than you have."[19]

Thus assured, Roosevelt called in a stenographer and sat on the edge of his desk, dictating a letter to be handed to Foreign Minister

Müller, outlining his needs. Around the first of December 1913, after completing his lectures, he intended to make his way north through the interior of South America, "especially with the purpose of seeing the great Amazonian Valley of Brazil." He asked that no advance notice be given of his plans, to avoid unwelcome hangers-on. His expedition would travel light. "I hope to have but little baggage. I will have a trunk meet me at Manáos with my civilized clothes."

He repeated the concern he had expressed to Zahm about getting "full information" on the overland march between the Paraguay and Tapajós rivers, where canoes were to be gathered to await the travelers.

For the descent of the Tapajós, Roosevelt asked for an interpreter to act as headman over the paddlers and to make arrangements for food and camping places en route. On reaching Manáos, he wanted a steam launch on hand and a guide to take his party up the Rio Negro to the sources of the Orinoco, from which point the Venezuelan government would take over.

De Lima recognized the public-relations value of having an American ex-president draw the world's attention to the little-known heart of the biggest nation in South America. Without waiting to consult his government, he offered the services of Colonel Rondon, Brazil's most experienced explorer, as a guide. A military engineer, Rondon was currently engaged in constructing a telegraph line across central Brazil. As soon as Foreign Minister Müller returned to Rio, orders would be sent to Rondon to prepare for Roosevelt's trip.[20]

The willingness of the Brazilians to provide such an escort lessened Roosevelt's worry about getting lost in the wilderness. "I quite agree with you that it looks as if we were going to have a first-class time," he wrote Zahm after seeing de Lima. If Zahm would be able to get the two motorboats he had spoken of, "it really will make our trip a delightful holiday . . . [with] just the right amount of adventure."[21]

By agreement with Zahm, no word was to be given out to the newspapers on their plans. "I do not want to talk about it in advance," T. R. explained in a letter to Arthur Lee, just before leaving for Arizona. It was, after all, "rather an ambitious trip for a stout, elderly, retired politician, who is no longer in good condition, and I may not be able to make it." He would be gone until the following May, and the only thing he regretted was "being so long away from Mrs. Roosevelt." But the burden of leading a failing third-party movement was cause for him to stay away longer. "I shall be glad to be out of the country for one reason," he told Lee, "and that is the Progressive Party. The temptation is for the

Progressives always to lie down on me, and in the unlikely event of the party continuing to exist, it has got to learn to walk alone."[22]

On July 7, 1913, the Colonel and his two youngest boys, Quentin, fifteen years old, and Archie, nineteen, boarded the Pennsylvania Limited for Chicago and the start of a cougar hunt and camping trip along the North Rim of the Grand Canyon. In Arizona, they were joined by one of T. R.'s cousins, Nicholas Roosevelt, who had arranged for the pack train and equipment. This was to be Roosevelt's last big North American hunting trip, and he took a personal interest in the preparations to make sure it went off without a hitch. During the preceding months, he had sent Nicholas instructions on choosing guides, the number of horses and mules needed, and the type of food and cooking utensils to purchase. No such attention to details would characterize the South American trip, which Roosevelt seemed to think would be far less physically demanding.

This was also to be T. R.'s last summer of vigorous health. Four months from turning fifty-five, he still had, in Nicholas Roosevelt's words, "the energy of a boy," although his weight—well over two hundred pounds—proved a handicap in keeping up with his sons as they scrambled down the steep canyon trails. Over the years, a too-heavy appetite had caused his waistline to grow bigger than his chest, which Nicholas described as "powerful and well-developed." Although T. R. was only five feet, eight inches tall, his heavy frame, bull-like neck, and powerful jaws suggested a big man, an impression heightened by his habit of throwing his shoulders back when he stood.[23] Adding to the quality of virility was a full head of stiff, light brown hair, parted high on the left and trimmed short. To look at Roosevelt's hair, a friend remarked, "one could understand how Delilah thought she would sap Samson's strength by shearing him."[24]

Roosevelt's seemingly inexhaustible strength was based more on willpower than on physical ruggedness. Like an athlete who had pushed himself to the limit, his body bore the scars of a lifetime of punishing activity. From Cuba he had brought back a touch of malaria, which erupted at intervals. By his middle forties, rheumatism had made him complain about feeling like "a worn-out and crippled old man!" unable to exercise as much as he liked.[25] The sight in his left eye was gone, the result of being struck during a White House boxing accident. Only his immediate family and close friends knew about it. Without his glasses, he could not recognize his own children at ten feet.[26] In public, T. R.

carefully hid the fact that he was depending on one eye, just as he kept secret a leg injury suffered in 1902, when his presidential carriage was rammed by a streetcar in Pittsfield, Massachusetts. Roosevelt had been thrown thirty feet from the impact, and a Secret Service agent riding with him had been killed. "I have never gotten over the effects of the trolley-car accident," he confided to Kermit in 1908. The doctors "had to cut down to the shin bone. The shock permanently damaged the bone, and if anything happens there is always a chance of trouble which would be serious."[27]

The task of working out an itinerary stretching through five South American nations now fell to Father Zahm. Armed with letters of introduction from Theodore Roosevelt, the white-haired priest became a familiar figure in the cool marble reception halls along Washington's Embassy Row. A bidding war soon developed among the various Latin American diplomats, each anxious to show off his country to the former American president. Zahm was not hesitant in asking them for favors. Perhaps thinking of his own health, he suggested that the Argentine government detail an army physician to accompany the expedition into the wilderness. The Brazilians, through their ambassador, Senhor da Gama, were baldly asked to provide "for the transportation of our boats, equipment, and scientific corps[!] from Cuyaba, or, if need be, from Corumbá, to [Santarem] on the Tapajós." In addition, Zahm requested "two or three pilots who are familiar with the Tapajós" and "one or two engineers to take charge of" the motorboats he was ordering. "I have assured the Colonel that your Government would leave nothing undone to help him make his journey through your great country with ease, comfort and dispatch."[28]

On a blisteringly hot day in early July, George K. Cherrie was relaxing under the shade of an apple tree on his Rocky Dell Farm, in southern Vermont, nursing a broken left arm and fractured wrist, the result of a bad fall, when one of his boys came running down from the house, waving a "New York" letter in his hand. It was from Frank Chapman at the American Museum of Natural History. Would Cherrie be interested in joining Theodore Roosevelt and a Catholic priest named Father Zahm on an expedition to South America in October? Besides trapping birds and mammals for the museum, Chapman went on, he would be in charge of the party's equipment and operate a motorboat on the rivers.[29]

One of Cherrie's sons, ten-year-old Hubert, recalled sixty-two years later the great excitement the family felt at "the prospect of 'G. K.' traveling with a man as famous as Mr. Roosevelt."[30] His father did not need much coaxing, although he had some momentary qualms about "camping with royalty."[31] "The trip with Colonel Roosevelt, as outlined by you, sounds good to me!" he wrote Chapman on July 16. He agreed to do all the trapping work, but admitted, "I have never felt that I was as successful with small mammals as I have been with birds."[32] He worried about the boat-handling chores in another letter: "I have some knowledge of gasoline engines—but think I would like some points about managing a launch." It was arranged that he would meet with Roosevelt in New York in September, after the Colonel returned from Arizona.[33]

Modesty was George Cherrie's most appealing characteristic. A naturalist friend, Paul G. Howes, described the forty-eight-year-old Vermonter as "the friendliest, most congenial and unassuming of companions." Nearly six feet tall, with "fine curling mustachios" and good-humored brown eyes, Cherrie liked to refer to himself as a "maple sugar rancher"—a reminder that besides raising Friesian and Holstein dairy cattle at Rocky Dell Farm, he ran a small maple syrup business on the side.[34] Howes, who had accompanied Cherrie and Chapman to Colombia in the spring of 1913, recalled that it was "truly astonishing the way Cherrie could make friends with people, and get us accommodations on the floor of native huts, or bunks in roadside posadas." Astride a mule, wearing a battered blue yachting cap and speaking fluent Spanish in a distinctive baritone, Cherrie projected an official air that opened all doors. The younger men nicknamed him "Old Thousand Percent" for his "way with the ladies of any age," as well as for his collecting abilities.[35]

Cherrie had begun his career as a naturalist indoors as a curator for the National Museum of Costa Rica and the Chicago Field Museum. By 1897, tired of having "stuffed too many thousands of birds for other explorers," he decided to go after his own specimens in Venezuela, Trinidad, and French Guiana as a freelance collector.[36] During these years Cherrie "took life as it came." Besides contracting yellow fever and being bitten by piranha on a shoulder and arm, he often found himself caught up in local revolutions. At times, he ran guns for rebel chieftains, earning the favor of one of them when he named a new species of ant thrush after him. Cherrie made his share of enemies as well. Once, near the Peruvian border, he was ambushed by a shotgun-wielding convict. The blast laid open his right arm, shattering the bones and severing most of the tendons. Medical help was a "horror" of a hundred-mile trip on foot and by canoe, and he spent half a year in the hospital recovering.[37] Miraculously, the nerves leading to his trigger finger had been spared, so he was still able to shoot a rifle and manipulate a scalpel, but his hand trembled uncontrollably. Despite this handicap, Cherrie was proud of the fact that he could skin and preserve birds twice as fast as any of his colleagues.[38]

Roosevelt took an instant liking to Cherrie when he met him in early September, after returning from Arizona. "There is no man in the world whom I would sooner trust in a tight place," T. R. would later write of the naturalist, "and I have had him by me in several tight places."[39] The fact that Cherrie had so far spent twenty-two years collecting in South America confirmed him on the spot. After discussing their plans, Roosevelt had turned back to the papers on his desk. Cherrie sat off to one side and lingered for a moment. He remembered that Roosevelt had the reputation for being a teetotaler. "Colonel, I think you should know a little bit about me before we start on this journey into the wilderness . . . I think you should know that I occasionally drink." T. R. whirled around in his chair and asked him what he drank. That depended, Cherrie replied, on what was available. "How much do you drink?" asked Roosevelt. "All that I want." With that, T. R. leveled his forefinger at the naturalist and said, "Cherrie, just keep right on drinking!"[40]

Cherrie's doubts about being able to handle all the scientific work himself were soon eased when another naturalist was added to the expedition's roster. If the Brazilian government "should lend a hand," Frank Chapman had written Zahm on July 14, "it might be possible to send a second man whose expenses we would pay to Cuyaba." He suggested a young mammalogist, Leo E. Miller, who was currently on assignment in British Guiana. Subject to Roosevelt's approval, he could join the party when their steamer touched at Bridgetown, in the West Indies, en route to Brazil.[41]

At about this time, Zahm had begun to make arrangements for the camping equipment, food, and boats the expedition would require. One day in New York City, he stopped in at the Rogers Peet store on Broadway at 34th Street and fell into conversation with the head of the sporting goods department, Anthony Fiala. As Zahm outlined his requirements, Fiala became intensely interested and told the priest, "I would give anything to go with you." "Come along," Zahm replied breezily. "I am sure Colonel Roosevelt will be glad to have you as a member of the expedition."[42]

Fiala was quickly accepted by Roosevelt and put in charge of equipping the party, as well as serving as its official photographer. "A better man . . . could not have been found for our purposes," recalled Father Zahm. A former Arctic explorer and skilled cameraman, Fiala had made two unsuccessful attempts to reach the North Pole earlier in the century. His second expedition in 1903 had gotten as far north as the eighty-second parallel, when their supply ship was crushed in the ice and sank with half of the provisions. Marooned for over two years, Fiala kept his men alive by a strict system of rationing and took the first motion pictures in the Arctic. When a relief ship finally found them in 1905, it brought news that Fiala's financial backer had died, thus ending his hopes for a third try at the Pole. He settled down in Brooklyn, married his fiancée, who had waited so long without word, and raised four children. In 1909 he organized the first sporting goods department at Rogers Peet, offering "everything from tents to frying pans."[43] He was forty-four years old in 1913, tall and angular, with close-cropped hair just beginning to gray at the temples. Facing middle age and still hungry for fame, Fiala found the chance to accompany Theodore Roosevelt to South America irresistible.

Acting under Zahm's instructions that "you are to have entire charge of equipment and of photographic work,"[44] Fiala proceeded to outfit the expedition using his Arctic experience and Zahm's suggestions. Rogers Peet Company disgorged a small warehouse of camping gear, which Fiala obtained at a 15 percent discount. Fifty thousand feet of motion-picture film was purchased to make a cinematic record of the expedition's progress. For surveying and mapping, Fiala provided compasses, a ship's chronometer for accurate time-keeping, a sextant for working out positions, and a sketching board with a wrist strap to keep it from being lost if a canoe tipped over.[45]

Providing a three-month food supply for the wilderness journey proved the biggest expense. Fiala had Austin, Nichols & Co., importers and wholesale grocers, prepare ninety watertight tin containers, each holding a day's rations for five men. Much of it consisted of canned meats and sausages, baked beans, and dehydrated fruits and vegetables, but there were also such luxuries as celery salt and Major Grey's chutney. To avoid monotony, Fiala arranged the food in seven different variations and numbered the outside of each lacquered container from one to seven to indicate which day of the week it was to be opened. Putting the daily bread ration in each can brought the weight to twenty-seven pounds—still light enough to float. The cans were then packed in wooden crates, with airtight empty tin cans inside to further guarantee floatability.[46] A youthful employee of the grocers, Thomas F. McCarthy, recalled later that "it was a very expensive packing."[47]

As additional insurance against starvation, Fiala ordered seventy-five U.S. Army emergency rations to be packed for the party. This food later proved to be of vital importance. His attention to detail was such that he sent Roosevelt samples of five different teas and asked him to choose his preference.[48]

All told, Fiala spent close to $4,000 (the equivalent of $40,000 today) outfitting the five-man party. The costs were split between Roosevelt and Father Zahm. As with his previous South American journeys, Zahm's traveling expenses were paid for by his close friend, the millionaire Catholic industrialist Charles M. Schwab.

Boats now had to be purchased to transport this mountain of equipment up the Paraguay River and beyond. Soon after he was hired, Fiala had ordered two Canadian freight canoes, canvas covered on a cedar frame, each capable of carrying a ton of cargo. By August, after prolonged negotiations, Father Zahm had signed a contract with the Rift Climbing Boat Company of Athens, Pennsylvania, for two of their steel-hulled motorboats, whose light draft and protected propeller (housed in a tunnel-like enclosure at the stern) were adapted to running in shallow streams. On August 16 Zahm asked the boat company's president, George S. Curtiss, to make further improvements:

> We did not speak of these last named things, but I trust, in view of the fact that our trip is going to be historic, you will wish to have the glory of fitting your craft from stem to stern without additional cost. It will be the best advertisement your Rift Climber will ever receive & I am confident you will see it in the same light as I do.[49]

No thought seems to have been given to how these eight-hundred-pound monsters, named *Edith* and *Notre Dame*, were to be transported over the mountains from the Paraguay River to the head of the Tapajós.

While Zahm was haggling over the Rift Climber boats, the Colonel's secretary, Frank Harper, was investigating an alternative. So far, T. R. had taken little interest in the details of equipage, but he let it be known that he wanted a "16 footer" for navigating the rivers in South America. Harper had dutifully made contact with the Mullins Company of Boston, builders of wooden dory boats. Writing to Zahm in mid-August, Harper quoted "the Mullins people" as having assured him that there was not a better type of boat to be found. "[They] are very enthusiastic about having this chance to supply these boats," which, Harper noted, were "equipped with air-tight compartments like lifeboats. They positively cannot sink." They also were cheaper. Was it possible, Harper asked Zahm, to cancel the Rift Climber order?[50]

"The price of the motorboat we shall use is quite secondary to safety and lightness of draft," Zahm replied the next day. He claimed to know South American rivers firsthand. The Mullins boats were heavier, and their propellers were completely unprotected, leaving them vulnerable in the shallow reaches of the Paraguay and Tapajós, where, he warned, "a breakdown would be fatal." Zahm suggested that Fiala be sent to Boston to inspect the Mullins boats before a decision was made and advised Harper not to bring the Colonel—then still hunting in Arizona—into the dispute. "All right about the boats," Harper conceded a few days later, knowing when he was outmaneuvered. "Whatever you and Mr. Fiala decide goes. I did not want you to let slip a fine opportunity with the Mullins people if the boats were suitable to your purposes."[51]

In the midst of this battle of the motorboats came a disturbing letter from Caspar Whitney, editor of *Outdoor World and Recreation*. Whitney, an old hand at exploring South American rivers, had learned from Frank Chapman of the expedition's plans. "Why attempt to use a motor boat?" Whitney asked Zahm. "I have always found that the simpler your equipment, etc., the better you get along. A motor boat would be strange to everybody who handled it, and if it turned over in the rapids, or a hole was stoved in . . . you would be up a tree; whereas with canoes, there you are."[52]

As September began, the Colonel had to turn down offers to speak at Progressive rallies in order to prepare for what he termed "my last trip of the kind."[53] To help pay for it, he would continue in his role as contributing editor for *The Outlook* by reporting on South American life and politics during the two-month lecture tour. *Scribner's Magazine* offered him $15,000 to write six to eight articles on the expedition's journey into the interior, with a $5,000 advance. Photographs taken and developed on the spot by various members of the party would enliven the Colonel's manuscripts. *Scribner's* editor Robert Bridges forwarded 150 sheets of carbon paper and a supply of blue, cloth-lined mailing envelopes for his use. Later, the magazine pieces were to be incorporated into a book to be published by Charles Scribner's Sons, who offered Roosevelt a generous 20 percent royalty.[54]

There were half a dozen speeches to write. In them, the Colonel would propound his Progressive Party philosophy, defend his presidential actions in building the Panama Canal, and interpret the Monroe Doctrine for a Latin audience. This last topic would prove to be the most controversial of all. Ever since 1824, when President James Monroe had declared the New World off-limits to further European colonization, South Americans had nervously viewed the Doctrine as a screen for North American domination of the hemisphere. In 1913 the Woodrow Wilson Administration had increased the tension between North and South by getting embroiled in an attempt to set up a stable government in revolution-torn Mexico. During the summer, talk of an imminent U.S. invasion of its neighbor seemed real enough to make Roosevelt consider canceling his trip, since he didn't want to be absent in the event of war. A lawyer friend, Lemuel Quigg, suggested he stay away from foreign policy subjects while visiting South America and predicted he would have "the damndest time explaining the Monroe Doctrine that any man ever had since Socrates undertook his [own] defense."[55]

The speeches, as written, were all submitted to the respective ambassadors for approval, which eliminated the possibility that Roosevelt would make any serious diplomatic blunder. Whether his words would have any useful effect seemed doubtful to him at the time. "As I speak in English, and nobody will understand it, the trip seems really pointless," he mused in a letter to Arthur Lee, "but our South American friends seem anxious that I should go."[56]

Roosevelt took the same casual attitude in making his personal preparations for the wilderness part of the journey. There was none of the intensive studying that had preceded his year in Africa. He was content to take with him only a handful of books about South America, including some natural histories of Panama and Colombia, places he would not be visiting. Nor did he consider it necessary to consult experienced explorers about the route he intended to take. He relied instead on Zahm's cheery advice and his own belief that nothing would happen to him. "I think we shall get through all right," he wrote confidently to Senator Lodge in late September, "and while it is of course no especial feat to perform, still it will be interesting . . ."

Lodge, like many of Roosevelt's friends, felt far less sanguine: "I hate to think of your going away on such a long expedition without a talk with you before you go. The trip you are considering seems to me much more serious than it appears to you."[57]

The Colonel's family was also worried. During the summer, Edith

Roosevelt had been kept in the dark regarding the details of her husband's plans to explore the South American interior. "I can but hope that the wild part of his trip is being more systematically arranged than is apparent," she confessed to Kermit. "Archie is a good deal troubled and I wish I could send him to look after Father, yet is not possible to take him away from college this winter. He really understands taking care of Father & tho' father & Sister [T. R.'s eldest daughter, Alice] distinctly feel that troops of negroes will be waiting, ready & competent to serve, the rest of us can't see it that way."[58]

Despite her misgivings, Edith did not try to stop her husband from going. She had sensed a deeper reason than his wanting to get away from the Progressive Party. "Father needs more scope," she explained to her daughter Ethel, "and since he can't be President must go away from home to have it."[59]

To this "best of wives and mothers" T. R. had grown even closer after 1912, when, with the children gone off married or to school, Sagamore Hill had become a lonelier place. "Mother and I have dear evenings together," he had written to Ethel in the spring of 1913, "but I wish I played cards and was more of a companion to her."[60] They had known each other since childhood and had married in 1886, two years after T. R.'s first wife, Alice Lee, had died tragically in childbirth. Quiet and reserved, with wavy chestnut hair and classical features, Edith Roosevelt was the perfect counterbalance to her impulsive, mercurial husband. "She personified order, duty and discipline," young Nicholas Roosevelt recalled.[61] Intensely private, Edith refused to give interviews and tried unsuccessfully to shield her family from public scrutiny. In her detached, analytical way, she was a shrewder judge of character than T. R., whose warmhearted, open nature tended to believe the best in people. He liked to joke that he was "the oldest and worst of her children!"[62] and that he lived under a form of domestic tyranny. At the dinner table, when his talk became too exuberant, she had only to call out, "Theodore!" and he would instantly grow meek and exclaim, "Why, Edie, I was only —."[63]

Although she had not fully recovered from a 1911 horse-riding accident in which she had been thrown to the pavement, Edith decided to accompany T. R. for the first two months of the South American tour, at least as far as Chile. She asked her young niece, Margaret Roosevelt, to be her traveling companion.

Two last-minute additions were made to the staff of the expedition as September ended. Frank Harper would come along to take the Colonel's dictation while touring the South American capitals and also help the

naturalists in the field. A short, slender man with a puckish grin, Harper
was ambitious in a well-mannered British way, unflappable under pressure, and a high-speed typist—"the best," he liked to boast.[64] So rapid
was his rise from penniless immigrant to T. R.'s right-hand man, that a
friend had remarked in 1909 that "it merely remains for you to marry
Miss Ethel Roosevelt, to become Mayor of New York, and subsequently
to succeed William H. Taft."[65]

While in New York, Zahm had been approached by a young, pipe-
smoking Swiss native, Jacob Sigg, who had heard about the expedition
and offered his services. Trained as a U.S. Army cook and practical
nurse, Sigg had also knocked around the world, sailed on square riggers,
mined for gold in the Andes, and run steam locomotives in Canada.
Besides speaking Spanish and Portuguese, he could pull teeth, amputate
a crushed finger, and operate a motorboat. Zahm had him write out a
contract on the spot, agreeing on $30 a month to work for Zahm "in
capacity of Valet, Cook, Nurse or Handyman any time occasion arises
and to be willing and Obeydient [sic] at all times during the trip."[66]

On Tuesday morning, September 30, the *New York Times* broke the
story that had so far been the best-kept secret of the summer:

ROOSEVELT SAILS SATURDAY
Heads Exploring Expedition of Amazon

For the next four days, Zahm and Fiala resorted to "the constant
use of the telephone and telegraph" to get the supplies and equipment
delivered to the dock in Brooklyn by the October 4 sailing date.[67]
Austin, Nichols & Co. worked around the clock to finish packing Fiala's
ninety food containers. The Rift Climber boats, on which Zahm had
expended so much energy, were temporarily lost between Pennsylvania
and New York City, and only arrived at the last moment to be loaded.

That same evening, the Progressive Party held a farewell dinner
for their departing chief. Some 2,350 Bull Moose supporters paid $3 a
head for admittance to the glass-roofed Garden of the Dance, on top of
the New York Theatre in Manhattan. Hundreds more had to be turned
away at the door or shunted noisily off into side rooms. Feeding such a
huge crowd would have delayed the speeches until after midnight had
toastmaster Gifford Pinchot not ordered the waiters out halfway
through serving and gotten the program under way. As each speaker
began, there were singsong cries of "Teddy! We want Teddy!" When it

came Roosevelt's turn to speak, the crowd stamped, cheered, and waved dinner napkins over their heads. "The Colonel has had many a great ovation," the *Times* reporter present noted, "but never so boisterous and hearty as this one."[68]

In a rousing speech, repeatedly interrupted by whistles and cheers, Roosevelt predicted great things for the party and denied rumors that he was secretly negotiating with the Republicans for the presidential nomination in 1916. He vowed to return in the spring from South America and "devote myself with whatever of strength I have to working with you for the success of the Progressive Party . . . I am with you for this cause, to fight to the end."[69]

His followers believed him heart and soul and made the glass roof of the dance hall rattle with their roar of approval. But many reporters came away curiously unconvinced: If Roosevelt was so devoted to the Bull Moose movement, why would he leave it rudderless by going away to South America for so many months?[70]

NOTES

1. Chapman, *Autobiography*, p. 215; Zahm, *South America's Southland*, p. 9. **2.** Chapman, Introduction to *Brazilian Wild.*, p. xiii. **3.** T. R. to J. A. Zahm, 6-10-13, *PPS.* **4.** Chapman, Introduction to *Brazilian Wild.*, p. xii. **5.** T. R. to Rómulo Sebastian Naón, 6-16-13, *Letters*, Vol. 7, #5855, pp. 731–32. **6.** *New York Times*, 6-13-13. **7.** T. R. to Ambassador da Gama, 6-19-13, *PPS.* **8.** T. R. to J. A. Zahm, 6-10-13, *PPS.* **9.** Carroll, "Mind in Action," *The Ave Maria*, (5-18-46), chapter XI, p. 623. **10.** T. R. to J. A. Zahm, 6-30-13, *PPS.* **11.** T. R. to Kermit Roosevelt, 6-23-13, *Letters*, Vol. 7, #5857, p. 733. **12.** Chapman, Introduction to *Brazilian Wild.*, p. ix. **13.** Frank M. Chapman to Henry Fairfield Osborn, 6-24-13, *AMNH.* **14.** Naumburg, Elsie M.B., "The Birds of Matto Grosso," *Bulletin of the American Museum of Natural History*, p. 3. **15.** Henry Fairfield Osborn to T. R., 6-25-13, *PPS.* **16.** Hellman, *Bankers, Bones*, p. 23. **17.** Frank M. Chapman to Leo E. Miller, 10-3-13, *AMHN; Forty-Fifth Annual Report of Trustees for 1913*, American Museum of Natural History, p. 29. **18.** de Lima, "Reminiscences of Roosevelt." **19.** Ibid. **20.** Ibid. **21.** T. R. to J. A. Zahm, 7-7-13, *JAZP.* **22.** T. R. to Arthur Hamilton Lee, 7-7-13, *Letters*, Vol. 7, #5863, p. 741. **23.** Roosevelt, Nicholas, *T. R., The Man*, pp. 13, 117. **24.** White, "Theodore Roosevelt," *T. R., A Profile*, p. 18. **25.** Wagenknecht, *Seven Worlds*, p. 28. **26.** T. R. to Henry Lewis Stimson, 6-23-08, *Letters*, Vol. 7, #5863, p. 741. **27.** Roosevelt, Kermit, *Happy Hunting Grounds*, p. 21. **28.** J. A. Zahm to "Your Excellency" (probably Ambassador da Gama), 1975, 9-25-13, *JAZP.* **29.** Cherrie, *Dark Trails*, p. 247. **30.** Cherrie, Hubert B., reply to author's questionnaire. **31.** Chapman, *Autobiography*, p. 214. **32.** George K. Cherrie to Frank M. Chapman, 7-16-13, *AMNH.* **33.** George K. Cherrie to Frank M. Chapman, 8-14-13, *AMNH.* **34.** Howes, *Photographer in the Rain-Forests*, p. 142. **35.** Howes, "Field Days with Chapman," *Explorers Journal.* **36.** Article on George K. Cherrie, *Des Moines Sunday Register Magazine*, 1-16-27. **37.** Cherrie, *Dark Trails*, p. 121. **38.** Letter to author from Paul G. Howes, 12-12-75. **39.** T. R. to Anthony Fiala, 7-8-15, *AMNH.* **40.** Cherrie, *Dark Trails*, pp. 248-49. **41.** Frank M. Chapman to J. A. Zahm, 7-14-13, *JAZP.* **42.** Zahm,

South America's Southland, pp. 11–12. **43.** Unnamed New York newspaper, 5-22-13. **44.** J. A. Zahm to Anthony Fiala, 9-5-13, *CAZA.* **45.** Invoices from Rogers Peet Co. and Austin, Nichols & Co., 9-13 & 10-13, *JAZP.* **46.** Fiala, Appendix to *Brazilian Wild.,* pp. 378–80. **47.** Letter to author from Thomas F. McCarthy, 7-14-76. **48.** Anthony Fiala to T. R., 9-5-13, *PPS.* **49.** J. A. Zahm to George Curtiss, 8-16-13, *JAZP.* **50.** Carroll, "Mind in Action," *The Ave Maria* (5-25-46), chapter XI cont., pp. 653–54. **51.** Ibid., p. 654. **52.** Ibid., p. 655. **53.** T. R. to Arthur Hamilton Lee, 9-2-13, *PPS.* **54.** Robert Bridges to T. R., 7-3-13, *SCRIB.* **55.** Lemuel Quigg to T. R., 9-24-13, *PPS.* **56.** T. R. to Arthur Hamilton Lee, 9-2-13, *PPS.* **57.** T. R. to Henry Cabot Lodge, 9-17-13, from Lodge, *Selections,* Vol. II; Ibid., Henry Cabot Lodge to T. R., 9-22-12. **58.** Edith K. Roosevelt to Kermit Roosevelt, 9-14-13, *KRP.* **59.** Edith K. Roosevelt to Ethel Roosevelt Derby (summer 1913), *TRC.* **60.** Hagedorn, *Roosevelt Family,* p. 333. **61.** Roosevelt, Nicholas, *T. R., the Man,* p. 20. **62.** Ibid., p. 23. **63.** Hagedorn, *Roosevelt Family,* p. 194. **64.** Harper, Troman, reply to author's questionnaire. **65.** W. Allard to Frank Harper, 6-9-09, courtesy Troman Harper. **66.** Carroll, "Mind in Action," *The Ave Maria* (5-25-46), chapter XI cont., p. 656. **67.** Zahm, *South America's Southland,* p. 14. **68.** *New York Times,* 10-4-13. **69.** *New York Times,* 10-4-13. **70.** "The Progressing Colonel," *North American Review,* Nov. 1913, pp. 597-99.

IV
A Feat Worth Doing

Four years after leaving the White House, T. R. could still command a large turnout when he made a public appearance, but the crowds filling Pier 8 on the Brooklyn waterfront this Saturday morning, October 4, 1913, showed none of the frenzied excitement that had surrounded his departure for Africa in 1909. On board the Lamport and Holt liner *Vandyck*, the ship's band played a lively selection of ragtime and Latin American dance music for the passengers lining the railings. Below, on the dock, a contingent of Progressives had brought its own brass band and chanted patriotic tunes while waiting for a last glimpse of the party's leader. Among the Colonel's family and friends on hand to see him off were Ted, Jr., and Ethel, Frank Chapman of the American Museum, and the ambassadors of the three South American countries where Roosevelt was to speak.[1]

Mixing unnoticed in the crowds were agents of the William J. Burns Detective Agency, hired by Roosevelt's family to protect him until he sailed. Less than a year had passed since the assassination attempt on T. R. in Milwaukee.[2]

At 11:40 A.M. the Colonel arrived accompanied by Edith and Margaret Roosevelt. They were preceded by two other automobiles loaded down with luggage and cans of motion-picture film. T. R. wore a gray business suit, a buff-colored soft hat, and a carnation in his lapel. An early morning session with a hotel barber had left his hair shaved quite close at the sides. As he stepped from the car, the dockhands started up a cheer for him. One strong-lunged longshoreman got a wave of the hat and a broad smile when he boomed, "Good boy, Teddy, shoot 'em in the eye."[3]

With the tide in, the *Vandyck* rode high above the pier, causing a delay in boarding while crew members adjusted the steeply pitched gangplank. As he mounted it, the Colonel reached for the rope railings and joked, "This is where I commence my mountaineering." On the inboard side, white-whiskered Captain Anthony Cadogan held out a hand to help him, but Roosevelt was too quick for him, "swinging in sure-footed fashion" to the deck and turning to help the ladies behind him. After posing briefly for the photographers, he pushed through crowds of admirers to his stateroom on B deck. There, as friends and relations milled around him, he sorted through the pile of cables and telegrams that had arrived, including one that asked for his help in locating two Americans who had disappeared in the Brazilian jungle.[4]

Leaving Edith and Margaret in the cabin to visit with family members, T. R. stepped across the narrow passageway into a reception room to face the newspapermen. He looked older, stouter, and somewhat subdued—"not the same strenuous Roosevelt of 1909," noted the *New York Tribune* correspondent. But he answered their questions in his usual "rapid-fire manner," saying that he was going down to South America to get into "fighting trim" in order to take an active part in the upcoming 1914 congressional and state elections. Returning on deck, he obligingly walked up and down for the newsreel cameras and then requested the photographers not to annoy him while he talked to his friends.[5]

The other members of the expedition were now arriving on board. Frank Harper had spent the morning painfully saying good-bye to his young wife, Dora, who was expecting their first child. While he was away in South America, she would stay with her Canadian family. To take his mind off leaving her, Harper busied himself arranging the Roosevelts' luggage.[6] For Anthony Fiala, this sailing day undoubtedly brought back memories of his own expeditions to the Arctic a dozen years earlier. As his four young children scampered around the deck of the steamer, Fiala explained to reporters how well equipped the Colonel's party would be; he had prepared for a six-month journey in the wilderness.[7] Father Zahm, with his passion for privacy, retreated to his cabin to avoid the press. A few days earlier, in an effort to keep his fellow priests at Notre Dame guessing, he had given out a playfully false report to the New York papers that his duties at Holy Cross Academy had prevented him from accompanying Roosevelt on the trip. Later, en route to Brazil, Zahm would write to his brother, Albert, "I presume the curiosity of some people is now near the bursting point."[8]

Literally the last man on board was George Cherrie, who had decided to so some last-minute shopping in Manhattan and misjudged the time. The "all ashore" gong had already sounded when a racing taxi screeched to a halt on the dock, and the expedition's senior naturalist bounded up the gangplank with a suitcase in each hand.[9]

As the *Vandyck* steamed southward, the Colonel found himself enjoying the sea voyage more than he had expected. "I think he feels like Christian in Pilgrim's Progress when the burden fell from his back," Edith wrote her sister-in-law, Anna. "In this case it was not made of sins but of the Progressive Party." She was happy to hear him laughing at the deck games "as I haven't heard him laugh for years."[10]

Shipboard life soon fell into a comfortable routine. Mornings, after breakfasting in their sitting room, Edith would retire to bed again in a dressing gown and cap to read or sew. The Colonel would take a few books with him to the relative privacy of the ship's bridge or else dictate articles for *The Outlook* to Harper. At noon, Edith and Margaret would go to luncheon, leaving T. R. to "virtuously walk up and down on the deck" for an hour, out of concern for his waistline. The truth was, he explained in a letter to his daughter Ethel, "I eat so much breakfast and dinner that I *could* not go to lunch." In the afternoons, Edith sat on deck, veiled to protect her complexion from the sun, and listened to Margaret reading aloud from Sir James Bryce's new book on South America, while the Colonel napped in a nearby deck chair.[11]

Roosevelt's ability to make friends anywhere was amply demonstrated on the way to South America. During a pause at one of the nightly ship's dances, he stepped out onto the floor and launched into an energetic version of the sailor's hornpipe, drawing applause and cries of "Encore" from his fellow passengers. In a tug of war between the bachelors and married men, Cherrie recalled that T. R.'s enthusiasm and 220 pounds at the end of the rope were "the deciding factors." A businessman told Cherrie that he had traveled ten thousand miles to vote against Roosevelt in 1912, but after meeting him on board and being charmed by him, was "ready now to travel twenty thousand miles to vote for him!"[12]

The chief topic of conversation at sea was always the expedition. Cherrie recorded that conferences "on the journey ahead of us" were held every day, during which the members of the party became better acquainted with one another and attempted to bring their individual plans into unison.[13] Roosevelt took a prominent part in the scientific discussions at these meetings. Father Zahm recalled being "often amazed by his broad and exact knowledge . . . of the fauna of the countries we were about to visit [and] also of the political and social histories of their people as well."[14]

There was no secret as to how Roosevelt had acquired this breadth of knowledge. Zahm noted that while on the steamer, T. R. would "devour two or three books a day, each on a different subject."[15] He also liked to cross-examine experts in their fields, storing away the information in a near-photographic memory. Cherrie learned to be "exceedingly careful" in answering Roosevelt's questions on zoological matters, "because he was apt to come back at me [later] and say 'Here, Cherrie, back [then] you told me this and that, and now you are telling me another story about the same thing.'"[16]

What the expedition could actually achieve remained a question in Roosevelt's mind. He was reluctant "to prophesy about results," he wrote his daughter-in-law Eleanor, "but if we have fairly good luck we ought to achieve a certain substantial amount of accomplishment. It is not exploration work exactly, but it is pioneer work, and the collections of birds and mammals ought to be of some value."[17]

On October 10 the *Vandyck* made its first port of call at Barbados, in the British West Indies, and dropped anchor off Bridgetown. While the Roosevelts were entertained at luncheon by the colony's governor, Harper, Fiala, and Cherrie went ashore to purchase supplies and a camping outfit for Harper. Afterward they rented a car "at this expedition's expense" and toured the island. When they got back to the ship, they found Leo E. Miller, who would serve as the mammalogist, waiting for them. At 4:00 that afternoon, the *Vandyck* departed Bridgetown; the next landfall would be Bahia, on Brazil's eastern coast.[18]

In spite of his youth, at twenty-six Leo Miller had already made a name for himself as a field naturalist with the American Museum.[19] Broad shouldered, with clean-cut good looks and neatly combed dark hair, Miller radiated self-confidence, energy, and an irreverent sense of humor. He fit in so well with Fiala and Cherrie that T. R. referred to them as his "Three Buccaneers."[20]

As an Indiana farm boy, Miller had avidly followed newspaper accounts of Roosevelt's 1909 African safari and daydreamed of going on such a trip. In 1911 Frank Chapman hired him as a novice assistant on an expedition to Colombia. Miller's agility at scaling cliff faces to get at rare birds' nests impressed Chapman, who had him stay on another eighteen months before sending him to southern Venezuela, some fifteen hundred miles up the Orinoco, to collect around the shadowy Mount Duida region. "Of this country, and of the people and animal life inhabiting its virgin wilds," Miller was to write, "very little was known."[21] It was said to be the setting for Sir Arthur Conan Doyle's best-selling novel *The Lost World*. Miller found no dinosaurs lurking there, but instead a rich diversity of birds and animals, which he had only begun to investigate when, in June 1913, the museum sent him into British Guiana. Two months later, at an isolated gold-mining camp on the Essequibo River, he received a message from Frank Chapman that he had been chosen as the second naturalist for Theodore Roosevelt's expedition.

A long shipboard conference was held on October 11, the day after Miller's arrival, in which he spoke of his work around Mount Duida and the collecting potential in southern Venezuela. From the start, Father Zahm had intended that the expedition go into Venezuela, despite Roosevelt's doubts of having enough time to do so. Zahm now found an unexpected ally in Miller, and the young naturalist's enthusiastic description of the Duida region apparently made an impression on Roosevelt. That evening, at T. R.'s request, Miller asked Chapman to send down an English translation of the early-nineteenth-century German explorer-scientist von Humboldt's travels in Venezuela, as well as good-quality maps of the upper Orinoco and its tributaries. By the time the *Vandyck* docked at Rio de Janeiro two weeks later, Miller could report to his museum superior that "Col. Roosevelt is greatly interested in Duida and it seems as if we shall all work there for some time, and then come down the Orinoco, and go to Caracas overland . . . working along the way . . . Our trip promises to be a great thing, and we are eager to start work."[22]

The arrival of the *Vandyck* in Brazilian waters on October 14 prompted Roosevelt to cable Foreign Minister Lauro Müller to alert officials in the interior of the expedition's requirements. "We shall need ox teams or whatever methods of transportation are necessary in order to get our boats across the divide," wrote T. R. Besides the two steel motorboats, they were bringing eight other boats and five tons of supplies and equipment. Fiala and Sigg would arrive at Corumbá in mid-November with the baggage train. Roosevelt would join them there with his naturalists a month later, and the expedition would then march overland to the headwaters of the Tapajós. "It is necessary that everything should be in readiness on the Arinos when I come," he informed Müller, "so that we will be able to make the trip in the time allotted me." In addition to Colonel Rondon's services, Roosevelt wanted "a patrone, a first-class man, with whatever assistants in the way of other pilots he deems wise," and thirty paddlers to take the party down the Tapajós. Another headman and crew of paddlers would be needed for the journey up the Rio Negro to the Venezuelan frontier.

In return for this help, Roosevelt offered to produce a sketch map of the Tapajós and make whatever studies of the Rio Negro the Brazilian government desired. "My hope is to make this trip not only an interesting and valuable one from the scientific standpoint, but of real benefit to Brazil, in calling attention to the ease and rapidity with which the vast territory can be traversed, and also to the phenomenal opportunities for development which she offers."[23]

To accomplish all this, it was essential that the expedition separate upon reaching Rio de Janeiro. The Roosevelts and Father Zahm would begin the speaking tour in the Brazilian capital, while Fiala, Sigg, and the two naturalists would proceed to Buenos Aires on the steamer and start immediately up the Paraguay. To clear the way for them, T. R. cabled a request to the U.S. minister to Argentina, John W. Garrett, asking that the Argentine customs officials treat the party's "elaborate outfit" as scientific in purpose and waive duty and inspection. Roosevelt was also anxious that not a word get out as to their destination. "I do not wish it advertised where we are going," he cautioned Garrett, "as I want particularly to avoid the chance of outsiders trying to follow me."[24]

The magnitude of their enterprise brought out Roosevelt's habitual caution. "Just what we can do of course remains to be seen," he admitted to Frank Chapman on October 15. "We have a difficult trip ahead of us. We will have all kinds of troubles, with waterfalls, showers, shallows, fevers, insects and the like, and we may not be able to get beyond the Amazon Valley . . . When we will get home I have no idea."[25]

On October 18 the *Vandyck* arrived at Bahia (now Salvador), Brazil's oldest city, and the first stop of what was to be an exhausting two-month round of official receptions and banquets honoring Roosevelt in South America. Reminiscent of T. R.'s European tour, the crowds on the dock surged forward with such enthusiasm that the visitors had to fight their way to the line of waiting government automobiles. Houses and public buildings along the route to the governor's palace were decked in bunting and intertwined American and Brazilian flags. "Everybody seemed to be in the street, or at the windows of the houses lining the thoroughfares through which we passed," noted Father Zahm.[26] At a champagne breakfast in the Municipal Hall, attended by the city's elite, T. R. spoke of the United States and Brazil as the future peace-keepers of the Western Hemisphere and predicted, as a result, that the twentieth century would be an era of universal peace.

As a prophet, Roosevelt was more hopeful than accurate, but his words created a controversy in Argentina, long a military and economic rival of Brazil's. *La Prensa*, the leading Buenos Aires daily, fumed editorially over this unintended insult to national honor. If Roosevelt did not take steps to retract his statement in Bahia, "he had better stop in Brazil." Argentina, it declared, "does not intend to play second fiddle to Brazil in the Pan-American concert."[27]

Bahia was also the scene of Kermit Roosevelt's reunion with his parents, after more than a year's absence. The Colonel did not think his tall, wiry second son, who had recently turned twenty-four, looked as healthy "as I should like to see him," and suspected malaria. On the positive side, Kermit seemed happy about having switched from railroad construction to bridge building. It was a job that required taking chances, which appealed to him. As traveling superintendent for the Anglo-Brazilian Iron Company, he earned $2,500 a year, already spoke Portuguese well, and talked about his work as if it had a future.[28] That future had nearly ended a few months earlier, when Kermit had dared to ride a ninety-foot-long steel beam as it was hoisted across a river gorge. Halfway over, the derrick had slipped, sending the beam and Kermit down some forty feet to the rocks and water below. Miraculously, he had survived the fall. Aside from two broken ribs, several broken teeth, and a partially dislocated knee, he was, in T. R.'s words, "practically all right again."[29]

Able to support himself, Kermit had recently proposed to Belle Willard, the daughter of the U.S. ambassador to Spain, and was waiting for her answer. He had not expected to join the expedition until Edith, full of foreboding, took him aside during the festivities at Bahia and told him that he "must go to manage the trip and take care of father," whose right leg, injured in the 1902 carriage accident, needed constant attention. The Colonel did not want his son to delay his wedding plans, but Kermit did not wish to be married in his father's absence and argued convincingly that "this semi-exploration business was exactly in his line."[30] Kermit's employer agreed to grant him a leave of absence, believing the experience would increase his value to the firm. "He thinks quite possibly that he will be able to make much of this trip with Father," Edith wrote Ethel afterward, "which of course lifts a great weight from me."[31]

Two days after leaving Bahia, the *Vandyck* arrived outside Rio de Janeiro, in 1913 the capital of Brazil and the second largest city in South America. Rough seas kept the steamer from entering Guanabara Bay until dawn the following morning, October 21. The Roosevelt family contingent and Father Zahm got up at 5:30 A.M. to watch the approach to the city and gaze around at the most scenic natural anchorage in the world. "The harbor is more beautiful than can be imagined," Edith wrote home to Ethel after arriving. "The white houses of the city run up the narrow valleys between the thickly wooded mountains. The shores are of soft sand of the finest & choicest sort."[32]

The weather was unusually cool, breaking a thirty-year record for what was normally the beginning of the hot months in the Southern Hemisphere. Cherrie complained in his diary about not having brought warmer clothing, noting that "my Fall suit is all but too light."[33]

There was nothing chilly about Roosevelt's reception in the Brazilian capital. It had, according to Father Zahm, "all the wild enthusiasm of a national holiday,"[34] beginning with a shipboard welcome from the American ambassador, Edwin V. Morgan, and his staff, and officials from the Rio Historical and Geographical Society. The Colonel was then escorted by boat with the rest of his party to the waterfront Plaza of November 15, a site that commemorated the bloodless 1889 revolution that transformed Brazil from a monarchy to a republic. Surrounded by waving crowds and blaring bands, Roosevelt reviewed an honor guard, bared his head as the two national anthems were played, and shook hands with cabinet ministers and the Rio diplomatic corps. A ladies committee presented Edith and Margaret with large bouquets of roses. After the ceremonies, the Colonel was driven to see the city's port works and principal boulevards, before rejoining Edith and the others in the guest quarters of the Guanabara Palace, a former royal residence of the daughter of Brazil's last Emperor, Dom Pedro II.[35]

"Just arrived here," Father Zahm jotted on a postcard to his brother, "after a most delightful voyage and am now in the palace of the Princess Isabella, the guest of the government . . . Everyone most cordial."[36] Within the white marble walls of the palace, the travelers found themselves overwhelmed by luxury: high-ceilinged rooms filled with tall mirrors, ornate gilt furniture, and thousands of exotic flowers and orchids. From the table in the immense dining room, one could look down a palm-lined avenue to the sparkling blue waters of Guanabara Bay half a mile distant, where the last royal occupant had been driven daily for her bath in the surf. The government also provided limousines, military escorts, and free use of a cable station.[37]

The Colonel barely had time to catch his breath before Ambassador Morgan dragged him off to pay a courtesy call to Brazilian president Hermes da Fonseca. The two statesmen conversed in French, a language T. R. spoke "without tense or gender" but with enough energy to be understood.[38] Da Fonseca wished him success in his travels.

From the presidential palace, Roosevelt moved on to another palace—the Itamaraty, the official residence of the minister of foreign affairs, Dr. Lauro Müller. Behind closed doors, in the plush velvet and leather comfort of Müller's office, the plans of the expedition were greatly changed.

In his 1912 book on South America, the British historian Sir James Bryce had observed that Brazilian politicians spent their time "absorbed in personal intrigues" instead of grappling with the enormous problems facing their country.[39] He would have made an exception in Lauro Müller's case. Distinguished looking in his swallowtail coat, trim mustache, and imperial, Müller was an enlightened public servant, formerly a military engineer and provincial governor before being named foreign minister in 1912. He had a charming, refined manner that reminded T. R. of his own secretary of state, John Hay. A fervent nationalist, Müller was keenly interested in developing Brazil's vast, unexplored interior and encouraging immigration to a country that, in 1910, numbered only twenty-two million inhabitants. He believed Roosevelt's expedition could be useful in spreading knowledge about Brazil to the outside world, and he took a personal interest in its plans. On the day the *Vandyck* sailed from New York—October 4—Müller had alerted Colonel Rondon, who was then deep in the interior, to make arrangements to meet the American ex-president's party on the upper Paraguay in December. A few weeks later, Müller telegraphed Rondon that Roosevelt planned to descend the Rio Tapajós and thence to the Amazon.

To a seasoned explorer like Rondon, going down a river as well known as the Tapajós seemed a pretty tame affair that "could not offer anything new to an Expedition whose object was to unravel the unknown aspects of our wilds." Accordingly, he instructed his clerks in Rio to draw up four possible itineraries for "our illustrious guest" when he arrived at the Brazilian capital.[40] Two of these routes followed Zahm's original plan to descend the Tapajós to its junction with the Amazon; another called for the party to voyage down the less well-traveled Rio Gy-Paraná and then down the Madeira to Manáos. The most interesting of the four choices involved the descent of a river whose headwaters Rondon had come upon in 1909, while surveying a route for the telegraph line in an unexplored part of Mato Grosso state, far to the west of the Tapajós. No one knew where this river went or how long it might prove to be. For these reasons, Rondon had given it the provisional name of Rio da Dúvida—the River of Doubt.

If Roosevelt was willing to accompany Rondon down this unknown river, Müller was prepared to offer the full cooperation of the Brazilian government, including the services of a botanist, a geologist, an army physician, and six officers trained in geographical exploration from Rondon's Telegraph Commission. Once explored, the river would be renamed in Roosevelt's honor. "Now, we will be delighted to have you do it," Müller concluded, "but of course, you must understand we cannot tell you anything of what will happen and there may be some surprises not necessarily pleasant."[41]

With hardly a second thought, T. R. "jumped at the chance,"[42] recognizing it as a matchless opportunity to contribute "to the geographical knowledge of one of the least-known parts of South America."[43] He did not dwell on the added risks he would be taking, probably because of the promised support of an experienced explorer like Rondon. It was "a feat worth doing, and I accepted," he explained afterward in a letter to Frank Chapman.[44]

Roosevelt's eagerness to descend the River of Doubt was matched by that of his companions, including Father Zahm, the oldest and least healthy member of the party. T. R. told them they were under no obligation to accompany Kermit and him on what was "a new and probably slightly more hazardous plan" than the Tapajós route would have been. But to a man "they all eagerly stated that they wished to go," Roosevelt proudly informed Chapman, adding that "if any two of them were more eager than the others, I should say it was Cherrie and Miller. They both believe that they may get collections for the museum which will be really worth while."[45]

Edith Roosevelt learned of T. R.'s decision after the fact and could only wonder what her adventurous but out-of-shape husband would face in going down an unexplored tropical river. Outwardly stoic, as she had been when he went to Africa, Edith let her unease slip through in a letter to Ethel: "Thank Heaven Kermit's going for though I don't think he is well, at least he is young and strong & Father Zahm already has constant falls by the wayside."[46]

The abrupt change in plans marked the end of Zahm's importance to the expedition he had organized. Besides his uncertain health (he tired easily), his reputation as an expert on tropical matters was found to be less than absolute. The Brazilian officials told Roosevelt that it would be "practically impossible" to transport Zahm's beloved pair of steel motorboats overland from the Paraguay River. They would have to be shipped around by sea to Manáos, to be used if the Rio Negro trip was actually made, or else given away. "Father Zahm is a perfect trump," T. R. wrote Frank Chapman, "but he knows nothing of any of the country which we have planned to go through, and in practice can give us no help or advice as to methods of traveling and what we will or will not be actually able to accomplish."[47]

Now there was no time to lose. The Colonel, about to plunge into seven weeks of speech making and receptions, said good-bye to the working members of his expedition, who sailed for Buenos Aires on October 22 on the *Vandyck*. Cherrie and Miller would leave the Argentine capital by train for Asunción, the capital of Paraguay, and begin collecting birds and mammals there. Fiala and Sigg would follow more slowly by boat up the Paraguay River, bringing the equipment. Roosevelt promised to rejoin them all at Corumbá around the middle of December. Before leaving Rio, Cherrie had been handed a letter signed by the Brazilian minister of the interior, who requested that all military and civil authorities assist the Roosevelt party and facilitate their work. Cherrie, wise to the ways of petty officialdom, noted in his diary: "Just how much it may mean to us of course remains to be seen."[48]

Word of what Roosevelt had decided to do fell like a bombshell at the American Museum of Natural History in New York. Henry Fairfield Osborn dropped his cool patrician manner when he learned that T. R. planned to go into an unexplored part of central Brazil where the climate alone was known to be deadly. Thoroughly alarmed, Osborn threatened to withdraw the museum's sponsorship of the expedition if Roosevelt insisted on going "to this particular region" and vowed to "not even assume part of the responsibility for what might happen in case he did not return alive."[49]

From Brazil, Roosevelt sent a stirring message back to Frank Chapman: "Tell Osborn I have already lived and enjoyed as much of life as any nine other men I know; I have had my full share, and if it is necessary for me to leave my bones in South America, I am quite ready to do so."[50]

NOTES

1. *New York Evening Post, New York Times, New York Tribune, New York Sun, New York World*, 10-5-13. 2. Ervin Smith to T. R., 5-23-14, *PPS*. 3. *New York Sun*, 10-5-13. 4. *New York Times, New York Sun*, 10-5-13. 5. *New York Times, New York Tribune, Scranton (Pa.) Times*, 10-15-13. 6. Harper, Troman, reply to author's questionnaire. 7. *New York Times*, 10-5-13. 8. *New York Evening Post*, 9-29-13; J. A. Zahm to Albert Zahm, 10-17-13, *CAZA* 9. Cherrie, *Diary*, 10-11-13. 10. Edith Roosevelt to Anna Roosevelt Cowles, 10-15-13, *TRC*. 11. T. R. to Ethel Roosevelt Derby, 10-8-13, *TRC*. 12. Cherrie, *Dark Trails*, pp. 255–57. 13. Cherrie, *Diary*, 10-11-13. 14. Zahm, *South America's Southland*, p. 19. 15. Ibid., p. 16. 16. Cherrie, *T. R., Memorial Meeting*, pp. 23–24. 17. T. R. to Eleanor Alexander Roosevelt (Mrs. T. R., Jr.) 10-8-13, *KRP*. 18. Cherrie, *Diary*, 10-11-13. 19. Frank M. Chapman to F. A. Lucas, 5-5-14, *AMNH*. 20. Fiala, *T. R., Memorial Meeting*, p. 14. 21. Miller, *In the Wilds*, p. 142. 22. Leo E. Miller to Frank M. Chapman, 10-11-13 & 10-24-13, *AMNH*. 23. T. R. to Lauro Severiano Müller, 10-14-13, *PPS*. 24. T. R. to John W. Garrett, 10-14-13, *PPS*. 25. T. R. to Frank M. Chapman, 10-15-13, quoted in Chapman's Introduction to *Brazilian Wild.*, p. x. 26. Zahm, *South America's Southland*, pp. 32–33. 27. *Buenos Aires Herald*, editorial, 10-24-13. 28. T. R. to Anna Roosevelt Cowles, 11-11-13, *TRC*. 29. Kermit Roosevelt to Belle Willard, 12-4-13, *KRP;* T. R., *Brazilian Wild.*, p. 4. 30. Kermit Roosevelt to Belle Willard, 11-14-13(?), *KRP;* T. R. to Eleanor Alexander Roosevelt, 12-10-13, *KRP*. 31. Edith K. Roosevelt to Ethel Roosevelt Derby, 10-25-13, *TRC*. 32. Ibid. 33. Cherrie, *Diary*, 10-24-13. 34. Zahm, *South America's Southland*, p. 53. 35. *New York World*, 10-23-13; *Buenos Aires Herald*, 3-8-14; *New York Times*, 10-22-13. 36. Carroll, "Mind in Action," *The Ave Maria*, (6-1-46), chapter XI, p. 687. 37. Wiley, *T. R.'s America* (Leo Miller quoted), p. 304. 38. Wagenknecht, *Seven Worlds*, p. 34. 39. Bryce, *South America*, p. 419. 40. Rondon, *Lectures*, p. 11. 41. *New York Times*, 5-27-14. 42. T. R., *The Geographical Journal*, p. 90. 43. T. R. *Brazilian Wild.*, p. 9. 44. T. R. to Frank M. Chapman, 11-4-13, *Letters*, Vol. 7, #5876, p. 754. 45. Ibid. 46. Edith K. Roosevelt to Ethel Roosevelt Derby, 10-25-13, *TRC*. 47. T. R. to Frank M. Chapman, 11-4-13, *Letters*, Vol. 7, #5876, p. 755. 48. Cherrie, *Diary*, 10-23-13. 49. Osborn, "T. R., Naturalist," *Natural History Magazine*. 50. Osborn, *Impressions* (chapter on T. R.), p. 179.

V

A Continuous Ovation

No one was more surprised than Theodore Roosevelt by the enthusiasm with which he was received during his seven-week goodwill tour of southern South America. Less than a year after his own countrymen had rejected his program of reform, he found himself hailed by a new audience as a political sage and inspiring leader. From Brazil to Argentina and across the Andes to Chile, his progress would amount to, in Father Zahm's grand phrase, "a continuous ovation as well as a triumphal march."[1] Diplomatically, the trip would prove to be a success, warming for a time the strained relations between the United States and the larger of its Latin neighbors. South Americans who expected to find T. R. brandishing the "Big Stick" were instead charmed by his friendliness and approachability. By the time the tour was over, Roosevelt had left behind more friends and admirers in South America than any visitor before or since.[2]

The Brazilians lived up to their reputation for lavish hospitality, reportedly spending $80,000 to entertain Roosevelt.[3] When Foreign Minister Müller handed him the official program of events, T. R. began to pick it apart, objecting to the excessive entertainment. He wanted to avoid the limelight and be left to his own resources. "When I was in Washington," Müller politely reminded him, "I followed every letter of the program presented to me by [Secretary of State] Mr. Bryan." "You should not have done that," Roosevelt replied with a laugh, and gave in.[4]

For a week Rio de Janeiro played host to the North American visitors. While Edith rested in bed in the mornings and wrote letters, the Colonel

met with delegations of schoolchildren, attended a session of the
Brazilian parliament, and inspected the military and naval institutes. In
the afternoons, there were excursions on the bay, drives up the forested
slopes of Tijuca Mountain and lofty Corcovado, and a nerve-tingling ride
in a swaying cable car to the top of Sugar Loaf Mountain, 1,383 feet above
the harbor. The evenings were filled with diplomatic receptions and
twelve-course banquets that dragged on past midnight. Edith's delight
in the French-style food was not shared by her husband, for whom
haute cuisine remained a mystery. "I could never tell what I was eating,"
he said to Leo Miller later. "They gave you something that looked like
a pork chop and when you cut into it green peas rolled out." He wanted
something recognizable, like "a mutton chop with a tail on it."[5]

Father Zahm came in for his share of entertainment as well. "The
fact that I have been traveling with T. R. has in no wise detracted from
the welcome accorded to myself personally," he assured his brother,
Albert Zahm.[6] The Rio Catholic Club hosted a reception for him,
attended by clergy and laity alike. His theological works were praised,
and he heard himself eulogized as "the greatest scientist and [Catholic]
apologist of the age."[7]

The glamour of Rio was not enough to make this a pleasant trip
for Edith Roosevelt. Living out of a trunk and coping with full dress
receptions were bad enough, but Lizzie, the maid she had brought
along, turned out to be forgetful and disorganized. "She can't see or
remember & would lose her head if it were not tightly attached to her
body," Edith complained to Ethel. The fact that her daughter was
undergoing a difficult pregnancy at home in her absence made Edith
feel guilty for having gone to South America. "I am all the time wishing
to be home & help you & caring little for all this except as my being
here affects Father & Kermit."[8]

On October 24, at the Government University, Roosevelt delivered
his first major address, "American Internationalism," in which he dis-
cussed the Monroe Doctrine without referring to it by name. The *New
York Times* dispatch reported that "All the notable men of Rio de Janeiro,"
from the president of the Republic on down, were there, many with
their wives.[9]

Speaking in his high-pitched, emphatic way, in which words seemed
to explode in syllables as they left his mouth, the Colonel told his audience that he regarded Brazil, Argentina, and Chile as standing on the
same level as the United States when it came to international dealings.

He called for hemispheric unity and joint action in keeping foreign intruders out of the New World. Looking ahead, T. R. predicted that North and South America would draw closer together and their trade increase with the opening of the Panama Canal. The most important event of the twentieth century, he believed, would be the "the growth and development of South America."[10]

On his last day in the Brazilian capital, a Sunday, Roosevelt saved a few hours for a bird walk in the cool, green forests of Petropolis, a mountain town thirty miles outside of Rio where the diplomats summered. It was springtime in South America, and the trees echoed with bird calls, many of which he was unable to identify. The loveliest of all came from "a shy woodland thrush" of dark coloring, which he observed made its nest in the thick undergrowth but sang high above in the branches. He wrote of it:

> At a great distance we could hear the ringing, musical, bell-like note, long-drawn and of piercing sweetness . . . at first I thought this was the song, but when it was possible to approach the singer I found these far-sounding notes were scattered through a continuous song of great melody. I never listened to one that impressed me more.[11]

At 8:00 that evening, Roosevelt boarded the night train for São Paulo, the next stop on the tour. "If kindness could kill," he told the large crowd gathered at the station, he could hardly have survived their hospitality. "I will remember the Brazilian people all my life."[12] Lauro Müller, who was standing nearby, thought of the expedition Roosevelt was soon to lead as he said good-bye to Father Zahm. "Your party is going to discover the interior of Brazil for us Brazilians."[13]

They reached São Paulo, picturesque with its lumbering ox carts and fields of green coffee plants, the next day, October 27. The Colonel celebrated his fifty-fifth birthday by visiting a snake farm where antitoxin serums were manufactured from the venom of live snakes. Here he made the acquaintance of "the most interesting serpent in the world," a five-foot-long, black-skinned mussurama, a nonpoisonous species that lived entirely on other snakes. In a laboratory experiment, Roosevelt let the friendly, seemingly harmless mussurama slither around in his arms and even poke its head into the armpit of his coat, before releasing it. Then he watched as it wiggled over to devour a deadly fer-de-lance at the other end of the table.[14]

The evening's official banquet got off to a lively start with a "Roosevelt March" performed by an orchestra. The menu covers featured a pasted-down oval photograph of T. R. in stern profile, set between the crossed flags of the United States and Brazil. Afterward, at the Municipal Theater, a polite but perhaps skeptical audience of coffee barons and industrialists heard Roosevelt sermonize on virtue in a speech titled "Character and Civilization."

The following day Kermit and his father made a sentimental side trip on a branch line to Pirajú, an agricultural town where Kermit had once supervised a bridge-building project. After inspecting the steel bridge his son had helped build, Roosevelt insisted on being taken to the hotel where Kermit had stayed and to the room he had slept in.[15] During the brief visit, the town's mayor managed to scare up a late-morning Brazilian breakfast for the distinguished visitors—"lunch we in our country would probably call it," noted T. R., who never did get used to Brazilian eating habits. Here he tried his first spoonful of *canja*, a savory native soup made from chicken and flaked rice, so tasty that he vowed to steal the recipe and bring it home to Sagamore Hill.[16]

South of São Paulo lay the three most southerly of the Brazilian states: Paraná, Santa Catharina, and Rio Grande do Sul. The government in Rio was eager to have Roosevelt see—and write about—this thinly populated region, only recently opened up by railroad service.

The Brazil Railway Company, Kermit's former employer, assembled a special train, complete with a dining car and an observation car. Accompanying Roosevelt as far as the border with Uruguay were railway officials, including Hugh M. Taylor, the line's general manager. Taylor had once held a strong dislike for Roosevelt's liberal political views. A long-distance but loyal subscriber to *The Outlook*, he had twice urged the magazine's publisher "to get rid of [T. R.] and give us the paper free from [his] influence." Taylor had undergone a change of heart after Kermit came down to work for him in 1912. Having met the son, Taylor wrote apologetically to T. R. in June 1913, "I know now the Father is a far more manly man than I ever thought and that I did you an injustice."[17]

Life on a crowded train did not cramp Roosevelt's remarkable capacity for work. "I always believe in going hard at everything," he once explained to Kermit.[18] By using every minute of his time, he was able to churn out practically an article a day for *The Outlook*. Coming in from visiting a cattle ranch or an immigrant settlement, he would immediately begin dictating to Harper, oblivious to the babble of conversations in English and Portuguese that filled the swaying car. He would work steadily until the train began slowing down again for another stop and someone called out, "You are wanted on the platform, Colonel." Roosevelt would jump to his feet, often in midsentence, and go out to meet the crowd gathered at the station. When the speeches and handshaking were finished, he would return to his seat and pick up where he left off, even as the band was still playing. Soon afterward, Harper could be heard pounding away at his Remington typewriter at a corner table.[19]

In his *Outlook* articles, Roosevelt paid tribute to the Polish, German, and Italian immigrants who were building new towns along the railway line. Meeting these bearded farmers, with their mud-caked boots and log houses, reminded him of his own younger days in the American West and how quickly a frontier filled up. "This whole country, from São Paulo to the Uruguayan line, is already developing with much rapidity, and offers a great chance for further development," he wrote with enthusiasm. There was "any amount of fine land" to be had by settlers of the right sort, and the climate was "well adapted for the white race."[20] A Brazilian businessman told Father Zahm, "Roosevelt is worth to our country a million dollars a day for every day he remains within our boundaries."[21]

For Edith, the heat and cinders and "a very jiggly road" made the railway journey south a nightmare of discomfort. She steeled herself to gracefully play the part of the Colonel's consort while all the time longing for a bathtub and privacy. Kermit's health continued to worry her. He had developed a painful abscess on his leg, which Edith had to dress in the bouncing coach. "Thank goodness it is all well now," she wrote in relief to Ethel on November 2, when the Brazilian tour came to an end. Her one consolation was that Margaret had turned into a resourceful traveler and was making up for the deficiencies of Lizzie, the scatterbrained maid.[22]

The tiny republic of Uruguay, squeezed in like a pebble between its giant neighbors, Brazil and Argentina, had not originally figured in the Colonel's speechmaking itinerary. An invitation came at the last minute, just as he was boarding the train at Rio de Janeiro for São Paulo. On November 3, at the border town of Rivera, his party was met by Uruguayan officials sent on a special train. Instead of soldiers standing at attention, a double line of schoolgirls dressed in white greeted the Colonel and Edith, throwing roses at their feet as they walked to the train. One of the young girls read a brief speech welcoming the American ex-president to Uruguay. Visibly moved, T. R. made a brief reply in English, thanking them.

A Uruguayan newspaperman who was present at the border meeting was struck by how Roosevelt looked close up. For one thing, he was not as tall as supposed, although strongly built. He carried his head high, suggesting pride, but his manners were extraordinarily simple, considering his rank. There was a lively, inquisitive quality to Roosevelt's blue-gray eyes, half hidden by the glint of his gold-rimmed pince-nez. His smile, dominated by a double row of glistening white teeth, was his most captivating feature. If this was the *real* Roosevelt, the reporter concluded, "it would be hard to find a face more clearly likeable and a person who with more ease subjugates and fascinates at first sight."[23]

Punctually at 9:00 the next morning, November 4, the express train bearing Theodore Roosevelt and party pulled into Montevideo's Central Station, where thousands of citizens were on hand for the one-day visit. As T. R. jumped down from his Pullman car, a group of mega-phone-wielding young men from the Y.M.C.A. greeted him with a touch of home—the Harvard Cheer, his alma mater's football yell. The official welcoming committee hurried through the necessary introductions and then steered the visitors past lines of mounted police to three waiting automobiles for the ride to the hotel. Before starting out, Roosevelt made it a point to shake hands with each of the chauffeurs, a characteristic act of courtesy.[24]

Arriving at the Hotel Oriental, Roosevelt pleaded for time to work on the evening's speech. An hour later, he emerged from his suite, and in the company of the American minister to Uruguay, Nicolay Grevstad, made a high-speed visit to El Cerro, the landmark hilltop across the harbor. According to legend, the first missionary to arrive had seen the five-hundred-foot-tall eminence from afar and cried, "Montem video!" ("I see a mountain!"), thus providing the city with its name. Unfortunately for the Colonel, the view on this day was obscured by mist. He had to satisfy himself with a hurried inspection of the old Spanish fort and lighthouse on the summit, before racing back to town at fifty miles an hour to be on time for a banquet hosted by the president of Uruguay.[25]

The luncheon at Government House was said to be the first social function President José Batlle y Ordóñez had agreed to hold since returning to office in 1911.[26] A stout, amiable figure with a drooping mustache and massive head, Ordóñez was a frugal chief executive, a socialist at heart, and perhaps the most truly democratic leader Roosevelt would meet in South America.

Now in his second term, Ordóñez had pressed for reforms practically identical to those of T. R.'s Progressive Party: the eight-hour workday, regulation of factory conditions, and a workmen's compensation law.[27] Finding a kindred spirit seated across from him, T. R. regretted not being able to speak Spanish. As Ordóñez did not speak English, the two had to resort to French. The linguistic barrier did not keep both men from carrying on an animated conversation. At one point, Roosevelt leaned over the flower-laden table and said to Ordóñez, "You and I belong to the same party."[28]

The Uruguayan leader chose the end of the luncheon to make a dramatic toast. Raising his glass in Roosevelt's direction, he praised him as "the defender of the Monroe Doctrine in the interests of the whole of [North and South] America."[29] This compliment forced T. R. to declare his position on the most provocative subject in Latin America at the time.

To many South Americans, the Monroe Doctrine was an outworn principle, a vestige of the time when the United States had been the only credible military power in the Western Hemisphere. That time had long since passed. By 1913, the three strongest democracies on the southern continent—Argentina, Brazil, and Chile—all possessed armies and navies capable of resisting European annexation of their lands. They resented the idea of being protected by "the great colossus of the north," and worried more about U.S. territorial ambitions than any other threat to their security.

Roosevelt's argument surprised them all. He denied that the Monroe Doctrine gave a one-sided advantage to the United States and argued that it was instead a framework for mutual defense. As soon as any nation in the hemisphere had achieved a sufficient amount of "orderly liberty" and "self respecting strength," it became a guarantor of the Doctrine.*

Foreign policy questions were absent from Roosevelt's lecture notes when he spoke that night at the Atheneum on "The Essential Virtues of a Democracy." Although the English-language *Montevideo Herald* called it "a striking and interesting address," it was actually a replay of the talk he had given at São Paulo, full of platitudes. His text was interpreted line for line into Spanish by an American Methodist

---

*"The visit has made for a better understanding here of American policy as regards Latin America," Minister Grevstad cabled the U.S. State Department a few days later.

pastor, which made for a long evening. Loud applause greeted the finish and Roosevelt's exit from the hall.[30]

At midnight, with another diplomatic triumph under his belt, Roosevelt boarded the cruiser *Uruguay* for the overnight passage across the wide estuary of the Rio de la Plata. Ahead lay Buenos Aires, capital of Argentina and the next phase of his South American tour.

Meanwhile, far from the champagne and caviar, the expedition's two naturalists had already begun collecting specimens for the American Museum of Natural History. On November 2, as the Colonel was traveling by train through southern Brazil, Miller and Cherrie departed from Buenos Aires on the newly opened Argentine Northwestern Railroad, bound for Asunción, Paraguay.[31]

They arrived two days later and were met by the American consul, Mr. Ferris, who arranged to get them gun permits from the police. The backwater capital had witnessed five revolutions in as many years, and the authorities were suspicious of armed strangers.[32] Housed temporarily in a nearly deserted hotel on the city's outskirts, Miller set out his traps and Cherrie roamed the nearby vacant lots with his shotgun. "Birds were not abundant and what there were, were wary," the latter noted in disappointment on November 7. That morning's hunt produced only seven birds. "I might . . . have added a few more specimens to what I had if the police had not interfeared [sic] and asked me not to shoot any more within city limits."[33]

There was better luck on the Rio Pilcomayo, some miles upriver from Asunción, on the fringe of a vast steaming wilderness of marshes, tall grass, and tree islands known as the Gran Chaco. For a week Cherrie and Miller worked and slept in a shed made of sheets of corrugated iron supported on logs and open on all sides. A toylike narrow-gauge railroad brought in a daily supply of food and jugs of fresh water. With the help of several Paraguayan naturalists, Cherrie and Miller caught a variety of birds, monkeys, weasels, and rodents. After being skinned, the carcasses of the larger mammals were thrown into the river, which swarmed with piranha. Miller recorded how ". . . instantly the ravenous hordes charged the spot and tore greedily at the bloody flesh; so great were their numbers that they threw one another out of the water in their mad struggles to reach the gory repast." Once, in a careless moment, Miller had a piece of his finger bitten off as he washed his hands in the river.[34]

Nothing in Cherrie's or Miller's previous tropical experiences had prepared them for the insect hordes of the Pilcomayo marshes. They would later report to Roosevelt that "never had they been so tortured" by mosquitoes, horseflies, and sandflies.[35] Cherrie wrapped a small towel around his head and neck and wore socks on his hands to keep from being bitten to death as he worked at his skinning table. As soon as the sun went down, the naturalists dove under the netting of their hammocks and sweated through the long night, the angry buzz of mosquitoes vibrating in their ears.[36] If a bare knee touched the netting during the night, the skin would redden from dozens of tiny bites.[37]

After five days of this living hell, word came that Fiala and Sigg had finally arrived by steamer at Asunción with the expedition's equipment. Returning there on November 17, Cherrie and Miller packed up the first crate of specimens for shipment back to New York—an impressive 150 birds and 50 mammals.[38]

"Considering the time we had at our disposal and the conditions under which we worked," Cherrie noted dryly in his diary, "I feel that the results were satisfactory." The next day, he and his three companions were steaming up the Paraguay River for Corumbá, where they would rendezvous with Roosevelt and Father Zahm sometime in December.[39]

Shortly after 8:00 A.M. on November 5, the cruiser *Uruguay* was intercepted by a flotilla of steamers and tugs, bright with flags and banners and packed with high-spirited members of the Argentine reception committee, headed by a group of American businessmen. With sirens hooting and whistles screaming, the escorts fell in behind the fast-moving warship. On its afterdeck, only Kermit Roosevelt could be seen standing by the rail with his cousin, Margaret. The brass band on the reception committee's boat struck up "The Star-Spangled Banner." As if on cue, a cabin door on the cruiser flung open, and out stepped Theodore Roosevelt, resplendent in frock coat and glossy top hat.

Roosevelt held his hat against his heart while the band played. Responding to cheers from the boats following behind, he started walking rapidly to the stern, where he stood with both arms raised over his head and teeth bared to show his delight at the music and the repeated American college football yells—first Harvard, then Yale, then Cornell—that were shouted over the water. He was soon joined by Edith and Father Zahm, who looked decidedly unpriestly in formal clothes and opera hat, with a binocular case hanging from his shoulder.[40]

On the cruiser's foredeck, sailors in dress whites held the salute during the playing of the American and Argentine national anthems.

As the martial tunes died away, the forward guns began methodically firing blank charges fifteen times in succession, then six times more, making a full twenty-one-gun salute due a visiting head of state—or, in this case, an ex-president of the United States. Far ahead, almost too distant to be heard, a squadron of Argentine warships returned the honorary salvos.

By 10:00 A.M., the *Uruguay* was making its way up the long, buoy-lined channel leading to the harbor of Buenos Aires. The warship slowly swung past the lighthouse guarding the entrance to the North Basin. As it did so, military bands on the wharf signaled the start of a wildly enthusiastic welcome by the largest city of South America. An enormous crowd—a quarter of a million people by Father Zahm's generous estimate—waited expectantly in the hot sun. Argentine Boy Scouts in short pants and stiff-brimmed hats handed out souvenir buttons bearing Roosevelt's picture and pamphlets printed in Spanish containing his biography. The large number of expatriate North Americans present made T. R.'s arrival something of a homecoming. Every known football cheer in North America was said to have been heard when he walked down the gangplank with his family.[41] Waiting at the bottom step was John W. Garrett, the U.S. minister to Argentina, along with other dignitaries. Once the dockside ceremonies were concluded, the visitors were driven to Garrett's legation residence, where Edith, for one, planned "to rest . . . for a week and try to get my clothes in some kind of order after all this travel."[42]

There was no rest for the Colonel at the American legation. Diplomatic friends and old Harvard classmates were waiting for him on the front steps. He waded into the impromptu reunion like a presidential candidate, recognizing familiar faces, tossing off jokes, and adding humorous details to shouted anecdotes. Over it all rang his laughter, deep-chested and spontaneous according to the *Buenos Aires Herald*, and "so good to hear."[43]

More proof of Roosevelt's appeal among the Argentines came later that afternoon when he returned with Minister Garrett from paying a courtesy call at the presidential palace. In the broad, tree-lined Plaza Mayo, the good-natured crowds threatened to engulf the former president's automobile. Delighted by the cheers and applause, Roosevelt repeatedly stood up and took off his hat, laughing uproariously whenever he saw something comical taking place in the demonstrations along the route. Flowers by the hundreds rained down on his open car, until the interior resembled a hothouse. At one point, a well-aimed bouquet of American

Beauty roses knocked his spectacles off. "I call that real good shooting," T. R. quipped as he readjusted his glasses and then quickly bowed with a grin to the young lady who had thrown the flowers.

Two blocks from the American legation, the motorcade slowed to a crawl as dozens of frenzied admirers clung to the door panels of Roosevelt's car and trotted alongside. Minister Garrett, riding in the car ahead, grew concerned at the slow progress and passed word to the chauffeurs to speed it up. When Roosevelt realized what was happening, he ordered his driver to slow down, worried that those chasing the car would succumb to the intense afternoon heat. One Argentine who spoke English overheard him and in gratitude began singing "For He's a Jolly Good Fellow." The refrain was immediately picked up by all the runners, whether they knew the words or not.[44]

On the day of T. R.'s arrival, the amusements page of the *Buenos Aires Herald* carried the following notice:

> *Colon*—The Management of the Municipal Theatre desires to announce that Mr. Theodore Roosevelt will give several lectures under the auspices of the Museo Social Argentino, the subject being "Democratic Ideals."[45]

This was in fact the title of Roosevelt's first address, which he gave two nights later in the gilded splendor of the Colon Theatre. It was a long speech, running to 109 small typewritten pages. On a stage built for grand opera, the Colonel spoke to a sold-out crowd of thirty-six hundred who came more perhaps to see him than to listen to him. He defended the Progressive philosophy and hammered away on the idea of judicial recall. The people should be able to decide what laws they want, T. R. asserted. He warned against judges becoming lawmakers, and cited the example of the New York Supreme Court striking down as unconstitutional a recently enacted Workmen's Compensation act. Edith Roosevelt, sitting in the balcony, supposed "one person out of about every hundred *may* have understood him."[46]

By this point, the hectic pace of the tour had begun to take its toll. "Father Zahm looks like a wreck of his former self," Edith reported to Ethel. "How he will get through the [wilderness] trip I can't picture to myself." She had similar doubts about Kermit. The abscess on his leg had healed, but he didn't look well, and she couldn't "make out whether it is the result of fever or what." Surprisingly, T. R. seemed to be thriving on the pressure. He seemed "perfectly well," Edith noted, "& scarcely sleeps & [likes] everything he does without any exception."[47]

The Argentine capital held no charms for Edith. "B.A. is a modern city," she pointed out to Ethel, "absolutely characterless—gay, clean, bright, lovely gardens, immense palaces, any amount of luxury—I never saw so many pretty women & fine clothes—I should hate to live here."[48]

The high point of Roosevelt's stay in Buenos Aires came on October 12, when he attended military maneuvers at Campo de Mayo, the big Argentine army training camp outside the capital. Drenching rains and high winds did nothing to lessen T. R.'s enthusiasm. Surrounded by a hundred staff officers, he was reported to be "as cheery as ever," taking the salute from infantry regiments that marched by singing patriotic songs. The bad weather did not prevent several primitive biplanes from circling overhead; one daring pilot buzzed the reviewing stand, causing everyone—including Roosevelt—to duck. Afterward, T. R. stood in the rain and chatted with those soldiers who spoke English, complimenting them on their spirit. At the officer's club, he presented his hosts with a bust of the American Civil War general Phil Sheridan—a gift of the United States Army officer corps. The sculptor was a then little-known artist named Gutzon Borglum, who thirty years later would carve Roosevelt's face in gigantic scale on a mountainside in South Dakota.[49]

Roosevelt gave his final speech in Buenos Aires that evening. The auditorium of the Colon Theatre was transformed into a huge dining room, level with the stage and decorated with evergreens, roses, and carnations. Besides those seated at the long rows of table, an estimated six thousand people had crammed into the aisles, galleries, and lobbies. By the custom of the day, only men were allowed on the main floor; their wives and daughters were restricted to the balconies.

The Colonel's entrance drew a standing ovation and cries of "Viva!" He made his way to the head of the stage, flanked by Dr. Frers of the Museo Social and Minister Garrett. "Mr. Roosevelt was one concrete smile," wrote the *Herald* reporter covering the night. The smile "seemed to be specially directed to every individual within its reach."[50]

Dr. Frers's soaring eulogy of Roosevelt dragged on for half an hour before he finally proposed a toast to "the Guest of the Evening." A children's choir in the galleries then sang the national anthem of Argentina, accompanied by the Municipal Orchestra. When it came time for Roosevelt to speak, a Latin admirer overcome with emotion grabbed him in a bear hug. It took a well-placed but friendly shove of T. R.'s fists to get free. A flash of the famous teeth brought the crowd to a roar.[51]

In "American Ideals," Roosevelt spoke of peace and brotherhood and his respect for Argentina's military might. He paid his audience the supreme compliment when he told them, "You are fit to champion your own Monroe Doctrine." This brought down the house and launched a shower of flowers from the balconies.[52] "I think I have been able under pressure to state the Monroe Doctrine in a way . . . so as to make it correspond exactly to the facts and to our national needs," a satisfied T. R. wrote Senator Lodge later.[53]

Kermit also had reason to be pleased at this time. On November 14, after returning from a horse ranch outside Buenos Aires with his mother and Margaret, he found a cable from Belle Willard, accepting his marriage proposal. "I had go to a big formal lunch, & a big formal dinner to-day, but I don't remember a word I said . . ." he wrote her in a daze of happiness. "I remember all I thought[,] for I was with you the whole time." Their wedding plans would have to be delayed until the following spring, as Kermit felt it was his duty to go on the expedition. "We have two good naturalists," he explained to his fiancée, "but the trip has not been well planned and I have been a good deal worried about father," the bad leg being the culprit. They expected to start into the interior by December 5, going by boat up the Paraguay, then by horseback across the high plains until they reached "a totally unexplored river," which either ran into the Amazon or ended in a lake somewhere. "Eventually," wrote Kermit, "we will come out on the Amazon & go to Manáos, the chief place on it; reaching there about the beginning of March."[54]

Pouring rain did not keep a large crowd of well-wishers from seeing Roosevelt and his entourage off from the Retiro Station on the morning of November 15. Ahead lay a six-day journey across Argentina, via the provincial capitals of Rosario, Tucumán, Córdoba, and Mendoza, before crossing the Andes into Chile. The American legation at Buenos Aires assigned its military attaché, Maj. James A. Shipton, as aide-de-camp to Roosevelt. A convivial, forty-six-year-old bachelor, Shipton left a detailed and humorous account of Roosevelt's progress across the Pampas, starting with a description of the "splendid special train" organized by the Argentine government.

There were eight cars in all, headed by the White Coach, the luxurious private car of the president of Argentina, which was reserved for the Colonel, Edith, and Margaret Roosevelt. The next coach in line, only slightly less ostentatious, held Father Zahm, Kermit, and Frank Harper. Behind them was a dining car, fragrant with roses and decorated with flags and paintings. This was followed by the kitchen car, whose chef Shipton thought turned out "the best food I have had in the Argentine." Several more coaches contained members of the Museo Social, railway officials, and newspaper reporters. A baggage car brought up the rear.

As the train clicked northward from Buenos Aires, Shipton learned that his primary duty was to act as "go-between" for Roosevelt and the Argentine Committee several cars back. All morning he scuttled back and forth from the White Coach, "finding out what [T. R.] wanted or did not want; who he would see or not see; when he would eat; whether he would step out at this or that station where crowds had assembled, etc, etc."

Just before 1:00, the train steamed into Rosario, the capital of Santa Fe province and the chief shipping port for Argentina's lucrative grain exports. The big event of the four-hour stopover was a waterfront cruise conducted by the chamber of commerce to show off six miles of stone wharves, grain elevators, and petroleum tanks. On the boat, according to Shipton, champagne was served every five minutes. Several times he had to interrupt T. R. from getting too engrossed in a scientific book and ask him to look at what the city fathers were pointing out. At the Stranger's Club, where tea was served, Shipton introduced Alfredo Benitz, an Argentine sportsman who had hunted big game in Africa. Roosevelt talked to him to the exclusion of everyone else and afterward thanked Shipton for letting him have a good time.[55]

Late in the afternoon the journey resumed. The next destination was Tucumán, five hundred miles away in the foothills of the Andes. Kermit spent the long hours in his coach drawing a map of the expedition's planned route, marked with rough dates for Belle's benefit. Earlier Edith had had another long talk with him on how to look after his father. "She's dreadfully worried about him," Kermit wrote Belle, "and there's nothing for me to do but go." For the first time, Kermit voiced his concern about Father Zahm's presence on the expedition. "There is an old priest going with us . . . I wish he weren't going for I'm afraid that he's going to get sick which makes complications, & things more difficult as far as father is concerned."[56]

Although he was the oldest member of the party, Zahm had no qualms about exploring an unknown river, telling his brother at one point to prepare their friends at Holy Cross Academy for "a few more 'thrills & jolts'" in the coming months, when the Colonel's *Scribner's* articles began appearing. He was pleased to be in T. R.'s company. "It would be impossible to have a more charming traveling companion . . ." he wrote Albert. "We are both most eager to begin the strickly [sic] scientific part of our trip"—putting on the map a river that was already being referred to as the Rio Téodoro.[57]

On November 16 they reached Tucumán, the sugar capital and birthplace of Argentina's independence from Spain. During the course of a long, humid, overcast day, the Colonel saw the historic shrines, then made a pilgrimage to Belgrano Park, the site of a pivotal battle against Spanish troops in 1812, where he laid a wreath at the victory monument. Shipton suggested he say a few words and compare the event to the battle of Bunker Hill. Afterward, someone else suggested Roosevelt shake hands with an elderly man standing nearby whose coat was covered in medals. T. R. greeted him exuberantly as a veteran of Argentina's bloody 1865 war with Paraguay. According to Shipton, this caused "much astonishment to the old man, and amusement to the bystanders, who knew him only as a member of the local labor union."[58]

That night Shipton escorted the Colonel and Edith—"looking lovely in evening dress"—to a banquet given by the provincial governor. It was a hastily arranged affair, without seat assignments, and everyone had to choose where to sit. Going in to dinner, the attaché noted how, in the absence of any instructions, T. R. "grabbed the best looking lady" in the room, not realizing she was the wife of the *ex*-governor. Seeing young Margaret Roosevelt standing alone in her street dress, Shipton gallantly offered his arm. Afterward, he rode back to the hotel with the Colonel and laughed with him as Edith imitated her husband's mangled French. The two men stayed up late talking Argentine politics.[59]

En route south to Córdoba on November 17, the Colonel stopped to visit several big sugar plantations. At San Pablo, he was escorted through the factory of Señor Nogués, then sat on a chair on a flat car for an open-air ride to a waterworks run by North American engineers. Nogués made T. R. an official landholder by presenting him with a deed for two and a half acres of mountaintop overlooking the sweltering cane fields. The ex-president took off his coat and planted a tree to commemorate the event.[60]

Evening brought a stop at Santa Ana, the biggest of the plantations. While Edith and Margaret stayed in the coach, the Colonel was met by "a fine young Frenchman," René Hileret, whose father had spent half a century building up a sugar empire.[61] Five thousand migrant workers

toiled here under the eyes of European overseers. Another Frenchman, Georges Clemenceau, had visited the Hileret plantation two years
earlier, in 1911, and had been appalled at the wretched conditions,
writing of "indescribable slums . . . dens rather than dwellings . . ." and
of children "moving about on all fours . . . scarcely distinguishable from
the little pigs which [were] grubbing in the rubbish-heaps."[62]

The factory was still operating at 9:00 P.M., and the Colonel's party
walked through the corrugated iron main building to watch the raw
cane come in one end and the various grades of sugar come out the
other. Unlike his workers, Hileret lived in princely style in a chateau,
surrounded by busts and statuary. Besides offering a late-hour dinner,
he gave the Colonel three of his best hunting dogs. As the party was
returning to the train, one of the factory workers, claiming to be an
American, appealed to Roosevelt for a ticket home. T. R. asked Shipton
and Kermit to investigate, but Hileret volunteered to take care of the
matter. "It looked like the fellow was a fake," noted Shipton, "so we
left it to Hileret, and started to Córdoba about 11 P.M."[63]

They reached the old colonial city of Córdoba the following afternoon and were met at the station by a big crowd and the Thirteenth
Infantry band. Edith and Margaret remained in seclusion on the train,
shades drawn, to the disappointment of the ladies committee on the
platform, who did not get, in Major Shipton's words, "so much as a
bow" from the window. The men in the Colonel's entourage were first
driven to the governor's palace and then to the three-hundred-year-old
University of Córdoba, where a formal reception took place. Bored by
the speeches, Shipton and Kermit sneaked outside to smoke cigarettes.
The inevitable banquet in the evening drew the leading families of the
city and the teaching staff of the university, which meant there was no
shortage of after-dinner speakers. It was midnight before the weary
travelers crawled back onto their train.[64]

The Argentine tour came to an end on November 19, at Mendoza,
in the far western wine country. After two days of tramping through
vineyards and visiting agricultural colleges, the Colonel departed for
Chile, minus Major Shipton, who would rejoin the party on its return.

"Wonderful day for crossing Andes," Edith jotted in her diary on
November 21, after the train had climbed the thirteen thousand-foot-
high Uspallata Pass.[65] Late in the evening they reached the Chilean
capital of Santiago, where, for the first time on his tour, Roosevelt
encountered hostile demonstrations. Several hundred Colombian and
Central American students from the university shouted "Viva Colombia!"

and "Down with the Yankee Imperialism" over the blare of band music, and then followed the Colonel's motorcade from the station to the city's Grand Hotel. Mounted police finally drove off the hecklers, who were said to have been whipped-up by weeks of anti-Roosevelt diatribes appearing in Colombian newspapers. The Chilean government apologized to the Colonel and quietly bought up and destroyed large quantities of Santiago newspapers that carried any mention of the disturbances.[66]

In Santiago, Roosevelt had one more occasion to defend the Monroe Doctrine, calling it "a living doctrine today as it ever was" and naming Chile as one of its co-guarantors. But the subject was becoming tiresome to many in the audience. A prominent Chilean asked an American journalist traveling with the Roosevelt party, "Why does he repeat here the speeches he made in the Argentine and Brazil?"[67]

From Valparaiso, on November 26, Edith and Margaret sailed for home via the Panama Canal. The Colonel and Kermit went out on a navy launch to see them off on the steamer *Orcoma*. "We're both feeling quiet and sad," Kermit wrote Belle that evening. Had it been a liner bound for Spain, he told her, he would have stayed on board.[68]

By now Roosevelt was eager to join the other members of the expedition on the upper Paraguay. He turned down an offer from his Santiago hosts to cruise to the tip of South America, deciding instead to travel south by train to Puerto Varas, in the Chilean lake district, and from there cross back into Argentina on horseback through one of the low passes in the Andes. After that there would be an automobile trip across the Patagonian Desert to the railhead at Neuquén, where a train would be waiting to take him back to Buenos Aires and then into Paraguay.

On the train ride south, a seventeen-year-old railroad steward, Eduardo Ibañez, had a chance to observe Roosevelt at close range. When not dictating to Harper or making a speech at one of the stops, T. R. spent much of his time sitting alone in the Presidential Car. The windows were all kept wide open, and he drifted at times from reading the book in his hands to watching the rolling farmland of central Chile flit by. Like many others, young Ibañez was surprised at the mildness of Roosevelt's expression, so different from the newspaper photographs. There was an abstract quality to his eyes, he remembered, "rather of a dreamer."[69]

On Saturday, November 29, the Colonel's train, blinds drawn down for privacy, pulled into Puerto Varas, a German settlement on the shores of Lake Llanquihue, where Major Shipton was waiting. Roosevelt admitted him to his car at once and proceeded to "tell all about the Chilean trip, then and there." The thumping beat of a marching band interrupted his monologue. After listening to a few welcoming speeches, T.R. and company marched down to the town's hotel, whose proprietor had laid on a huge breakfast, featuring Westphalian ham and Strasburg pâté, washed down with beer and wines.

At 10:00, they got away on a lake steamer, after having been followed to the landing by most of the town's population. The Colonel's party now numbered more than two dozen—besides the four North Americans, there was a fifteen-man Chilean committee that had tagged along since leaving Santiago, as well as Shipton's six-member Argentine delegation, which included a newsreel photographer. On the way across the lake, T. R. alternately chatted with Shipton, dictated to Harper, and admired the snow-clad volcanic peaks rising majestically above the shores of the lake.

Saddle horses were waiting for the party at the other side. Roosevelt, now dressed in hunting clothes, leggings, and a soft hat, led off at a gallop for the six-mile ride to the next one of four mountain lakes that had to be crossed. Only Shipton and Kermit were able to keep up with him. Father Zahm and an elderly member of the Argentine contingent made the trip more sedately in a creaking buckboard.

At Lake Esmeralda, aptly named for its ring of forest and emerald green water, the horses and wagon were led onto a barge tied behind the motorlaunch *Volcan*. Once under way, the Colonel hardly glanced at the scenery and locked himself up in the cabin to work on his *Outlook* article. Major Shipton stood guard outside the door to keep him from being interrupted. Tired from the brief horseback ride, Roosevelt nodded off to sleep in the middle of dictating. Harper sat quietly beside him for two hours, pencil in hand, waiting for the finish of the sentence.[70]

From a village on the eastern side of Lake Esmeralda, the party struck out again on horseback the next morning, November 30. Leaving before sunrise, they rode into the light, through a forested gorge filled with wildflowers. Delighting in his newfound freedom, T. R. cantered on ahead, singing cowboy songs and stopping only to ask questions about a tree or flower that caught his interest. He told one of his Argentine escorts, Ruiz Moreno, that these were the happiest two days he had spent since arriving in South America, because he had been left to do what he pleased. He said he felt the way he had as a young man in the American West.[71]

The party had two more scenic lakes to cross that day before reaching Bariloche, a frontier outpost just inside Argentina. From this point, a four-hundred-mile dash by automobile to the railroad at Neuquén began at sunup the next morning, December 1. The Argentine government provided three open-top Mercedes touring cars for Roosevelt's group, now reduced to seventeen, as some of the Chileans had gone home. A fourth car, a Fiat, carried the luggage. Two days were allotted to cross what was a largely uninhabited sandy wasteland stretching across southern Argentina.

Nothing seemed to go right on this journey, a prelude to the mishaps that would later plague the expedition. A police chief who supposedly knew the country had been recruited as a guide. "He had us in mud-holes or sand banks all day," groused Major Shipton.[72] The road was little more than ox-cart ruts, some so deep that the drivers had to detour to avoid getting stuck. They lost two hours when the rear car became mired in mud crossing a steam. Everyone got out and gathered stones to build a ramp beneath the wheels. At another place, the car in front sank to its shafts in soft sand. A party of gauchos was passing by, and two of them tied ropes to the car's fender and pulled it out backward.

By 2:00 P.M., the now-ravenous motorists reached the sheep-ranching settlement of Pilcaniyéu, where they had been expected five hours earlier for breakfast. The aroma of lambs roasting on open spits drifted over to the cars, and without waiting to be served, Roosevelt called for a knife, fork, and plate and carved himself a thick slab of ribs and flank, including a kidney. He went back for two more helpings and had one of the haunches wrapped in cloth to take with him.

To make up for lost time, the four-car caravan drove on into the night until an approaching storm made it necessary to find shelter. It was past 10:00 when the glare of the headlights picked out an adobe-walled rural store at the roadside. The hungry travelers hammered on the door, roused the owner, and soon were dining on boiled eggs, coffee, and cold joint of lamb. Being a light sleeper, Roosevelt offered to be the group's alarm clock. The cleanest bed in the house had been made up for him, but he rejected it in favor of sleeping on the dirt floor like most of his companions, wrapped in a blanket, with an automobile cushion for a pillow.

Four hours later, at 3:30 A.M., Roosevelt wakened the sleepers with a spirited rendition of a Sioux war cry: "Whoo-oo-oop-ee!" He was already dressed, in a cheerful frame of mind, and loudly asked for a cup of coffee.[73]

Half an hour later, when it was light enough to see the road, they were off again, for the final 225 miles to Neuquén. "The sunrise was glorious," T. R. wrote of this departure. "We came out from among the hills on to vast barren plains and drove at speed over them."[74] Ten hours later, they stopped at another store, kept by, of all people, a Syrian immigrant, and they lunched on eggs, cold lamb, and bread. Sometime later they saw rheas, the South American ostriches, in the distance, and Roosevelt asked for a halt to try his hand at shooting. As the occupants of the four cars watched, he walked for a considerable distance over the muddy fields and fired several times with his Springfield but failed to hit a single bird, probably because of his poor vision. His mood had changed when he got back into the car. Depressed by his failure, he was silent for hours.[75]

At dusk they reached the floating dock at the Rio Limai, still some miles from Neuquén, just as a violent storm erupted. The ferryman was afraid to take such a heavy load across with the wind blowing so hard. The hauling cables running across the water groaned under the pressure. A few months earlier, another ferry had been carried away by the swollen current when its cables snapped, drowning the operator. The Argentines in the party were willing to wait, but after eighteen hours on the road and a train to catch, Roosevelt was in no mood for delay. He demanded to be taken across the river, storm or no storm. Shipton offered to go over first with the four cars, in hopes that the wind would die down afterward. But T. R. insisted that he would go first and grew increasingly ill-tempered at being held up. Finally a compromise was reached. The ferry operator was persuaded to make three trips—the first one taking the Colonel and one of the cars, the second trip another of the cars and the other North Americans, and the third the other two cars and the rest of the party. "It would have been prudent to wait a couple of hours," Ruiz Moreno later recalled, "but Mr. Roosevelt proved unopposable."[76]

Once across the river there was a mad dash over sand hills and rutted roads to get to the station at Neuquén on time. With five minutes to spare before the scheduled 10:00 P.M. departure, the Colonel and his companions were seated in the dining car, ordering supper. Two days later, on December 4, he was back in Buenos Aires, wrapping up his tour of Argentina and saying good-bye to Major Shipton.

On December 6 T. R. boarded the International Express, bound for Asunción, Paraguay, with Kermit, Father Zahm, and Harper. Within a few days they would meet Colonel Rondon and the Brazilian half of the expedition, and higher up on the Paraguay, at Corumbá, there would be a reunion with Cherrie, Miller, and Fiala and the start of the long journey to the River of Doubt. "That we shall have a horribly uncomfortable time there is no question," T. R. predicted to Senator Lodge, "for we are going into a country where men literally cannot live without mosquito nets . . . There will also be undoubtedly a certain amount of fever and dysentery, and there may be unpleasant surprises for us when we get over the ridge and come down some affluent of the Amazon. But I am inclined to think we shall come through all right."[77]

NOTES

1. J. A. Zahm to Albert Zahm, 12-12-13, *CAZA*. 2. Zahm, "Roosevelt's Visit to South America," *Review of Reviews*, p. 85. 3. *New York Times*, 3-23-14 (letter from Anthony Fiala to his wife). 4. De Lima, "Reminiscences of Roosevelt." 5. Wiley, *T. R.'s America* (quoting Leo Miller), p. 304. 6. J. A. Zahm to Albert Zahm, 12-12-13, *CAZA*. 7. Carroll, "Mind in Action," *The Ave Maria* (6-1-46), chapter XI, p. 687. 8. Edith K. Roosevelt to Ethel Roosevelt Derby, 10-25-13, *TRC*. 9. *New York Times*, 10-25-13. 10. Ibid. 11. T. R., *Brazilian Wild.*, pp. 32–33. 12. *New York Times*, 10-27-13. 13. J.A. Zahm to Albert Zahm, 12-12-13, *CAZA*. 14. T. R., *Brazilian Wild.*, pp. 22–26. 15. de Lima, "Reminiscences of Roosevelt." 16. T. R., "São Paulo, an Old City That Is Carving New Ways," *The Outlook*, p. 267. 17. T. R. to Kermit Roosevelt, 6-23-13, *Letters*, Vol. 7, #5857 (footnote quoting Hugh Taylor's apology), p. 732. 18. Wagenknecht, *Seven Worlds*, p. 3. 19. Zahm, "Theodore Roosevelt as a Hunter-Naturalist," *The Outlook*, p. 435. 20. T. R., "In Southern-most Brazil," *The Outlook*, p. 361. 21. Zahm, "Roosevelt's Visit to South America," *Review of Reviews*, p. 85. 22. Edith K. Roosevelt to Ethel Roosevelt Derby, 11-2-13, *TRC*. 23. *El Tiempo*, 11-5-13. 24. Ibid. 25. *Montevideo Herald*, 11-5-13. 26. Report of U.S. minister to Uruguay Nicolay Grevstad to U.S. State Dept., 11-10-13, Misc. State Dept. Communications. 27. Pendle, *Uruguay*, p. 26. 28. T. R., "Montevideo," *The Outlook*, Vol. 106, 2-28-14, p. 476. 29. Report of Nicolay Grevstad to U.S. State Dept. 30. Ibid. 31. Miller, *In the Wilds*, p. 199. 32. Ibid. 33. Cherrie, *Diary*, 11-7-13. 34. Miller, *In the Wilds*, pp. 205–6. 35. T. R., *Brazilian Wild.*, p. 39. 36. Miller, *In the Wilds*, p. 206. 37. T. R., *Brazilian Wild.*, p. 40. 38. Cherrie, *Diary*, 11-7-13. 39. Ibid. 40. "T. R. at Buenos Aires," *Literary Digest*; *Buenos Aires Herald*, 11-6-13. 41. *Buenos Aires Herald*, 11-6-13. 42. Edith K. Roosevelt to Ethel Roosevelt Derby, 11-7-13, *TRC*. 43. *Buenos Aires Herald*, 11-6-13. 44. Ibid. 45. Ibid., 11-5-13. 46. Edith K. Roosevelt to Ethel Roosevelt Derby, 11-7-13, *TRC*. 47. Edith K. Roosevelt to Ethel Roosevelt Derby, 11-3-13, *TRC*. 48. Edith K. Roosevelt to Ethel Roosevelt Derby, 11-7-13, *TRC*. 49. *Buenos Aires Herald*, 11-13-13. 50. Ibid. 51. Wells, "What the South Americans Think of Theodore Roosevelt," *Harper's Weekly*. 52. *Buenos Aires Herald*, 11-13-13. 53. T. R. to Henry Cabot Lodge, 12-13-13, *Letters*, Vol. 7, #5878, p. 756. 54. Kermit Roosevelt to Belle Willard, 11-14-13, *KRP*. 55. Shipton, *Diary*, *TRC*. 56. Kermit Roosevelt to Belle Willard, 11-14-13, *KRP*. 57. J. A. Zahm to Albert Zahm, 11-16-13, *CAZA*. 58. Shipton, *Diary*, *TRC*. 59. Ibid. 60. Ibid. 61. T. R., "In the Argentine," *The Outlook*, p. 803. 62. Clemenceau, *South America To-Day*, p. 197. 63. Shipton, *Diary*, *TRC*. 64. Ibid. 65. Edith K. Roosevelt, *Diary*, 11-21-13. 66. "The Colonel in Chile," *North American Review*, p. 337. 67. Wells, "What the South Americans

Think of Theodore Roosevelt," *Harper's Weekly.* **68.** Kermit Roosevelt to Belle Willard, 11-26-13, *KRP.* **69.** Ibañez, "Roosevelt Recuerdos," *Y Sur.* **70.** Shipton, *Diary, TRC.* **71.** Moreno, "At Lake Nahuel Huapi," *Annales del Museo.* **72.** Shipton, *Diary, TRC.* **73.** Zahm, *South America's Southland,* p. 378. **74.** T. R., "From Ox Cart to Motor Car in the Andes," *The Outlook.* **75.** Moreno, "At Lake Nahuel Huapi," *Annales del Museo.* **76.** Ibid. **77.** T. R. to Henry Cabot Lodge, 12-12-13, *Letters,* Vol. 7, #5878, pp. 756–57.

VI
Everything Possible
Is Done for My Comfort

"We have started on our naturalist's trip; but as yet we are only in the preliminary and purely pleasant part," the Colonel wrote his daughter-in-law Eleanor on December 10, a day after leaving Asunción. The Paraguayan government had provided them "a clean comfortable river steamer—nominally gunboat, really armed yacht," the *Adolfo Riquelmo*, for the voyage up the Paraguay River. In six days they would reach the Brazilian town of Corumbá, where the full expedition would assemble. Meanwhile, after weeks of banquets and speeches, T. R. was "enjoying the rest, and the strange, hot landscape."[1] By noon the temperature would climb over one hundred degrees, but canvas awnings stretched over the deck protected the travelers from the fierce sun.

The three hunting dogs donated by Hileret lent a domestic touch to the shipboard scene. "You would like them," Kermit wrote Belle, "for they're big good natured fellows, and I think [they] will be fine for hunting." The dogs had clearly chosen Kermit as their master. Whenever he walked away from them, they "all howled dismally." His favorite was Trigueiro—"the brown one"—who had a habit of worming his head out of his collar and running over to plant his paws in Kermit's lap.[2]

The Colonel had mixed feelings about having Kermit along. He felt closer to his second son than to his other children, and recognized how much alike they were. Kermit shared his father's love of hunting and natural history and had his flair for making friends, but he lacked T. R.'s self-discipline. A moody, sensitive, and headstrong young man, Kermit was more interested in pursuing adventure than in buckling down to a career. His father thought marriage would steady him and felt guilty about keeping Kermit from his intended. "I wish he would have gone straight to Belle," T. R. admitted to Ethel, "but he did not wish to be married when I was not present, and I found that his feelings would really have been hurt if I had not let him come on this trip."[3]

For three days the gunboat steamed northward on the broad, placid river, still inside the borders of Paraguay. From the comfort of the shaded deck, the Colonel looked out upon a wealth of wildlife.

> On the mud-flats and sand-bars, and among the green rushes of the bays and inlets, were stately water-fowl; crimson flamingoes and rosy spoonbills, dark-colored ibis and white storks with black wings. Darters, with snakelike necks and pointed bills, perched in the trees on the brink of the river. Snowy egrets flapped across the marshes. Caymans were common, and differed from the crocodiles we had seen in Africa in two points: they were not alarmed by the report of a rifle when fired at, and they lay with the head raised instead of stretched along the sand.[4]

Roosevelt took an almost morbid interest in piranha—"the fish that eats men when it can get the chance." Peculiar to South American rivers, this most dangerous of freshwater fishes was practically unknown to the general public until T. R.'s *Scribner's* articles were published in 1914. The Paraguay River teemed with them. When the gunboat stopped to take on wood and provisions, the fishermen on board tried catching some, only to find their steel hooks and copper wire leads were bitten clean off by the piranha's razor-sharp teeth. Those that were landed flopped furiously on the deck and squealed loudly until they died. "As they flapped about," wrote T. R., "they bit with vicious eagerness at whatever presented itself. One of them flapped into a cloth and seized it with a bulldog grip. Another grasped one of its fellows; another snapped at a piece of wood, and left the teethmarks deep therein." Their only redeeming quality, he discovered, was that they were "fairly good to eat, although with too many bones."[5]

Higher up on the Paraguay, where the Rio Apa joins it from the east to form the southern boundary of Brazil, Col. Candido Mariano da Silva Rondon, the head of the Brazilian Strategic Telegraph Commission, paced the worn wooden decks of the old paddle wheeler *Nyoac* as he awaited Theodore Roosevelt's arrival. Rondon, a short, bandy-legged figure with the bronzed, impassive features of an Indian chief, stopped now and then to focus his binoculars through the heat haze. He scanned the broad expanse of water to the south, searching for signs of a steamer. By midmorning on this December 12, the lookout at the masthead reported seeing smudges of brown funnel smoke downriver. Soon after, the Stars and Stripes and the blue and red Paraguayan ensign were spotted at the masthead of a vessel moving rapidly upstream.

Before noon, the *Adolfo Riquelmo* drew up alongside the tubby *Nyoac* and dropped anchor. Rondon and his officers, in high-collared white dress uniforms, promptly boarded the gunboat. The two colonels exchanged pleasantries awkwardly in French and posed for photographs. Rondon sniffed the diplomatic air on board and guessed that the Paraguayans would be offended if they could not keep Roosevelt on their boat a while longer. In a conciliatory gesture, he arranged that the two vessels would steam in company for the rest of the journey to Corumbá.[6]

Two hours later, another halt was made, so that Roosevelt could cross over to Rondon's steamer for tea and more conversation. The future plans of the expedition were sketched out at the open-air table on the *Nyoac*'s stern. After arriving at Corumbá, the party would spend several weeks hunting for jaguar and wild boar at outlying fazendas, or plantations. Following that, the travelers would continue ascending the Paraguay and its tributaries to Tapirapuan, the headquarters of Rondon's Telegraph Commission; from there they would begin a month-long march by mule train to the unknown river.[7]

Having worked out a rough itinerary, Roosevelt and his Brazilian guide turned to swapping hunting and exploring tales. Kermit's grasp of Portuguese enabled Rondon and his officers to comfortably slip back into their native language. When the subject of piranha came up, T. R. found that his companions "had story after story to tell of them." Rondon himself had lost a toe one time while testing the temperature of the water before taking a river bath. During one of his expeditions, after running out of food, he had had a small stream dynamited for its fish. A desperately hungry assistant had lost a piece of his tongue and nearly bled to death when he put a supposedly stunned piranha in his mouth while reaching for another one.[8]

From their first meeting, Roosevelt was satisfied that Rondon was "all . . . that could be desired" in a guide. "It was evident that he knew his business thoroughly." A native of Mato Grosso, the forty-eight-year-old Rondon was half Indian on his mother's side and pure Portuguese on his father's. He had spent a quarter of a century building roads, bridges, and three thousand miles of telegraph lines to link his isolated region with the rest of Brazil.[9] In that time, his expeditions had produced the first accurate maps of northwestern Mato Grosso, a region of some two hundred thousand square miles. The naturalists who had accompanied him had collected thousands of plant and animal specimens and documented their studies in sixty-six volumes published by the Brazilian government. Through Rondon, Brazil for the first time had made a national effort to explore its interior without depending on foreigners.[10] Strangely enough, as late as 1913, Rondon's work was barely known outside South America. Roosevelt was astonished to learn that Rondon had received no recognition in the United States and Europe, a defect he remedied by bringing Rondon's career vividly to life in his *Scribner's* articles.[11]

Rondon had all the makings of a martyr. He was highly disciplined, ascetic, and fanatical in carrying out his duties. His expeditions were so notoriously hard that civilian workers had to be paid seven times their ordinary wages to accompany him.[12] At the same time, he was a tolerant and humane commander who shared his soldiers' bivouacs and wept openly when they died. For young Brazilian officers, service in Rondon's Fifth Battalion of Engineers represented the best chance for promotion in a peacetime army. They worshipped him and signed their reports as "your friend, comrade, subordinate and admirer."[13] Rondon took no personal credit for his achievements. "What have I done? Nothing by myself," he once remarked. "My colleagues did all the work."[14]

Rondon's greatest challenge came in 1907, when the Brazilian government ordered him to build a telegraph line from Cuiabá, the capital of Mato Grosso, all the way west a thousand miles to the Madeira River. Three successive expeditions were needed to survey the route, each one more punishing than the last. Finally, in 1909, Rondon reached the Madeira after marching for 237 days and losing all his pack animals in the process.

Work on the telegraph line had begun soon after the first surveying reports were available. By 1909, 366 miles had been strung. In 1913 the completion of the line was in sight, and two years later, in 1915, it opened for service. Until the 1940s, when air service began, Rondon's telegraph line would remain the sole means of communication in the vastness of Mato Grosso.[15]

It was during the 1909 expedition that Rondon had discovered the headwaters of the unknown river. In July of that year, several days' march beyond the then most-westerly telegraph station of José Bonifácio, he came upon a fast-flowing stream not even suggested on his map, and with so many twists in its course that he could not guess its probable direction. It might be a feeder stream to a larger, already-known river, such as the Gy-Paraná on the west or the Tapajós on the east. Still again, it might develop into a major river in its own right, gradually swelled by tributaries, and seeking its outflow into the lower Madeira, or the Amazon, hundreds of unmapped kilometers to the north. Rondon had explored a dozen rivers in his career, but none "occasioned more numerous and continuous doubts" than the one he had chosen to call the Dúvida.[16]

To complicate this geographical mystery, Rondon had also discovered the headwaters of another, smaller river several days' march to the west of the Dúvida. He gave it the name Ananás, or Pineapple, for the fragrant wild pineapples that grew on its banks. There was a possibility that it flowed into the Dúvida, but in any event, both streams would eventually have to be explored. Of the two, the Dúvida appeared to Rondon to be the most challenging.

Rondon had drawn upon his best officers in the Telegraph Commission to accompany the expedition. With him on the *Nyoac* was an old comrade, Capt. Amilcar de Magalhães. An alert, thickset man with a brush-cut mustache, Amilcar had the toughest assignment of all—overseeing the pack trains on the overland march to the unknown river. A geologist, Dr. Oliveira, also joined the party at this time. Later, the Brazilian contingent would be expanded by a navigator, a botanist, and two medical doctors. The assignment of such men convinced Roosevelt that the Brazilian government wanted to make his expedition "not merely a success, but a success of note."[17] He noticed that all the baggage piled up on the *Nyoac*'s deck had been stenciled "Expedição Scientifica Roosevelt–Rondon," henceforth the official designation.[18]

Rondon's arrival brought an end to Father Zahm's influence on the course of the expedition. Roosevelt now looked to his Brazilian fellow colonel to manage the day-to-day operations.

In spite of the changed circumstances, Zahm remained optimistic in his letters to his brother, Albert, and fully expected to descend the River of Doubt and study the primitive tribes of the Mato Grosso. "I have all kinds of presents for these children of the forest," he wrote, "& I am sure we shall at once become the best of friends." Zahm expected the results of the trip would fill fifteen volumes. "Everyone says that ours is the most important scientific expedition that has ever come to South America . . . All [of us] are in high spirits, & realize that [we] are taking part in an epoch-making enterprise."[19]

As the two ships steamed up the Paraguay, the landscape grew luxuriantly tropical. Roosevelt marveled at "forests of palms that extended for leagues, and vast marshy meadows, where storks, herons, and ibis were gathered, with flocks of cormorants and darters on the sand-bars, and stilts, skimmers, and clouds of beautiful swaying terns in the foreground."[20] In places along the shoreline, the trees and bushes were stained white with excrement, marking the rookeries of thousands of water birds.[21]

Caiman were now so plentiful that the passengers shot them for target practice. They were despised by the Brazilians as cattle killers, and no one on board objected to this sport.[22] The scaly reptiles were easy targets, lying exposed in rows on the mud banks, their heads raised and mouths vacantly open in the steaming sunshine. "Shot 4 crocs," Roosevelt noted coolly in his diary on December 13, but he missed as many more—"a throbbing boat does not improve one's aim." A few days later, he took time to record how caiman died:

> Sometimes they ran into the water erect on their legs, looking like miniatures of the monsters of the prime[val]. One showed by its behavior how little an ordinary shot pains or affects these dull-nerved, cold-blooded creatures. As it lay on a sand-bank, it was hit with a long 22 bullet. It slid into the water but found itself in the midst of a school of fish . . . It seized fish after fish. . . [until] a second bullet killed it. Some of the crocodiles when shot performed most extraordinary antics.[23]

Roosevelt drew the line, however, when it came to the wanton shooting of birds, which he loved above all other creatures. One day, while sitting with Father Zahm, he was outraged to learn that a crew member on the steamer had just shot a cormorant. He ordered the man to get into a rowboat and retrieve the dead bird so that the naturalists could prepare it as a specimen. After that, no one dared shoot a bird without his permission.[24]

By December 14, still a day away from Corumbá, the steamers

entered Brazilian territory. As evening came, the wide river turned eastward, toward a gathering storm. "This last sunset on the river was too glorious," a homesick and very much in love Kermit wrote Belle that night, "the purple of the mountains, and the reflection of the west making a veritable path of molten gold behind us along the river. Father and I stood watching it, and I guess he was thinking of Mother, and I know that I was thinking very little about the sunset and a very great deal about you. And when the moon rose, and a winding of the river made us sail right toward it I was just wishing that we would go right on that way straight to you."[25]

"The first view one has of Corumbá is rather pleasing," Cherrie had recorded after arriving with Miller on November 23, "but the place does not bear acquaintance." Built on limestone bluffs on the western side of the Paraguay, Corumbá had a commanding sweep of the river and few other charms. Hot, dusty, and somnolent, its proximity to the Bolivian border made it a refuge for outlaws on the run. Murder and robbery were so common in the back streets that most of the male citizens packed revolvers or carried long knives in their belts for protection. Cherrie was surprised to find that with a population of ten thousand, the town had no central market or streetcars. "There is not a single carriage for hire!" he complained. While looking for a suitable place to work in the countryside, he and Miller had stayed at the Hotel Galileo. "This is doubtless the best hotel in the city," Cherrie decided, "but the waterclosets consist of a hole in the floor that one must straddle— and incidentally furnish your own paper."[26]

While waiting for Roosevelt to join them, the naturalists spent three profitable weeks working at Urucúm, a village twenty miles outside of Corumbá. A wealthy sugar planter offered them the use of a large, airy cottage, with the added luxuries of shower baths and servants. Miller found Urucúm "a garden spot" for collecting. In the surrounding marshes and forests, he trapped vampire bats, hairy armadillos, and "a good specimen" of one of the rarest of South American mammals, the red wolf, known to Brazilians by the jawbreaker name of *guaraguasú*. Keeping Miller company as he skinned his catches was a tame owl that he had bought at the market in Asunción, "a forlorn and hungry little creature" he named Moses. It promptly became the expedition's mascot. Miller let Moses explore the rafters of the cottage, noting how "he walked about gravely overhead and came down only when hungry or when the half-filled wash-basin lured him to the delights of a cool bath."[27]

Cherrie was less enthusiastic about the stay at Urucúm. Birds were abundant there, so much so that he soon ran out of storage space in his specimen trunks. But he regretted how many birds were already in the post-mating stage and molting, which made for poor-looking specimens. "We seem to have gotten here at the wrong season," he lamented soon after arriving. The extreme heat and humidity made it difficult to prepare skins properly. "As I sit working at the table perspiration drips from my nose and chin! And I have constantly to dry my hands with [corn] meal in order not to wet the plumage of the birds I am handling."[28]

Chronic diarrhea and a sore wrist added to Cherrie's woes. In this irritable mood, he unburdened himself to his diary about his fellow explorers:

> I have not written anything about the organization of our expedition, but now I'm going to record my opinion that a *greater lack of organization seems hardly possible!* There is no head, no chief of the expedition. Fiala in a way is the temporary head but utterly incompetant [sic] for the work he has to do without previous experience in the tropics [and] without any knowledge of the character of the people with whom he must treat, and the almost insurmountable handicap of *not having any knowledge* of the language.[29]

A primitive telephone system linked Urucúm with Corumbá. On December 15 Cherrie was summoned to the sugar planter's house and heard Fiala's faraway voice saying that Colonel Roosevelt had arrived. T. R. wanted to see both of his naturalists and asked that one of them accompany him on a "tiger" hunt the next day. As Miller was the mammalogist of the party, he got the assignment. Cherrie agreed to stay at Urucúm for another three weeks collecting birds.[30]

Word of Roosevelt's coming had reached Corumbá in time for its leading citizens to crowd themselves into small craft decked with flags and bunting and sail off to meet him as his steamer approached the town on December 15. T. R. had not expected a formal reception in such a remote spot and was embarrassed to be found dressed in khaki hunting clothes and hobnailed boots. But the bands and the cheering passengers on the escorting boats had all the infectious enthusiasm of one of his presidential tours, "just as if we were nearing some town on the Hudson."[31]

At Corumbá, Roosevelt was pleased to find that in five weeks of work, Cherrie had collected more than 600 birds and Miller about 175 mammals. During this same time, Fiala and Sigg had managed to shepherd the expedition's mountain of equipment and supplies by boat from Buenos Aires without losing so much as a duffel bag. Proud of his quartermaster's skills, Fiala stood by as T. R. asked Rondon to inspect their outfit. All went well until Rondon looked over Fiala's pair of canvas canoes and shook his head over whether such apparently frail craft could survive South America rapids. Using Kermit as a translator, Fiala put up a spirited argument for their use, and the canoes for the time being were kept.[32]

While at Corumbá, Roosevelt dispatched the second of his articles for *Scribner's Magazine*, entitled "Up the Paraguay." "I can not tell whether it is satisfactory or not," he wrote his editor, Robert Bridges. "This is all so different from my African trip! But to me it is all interesting; this country will soon have a great development." The manuscript, written in indelible pencil, was accompanied by nearly eighty photographs taken by various members of the party. Kermit had worked until midnight to develop them in time. Among T. R.'s suggested captions were "Maneating fish; see his teeth!"; "Palms on river bank"; and "Corumbá family of poor people in Sunday clothes." Still more photographs were to follow, "by the steamer next week."

Had Bridges been able to communicate with Roosevelt at this time, he could have put his mind at ease. *Scribner's* was in fact "very much pleased" with the quality of the articles, and believed the readers would be, too, when the series began appearing on newsstands in April 1914. The only difficulty Bridges's editorial staff found was deciphering T. R.'s handwriting, especially when it came to names of unfamiliar South American birds and animals.[33]

It was important that Roosevelt's party reach the unknown river by late February, to be sure they could navigate it in dugouts before the rainy season ended. This left only a few weeks during which to secure jaguar, tapir, and other mammals wanted by the American Museum of Natural History. On December 17, after saying good-bye to his Paraguayan friends, the Colonel embarked on the *Nyoac* with Rondon, Kermit, and Miller for a week-long hunt at Las Palmeiras plantation on the Rio Taquary, a tributary of the upper Paraguay.

Bad luck attended their departure from Corumbá. Rondon had earlier tried to hire the *Nyoac*'s cook to come with them. Well aware of Rondon's reputation as an explorer, the man exclaimed to him, "Senhor,

I have never done anything to deserve punishment!" and wisely jumped ship before dawn.[34] A few hours later, some of the *Nyoac*'s crew started shouting that the small steam launch being towed behind had disappeared. Only a few sticks of firewood could be seen floating on the water. While rounding a sharp bend, the launch had tipped over and sunk. Rondon spent several fruitless hours trying to drag the submerged craft to shore before giving up.[35]

While ascending the Rio Taquary, the Colonel divided his time between shooting at caimans—"we killed scores of the noxious creatures"—and admiring the flocks of elegant, long-legged jabiru storks that "whitened the marshes and lined the river banks."[36] Late afternoon brought a chance to try out Kermit's hunting dogs. A giant anteater was spotted loping through the yard-high grass onshore. Rondon at once ordered a boat lowered, and the hunters set off in pursuit. About the size of a small bear, the ungainly mammal was soon cornered by the yapping dogs. T. R. dropped it neatly with a single shot from his favorite rifle, an army-issue Springfield, thereby redeeming his reputation as a marksman. By then the light had grown too dim to take a photograph of the strange-looking creature, with its elongated snout and oversized curving foreclaws. As soon as it was hoisted aboard the *Nyoac*, Miller had to work quickly, measuring and skinning the animal before decomposition set in. The gray-furred pelt, six feet long and thick with flies, was stretched on the upper deck to dry.[37]

The brief tropical twilight had faded into darkness by the time the steamer drew up at the landing place of the Palmeiras plantation. On the riverbank a group of cattleherders huddled just beyond the heat of a campfire, strumming their guitars and singing dolefully. Roosevelt's party spent the night on board, trying to sleep in stifling cabins or under netting on deck. In his first diary entry of the trip, Kermit used a minimum of words to describe their acute discomfort: "Hot and dreary, mosquitoes & insects."[38]

At sunrise the next morning, December 18, the party mounted small, wiry ranch horses for the twenty-mile ride to Palmeiras. Much of the route lay through palm-studded marshes and bogs, where the little horses struggled to keep from sinking into the muck. The rains were late this year, and many of the lagoons were drying up. Thousands of fish churned and flopped in the shrinking pools of muddy water, and thousands more dead or dying fish covered the banks, creating a stench described by Miller as "almost overpowering."[39] Water birds beyond count sat gorging themselves on the unexpected bounty. Miller noticed many species entirely different from those he and Cherrie had observed at Urucúlm, eighty miles to the south. He stopped frequently to collect specimens and reached the plantation hours after the others, with enough skinning work to last into the night.

The Fazenda das Palmeiras—Ranch of the Palm Trees—was a huge establishment, a virtual state within a state owned by Senhor de Barros, one of the great landholders who made up Brazil's ruling class. On its vast, unfenced range, thirty thousand head of half-wild cattle grazed freely. The home ranch consisted of a quadrangle of one-story buildings in which the field hands, cattleherders, and hunters lived in feudal style with their numerous children and farm animals. The humid papyrus swamps and palm forests surrounding the ranch represented prime jaguar country.[40]

Trackers had been sent out searching for jaguar before Roosevelt's arrival. On December 20, one of them came in to report finding fresh tracks nine miles from the ranch.

The next morning, T. R., Kermit, and Rondon awoke at 2:00 A.M. and an hour later set off on a jaguar hunt. They rode mules and horses, and in addition to Kermit's dogs, they were accompanied by a motley collection of ranch dogs judged by Roosevelt as "well-nigh worthless" because of their lack of obedience. He put his faith in two jaguar hounds borrowed from a neighboring fazenda, "lean, half-starved creatures with prick ears and a look of furtive wildness."[41]

The stars blazed in a coal-black sky as the hunters trotted away from the ranch compound. While crossing a shallow stream, the splashing of horses' hooves and dogs' paws did not seem to disturb a sleeping alligator, a jacaré-tinga. As morning approached, the light came up ghostly gray. Monkeys began to howl in the forest, and birds awoke. "Macaws, parrots, [and] parakeets screamed at us and chattered at us as we rode by," wrote T. R. "Ibis called with wailing voices, and the plovers shrieked as they wheeled in the air. We waded across bayous and ponds, where white lilies floated on the water and thronging lilac-flowers splashed the green marsh with color."[42]

By 6 A.M., the trackers found jaguar prints in the damp earth, and the chase was on. The dogs were unleashed and they took up the scent, whining and yowling as they lunged through the marsh grass. The jaguar, a large female, was found perched in the forked limbs of a taruman tree. Half hidden by the dense foliage, the big, spotted cat snarled down at the encircling pack of hounds. Roosevelt did not trust the dogs to hold it at bay should it decide to come down. He fired just once, at a range of seventy yards, "a very pretty shot" in Kermit's opinion, and a lucky one at that, considering T. R.'s bad eyesight.[43] The jaguar fell "like a sack of sand" through the branches to the ground, then rose and staggered some twenty yards before finally sinking for good under a palm tree.[44] Rondon knelt beside it and lifted up the huge head, baring the sizable fangs for Kermit's camera. Afterward, they carefully peeled the skin away from the body and saved the meat to eat.[45]

Kermit had his turn the following day, when he put a Winchester 405 round behind the shoulder of a big male jaguar, a magnificent, powerfully built animal with a sleek, gold coat dotted with dark brown spots. Killing it was the culmination of a pursuit that lasted eleven hours. At one point Kermit had to use his horse to stamp a passage through a long bayou choked with aquatic plants so that the men and dogs could keep up with their fleeing prey. "Our . . . dogs nearly finished by thirst on way back," he noted in his diary afterward.[46]

Roosevelt and his son, in Cherrie's absence, also tried their hand at bird collecting. Using his trusty Springfield rifle, T. R. shot a wood ibis "on the wing," but then "lost all the credit I had thus gained by a series of inexcusable misses, at long range," while trying to kill a stately jabiru stork. At much closer range, Kermit blasted away at another slender-legged jabiru with his heavy-caliber Luger pistol.[47] "These birds are in horrible condition and I was ashamed to skin them," a disgusted Miller wrote his chief, Frank Chapman, "but the Col[onel] wanted me to, so I did. I hope you will not consider them when judging my general work."[48]

Even with Kermit's help, Miller worked sixteen hours a day to keep up with the hunters. The larger skins were cleaned on the dirt floor of a ranch outbuilding, where Miller had to contend with chickens and ducks running in and out chasing flies. "As fact of one day's work," he reported to Chapman, "I skinned and made up ten hyacinthine macaws besides a large anteater and a good deal of smaller stuff." He did not have time to do any trapping on his own and complained that he was doing more work than he had originally signed on for. Not all the specimens, he discovered, were destined for the museum's display cases. "I did not know that I was expected to act as preparator to Col. Roosevelt and Kermit on this trip or I should have made special arrangements beforehand. But of course I can't say anything now . . ."[49]

The successful stay at Palmeiras was followed by an invitation for Roosevelt to hunt for a week at the Fazenda São João, the estate of the governor of Mato Grosso. Only the sudden advent of the rainy season led T. R. to cut this visit down to just two days. As Kermit explained to Belle, with the rains "coming on so fast . . . we must get started as quickly as possible with our mule caravan before the rivers become impassable." To Kermit, his father's decision was a blessing. "I felt, Belle, just as if five days had been added to my life, for it means that I'll be with you just five days sooner, my dearest heart."

In this same letter, Kermit tried to ease Belle's mind about his safety. "You must be sure to realize that there's not the slightest danger for me in this trip[,] for the tropics agree with me." He was more concerned about his father's health, and although he was sure that "everything [was] going to come out all right," he could not hold back his resentment against Father Zahm—"a foolish well meaning little fellow, who mislead [sic] father greatly as to the conditions of travel and life down here, for he had never been off the beaten track and saw everything through a golden haze."[50]

The Colonel was just as homesick as Kermit but characteristically put the best light on their situation when he wrote Edith on Christmas Eve 1913, on the way back to Corumbá:

> Darling Edie,
> Kermit is now in first rate shape, and as tough as hickory, and I never felt in better health—in spite of being covered with prickly heat—so if you do not hear from me to the contrary you can safely assume that this condition of things is permanent. Of course we have not really begun the expedition proper as yet, and there will be many extremely disagreeable experiences; but we are being hardened under exceptionally pleasant conditions, and so far have had no hardships whatever. Kermit, Harper, Miller and I, with some of the Brazilians, who are capital fellows and great chums of Kermit, are returning from a delightful week at a huge ranch in the marshes of the Taquary River . . . the weather was hot but clear; the food was good; and we were in the saddle eight or ten hours a day. We each killed a jaguar, his being an exceptionally large one and mine a good average one; together with other game. The bird life, especially as regards the big waders and the macaws, was marvelous . . . Kermit is his own mother's son! He is to me a delight-

ful companion; he always has books with him; and he is
a tireless worker. He is not only an exceptionally good
and hard hunter, but as soon as he comes in he starts at
his photographs or else at the skins, working as hard as
the two naturalists. Indeed of our whole expedition every
one works hard except good little Father Zahm . . .

We are very much pleased with Col. Rondon. He is
very hardy, and fitted for this kind of business by
twenty five years experience, and is evidently agree-
ably surprised by our conduct; and he is most anxious
to do all in his power for us. Everything possible is done
for my comfort, in the little ways that mean so much to
a man of my age on a rough trip.

I shall send you a Xmas cable from Corumbá, this
evening; we are now on a hot little sidewheel steamer
jammed with men, dogs, bags and belongings, partially
cured and rather bad smelling skins [and] the like. *I*
enjoy it; but my dainty sweetheart most certainly would
not. I am drenched with sweat most of the waking
hours, and the nights are too hot for really comfortable
sleeping as a rule; but there are exceptions. In ten days
we shall be at the last post office, São Luis de Cáceres;
and then we shall go into the real wilderness.

Kiss Ethel and Eleanor for me; I think of them very,
very often, and of you all the time; and it is a real comfort to think of Ted, so hardworking and trustworthy
and efficient. Archie and Quentin are also always in my
thoughts . . . I am sure we shall love Belle greatly.

Your own lover,[51]

By late afternoon, the *Nyoac* reached Corumbá, where the rest of
the expedition was waiting, including Father Zahm, who had spent the
week at a Catholic mission. There were three new faces on the Brazilian
side. Dr. Cajazeira, the portly, serious-minded head of the military hospital at Corumbá, had been assigned as the party's chief medical officer.
His first act was to see that everyone began taking quinine daily to
ward off malaria. A young civilian physician, Dr. Soledade, would be
responsible for the muleteers and soldiers. And to assist the naturalists,
Rondon had recruited an Austrian-born taxidermist by the name of

Reinisch. Missing from the group was Sigg, who had started upriver the day before for São Luis de Cáceres, in charge of the heavier equipment and food.

Roosevelt was anxious to get started, and Cherrie and Fiala worked quickly to round up the personal baggage and turn the trunks of specimens over to the steamship agent for transport to New York. By 7:00 P.M., everything was aboard, but the sailing was held up for Kermit, who was still at a photographer's shop developing pictures for the Colonel's *Scribner's* manuscript. Finally, at 10:00 P.M., the *Nyoac's* steam whistle screamed into the hot darkness and the decks began vibrating as the paddle wheels churned the harbor water. "What a Xmas eve!" Cherrie recorded that night. "Could anything be less Christmas like. How I wish I might be at home tonight."[52]

Christmas Day of 1913 saw the bluff-bowed *Nyoac* beating north against the yellow-brown flood of the Paraguay, en route for the Fazenda São João. The plantation lay four days' steaming time up one of the lesser tributaries of the Paraguay, the Rio Cuiabá. While there, Roosevelt hoped to hunt for more varieties of jaguar and obtain specimens of tapir and white-lipped peccaries, the other two principal South American game animals.

The Brazilians, meanwhile, tried to create a festive atmosphere on board. In the afternoon, the steamer stopped so that the crew could scythe down grass for the flock of sheep Rondon was transporting to one of the telegraph camps. The ship's stewards came back with armloads of palm fronds and green branches and wove them into the railings on the awning-covered afterdeck, where a long table was set up. One of Rondon's more artistically inclined assistants, Lieutenant Reis, wrote out greeting cards in English, Portuguese, and French, using different-colored inks. But all this failed to put the homesick North Americans in the holiday spirit. Perhaps it was the 110-degree heat in the cabins and the strange surroundings. That evening they stood up with their Brazilian colleagues to drink the health of Woodrow Wilson and Hermes da Fonseca, and then dug their forks into canned turkey and plum pudding.[53] Cherrie reflected the general mood when he wrote, "My thoughts have been with loved ones at home very often today."[54]

The Paraguay River was left behind on December 26, as the *Nyoac* pushed on up the dark waters of the Rio São Lourenço for a day, and then up the smaller, lemon-colored Rio Cuiabá. On the twenty-eighth,

gaily decorated steamboats carrying two generations of Gov. Costa
Marques's family escorted the Colonel's steamer the last few miles to
the Fazenda São João. At the landing place, an honor guard of perspiring
soldiers stood in front of the low, whitewashed ranch buildings and
presented arms. Near them, shaded by towering royal palms, were two
flagpoles, one of which flew the green and gold Brazilian national colors.
As T. R. stepped off the gangplank, a brass band struck up "Hail, Columbia" and the Stars and Stripes were quickly run up the other flagstaff.

Roosevelt called São João "the finest ranch-house in Mato Grosso"
and was charmed by his host's old-fashioned, patriarchal courtesy.[55] But
the traditional early-morning cup of black coffee and piece of bread
were not enough nourishment to keep T.R. going until the distant
breakfast hour. On the second morning of the visit, Kermit passed the
open door of the dining room and noticed that platters of cold meats
and salads had been laid out ahead of time. He hurried back to tell his
father. They tiptoed down the stairs and quietly shut the door behind
them. They were wolfing down a plate of sliced chicken when they
heard voices, and Gov. Costa Marques stuck his head into the room. T. R.
said afterward that he and Kermit "felt and looked like two small boys
caught stealing jam in the pantry."[56]

Monsoonlike rains ruined the Colonel's chance to bag another
jaguar, but he did succeed in realizing a twenty-year-old dream of
"killing peccaries with the spear" when the dogs ran a wild boar into a
hollow tree stump. In the tangle of vines and branches, T. R. could not
get a clear shot with his rifle. He borrowed a hefty jaguar spear from
one of his companions, closed in, "and killed the fierce little boar
therewith."[57] Such moments unleashed some primitive element in
Roosevelt's personality. A fellow hunter once recorded how, after T. R.
had shot a mountain goat, "the yell of delight he let loose could have
been heard for two miles . . . He rubbed his hands together, in the way
he had when he was greatly pleased with anything, and fairly danced
around with joy."[58]

On December 30, the *Nyoac* started back down the Rio Cuiabá for
the Paraguay, but the lure of hunting more jaguars was strong enough
to make Roosevelt stop for several days en route. He rang in the new
year of 1914 with a 5:00 A.M. breakfast of hardtack, ham, sardines, and
coffee before setting out on a walking hunt for the big cats.

The hunting party, consisting of T. R., Kermit, Rondon, and four
dark-skinned ranch hands from São João, crossed the river at 6:00 A.M.

and immediately found fresh tracks, indicating that two jaguars were prowling in the vicinity. Roosevelt's poor opinion of Brazilian hunting dogs was confirmed when the pack began whimpering and refused to follow the scent more than a few yards in front of the hunters. Fear spread as well among the camaradas, as the native helpers were familiarly known, even though they carried jaguar spears. It was up to Kermit, the youngest of the group and having the best eyesight, to take the lead; he caught up with the nervous dogs every few meters and urged them on. His two spear men, panting in the heat, barely kept pace with him.

For an hour the party pushed through dense jungle, "where the machetes were constantly at work," then slogged through marshes, where they waded at times up to their hips in water. They were bitten by fire ants, mosquitoes, and wasps and tore their hands and clothing on needle-sharp clusters of thorn palms. Twice they had to swim across bayous too deep for wading, holding their rifles and cartridge belts aloft while struggling to keep from becoming entangled among the slimy stems of water lilies. One casualty of the swim was Roosevelt's pocket watch, a survivor of Cuba and Africa, which "came to an indignant halt." By noon he could only go ahead at a slow walk, at which point Rondon suggested they start back to the river. Kermit by now had disappeared across the marshes with his dogs and spear men, still pursuing the elusive jaguar; there was no point trying to keep up with him.[59]

By 4:00 P.M., the worried captain of the *Nyoac* had begun sounding his steam whistle at intervals and cruising up and down the river, looking for the overdue party. As the steamer rounded a bend, Miller heard a familiar voice singing loudly across the water. A boat was sent out to pick up the hunters. "Are you all right, Colonel?" Fiala called out as they came back. "I'm bully," replied T. R., getting up rather stiffly to reach for the railing. For someone who had walked in the sun for eleven hours, he was bubbling with good humor, calling out "Happy New Year!" in French to the Brazilians and joking that he was just in time for afternoon tea. Rondon, by contrast, could barely drag himself up the ship's ladder.[60]

Once on board, Roosevelt pulled off his muddy boots and sat down to a long-delayed dinner. Between mouthfuls he cheerfully related how many times he had blindly walked into the nests of maribundi wasps when his eyeglasses had steamed over in the humidity. To Miller, sitting across the table, Roosevelt seemed "as fresh in spirit as when he started" that morning. But what a sight he was, sitting there in his stocking feet, clothes muddied and torn, his hair rumpled, and red welts and bumps rising everywhere on his hands, face, and neck. "Good heavens," Miller said to himself, "there sits an ex-president of the United States and I have never seen a more dilapidated individual."[61]

Kermit had tracked the jaguar all afternoon, until his dogs gave out and no amount of sluicing them with hatfuls of water or pushing their noses into the scent could rouse them. He reached the river at dusk, empty-handed and exhausted, having been sustained for twelve hours on nothing more than a cup of coffee and his family's amazing brand of vitality.

"We're on our way to São Luis de Cáceres at last," Kermit wrote his mother on January 3, 1914, as the *Nyoac* resumed working its way up the Paraguay. Two weeks of hunting had proved to be an agreeable interlude.

> Father's in fine shape; and seems to be sleeping fairly well. Yesterday he hurt his knee jumping off the boat, but as soon as we get to Sigg who went on ahead from Corumbá with the baggage, I shall make him massage it. So far we have been living very luxuriously and Rondon has warned us that after São Luis, we leave all that behind. A little less to eat and drink won't hurt anyone, and will improve father's figure. How long this trip will take seems to be getting more doubtful every day; tho I think Rondon is putting an outside estimate on everything so as to have Father prepared for the longest & worst.[62]

Rondon estimated that it might take from one to four months to find the outlet of the River of Doubt. Regardless of how long it took, or the hardships involved, Roosevelt told Captain Amilcar, he had "absolutely decided" to go ahead with the exploration. It would be the last thing he could do in a strenuous way, for he was "an old man" now.[63]

Roosevelt and Rondon had earlier decided that the expedition could achieve greater results if it split into two groups upon reaching the unknown river. The larger of these two groups, consisting of T. R., Rondon, Kermit, Dr. Cajazeira, Cherrie, and possibly Fiala, would descend the River of Doubt. The other party, led by Father Zahm and including Miller, Amilcar, and Harper, would go down the Rio Gy-Paraná, a river Rondon had explored some years earlier and wanted mapped. The rendezvous point for both parties would be the rubber capital of Manáos.

From his letters, Zahm seems to have taken being relegated to the second tier of exploration with good grace, perhaps realizing that he could not make a contribution to a real wilderness trek, such as Roosevelt and Rondon were about to begin. But once down the Gy-Paraná, he still had big plans, as he explained to his brother:

> If my health permits it, I shall take my part of the expedition from Manáos to Caracas, via the Rio Negro . . . [and] the Orinoco . . . I shall thus realize a dream of many years of making a journey through the heart of South America from Patagonia to the Caribbean. It will be the first time the trip has ever been made, & will in the estimation of every one that has heard of it be an extraordinary achievement & one that will contribute more towards making the southern continent known to the world than any similar undertaking in South American history.

Zahm held no resentment toward Roosevelt for the way the expedition's purpose had changed. "T. R. is a splendid traveling companion, always generous, considerate, & unselfish," he told Albert Zahm. "We talk literature & science by the hour, but you will be surprised to learn that we have never yet touched politics, even indirectly . . . You would think he never had any interest in politics or politicians . . . How few people know T. R. as he is in reality!"[64]

For all the comradeship, Zahm realized that Roosevelt would return to New York as soon as the exploration of the River of Doubt was completed. Still determined to reach Caracas, Zahm asked Miller to accompany him through Venezuela and offered to let him collect as much as he wanted. Miller, however, had his heart set on resuming his work around Mount Duida on the upper Orinoco and turned down Zahm's proposal. "It would be an absolute waste of time," the young naturalist wrote Frank Chapman, for Zahm "would not stop en route and has neither the facilities or the means to let me remain at Duida." Besides, Miller had a better offer for the museum. He had succeeded in getting Roosevelt to promise to donate $1,000 of his own money to support Miller's work at Duida and raise another $4,000, "which he says he can easily do." That would allow for an extensive exploration not only of Mount Duida but also other places along the Orinoco. "I saw the possibility of raising funds and took advantage of it," Miller explained. Roosevelt later grew so enthusiastic about the subject that he agreed to raise another $5,000 to keep Cherrie in the field as well.[65]

The enormous population of water birds inhabiting the marshes of the upper Paraguay made collecting a bountiful operation for Cherrie and Miller. During a stop at a ranch house where a steer was butchered for the party, the two naturalists went ashore with their shotguns and brought in nearly fifty birds, some eight or ten of which were species new to Cherrie's list.[66]

Roosevelt took a consuming interest in the work of his naturalists. Cherrie had never met anyone so hungry for knowledge about natural history.

> Day after day the Colonel would ply me with questions regarding the birds and other animals that were being collected and preserved. And he wanted to know all about them; their technical relations to one another, their geographical distribution, their food, their voices, their songs and calls, and their habits—especially the last. In short he wanted to know their life histories from "a" to "z."[67]

On January 5, the expedition reached São Luis de Cáceres, the last settlement on the upper Paraguay. Kermit described it to Belle as "a queer little frontier town." The riverbanks were lined with women and girls washing clothes, and children splashed naked in the shallows. The high grassy hills behind them were carpeted with a rainbow of drying clothes. At the waterfront, all the men gathered to greet Roosevelt with a daytime fireworks display and the inevitable brass band.[68]

Here another of Rondon's loyal lieutenants, João Salustiano Lyra, joined the expedition. Though a young man, Lyra was a veteran of many of Rondon's wilderness campaigns and a trained astronomer. He would serve as navigator—a role Fiala had once planned to play—and would assist Rondon in charting the unknown river. With Lyra came the final member of the Brazilian contingent, Frederico Hoehne, a botanist and zoologist.

Cáceres was the last point from which specimens or letters could reliably be sent back to New York. Roosevelt wired Lauro Müller at Rio de Janeiro that the trip had so far been "a marvelous success."[69] To Henry Fairfield Osborn of the American Museum, T. R. reported that Cherrie and Miller had collected more than a thousand birds and mammals—all in the short space of six weeks. He wanted their work recognized in a lasting way and asked Osborn to take the unusual step of letting the two naturalists publish their own observations on Brazilian faunal life in book form, under museum sponsorship. "It seems to me a matter of justice that the men who undergo the hardship and discomfort of work in the field should be permitted themselves to describe the animals they have collected, and to give their life histories. The man at home cannot adequately give the life histories."[70]

Above Cáceres, only 120 miles of river stood between the Colonel's expedition and the pack trains waiting at Tapirapuan. By steaming all night on January 6, the *Nyoac* reached a cattle ranch called Porto do Campo some 70 miles up the shallow Rio Sepotuba. Beyond this point, only light draft boats could proceed. Rondon had arranged for a gasoline-powered launch—improbably named *Angel of Fortune* and towing a pair of flat boats—to carry the equipment and supplies the remaining 50 miles to Tapirapuan. Cherrie and Harper were among the advance party that departed late on the seventh, leaving Roosevelt and the others to wait for the launch to return for them, a week later.

At Porto do Campo, the travelers for the first time slept under canvas. Military routine set the tone at this first of many wilderness camps. At sunrise and again at sunset, the entire company stood at attention while the colors were raised and lowered to the silvery sound of a bugle. Reveille call came at 5:00 A.M., a full hour later than Brazilian army practice, after T. R. had complained to Rondon about a too-early wakeup. At 8:00 P.M., the bugler sounded retreat inspection, and half an hour later came the call for silence.[71]

During the week-long stay, the Colonel added white-lipped peccaries, bush deer, and tapir to the list of mammals obtained for the American Museum. Father Zahm reported him "as happy as a schoolboy on a picnic" after these hunting forays.[72] The priest reminded him that when they had first spoken of going to South America six years earlier, Roosevelt had been most excited at the prospect of killing jaguar and tapir. "Well," said Zahm, "now you've shot them both!"[73]

At Cáceres, Kermit had come down with what he had thought was a heavy cold, but which gradually worsened into a serious bout of malaria. It left him prostrate in his hammock for four days, unable to stomach food and burning with a 102-degree temperature.[74] He had contracted the disease soon after arriving in Brazil, had dosed himself with quinine at each outbreak, and when the symptoms disappeared, had thought he was cured for good. Dr. Cajazeira tried to impress upon him the need to take quinine regularly, to avoid a relapse, but Kermit hated the bitter taste of the medicine and believed it had harmful side effects. Until the fever broke, on January 12, the Colonel felt "utterly miserable with worry," as he wrote his youngest son, Quentin, not least because it was so hard to get Kermit "to take any care of himself."[75]

On January 12, the little *Angel of Fortune* returned from Tapirapuan with a houseboat strapped to its side and picked up the remaining thirty men, their five dogs, and the baggage. During the journey upriver, Roosevelt and Father Zahm slept on the launch under a canvas awning. Kermit slung his hammock on the side boat, at the stern of which the cook held forth over an improvised fireplace made of earth taken from a deserted anthill. The crew, whom T. R. described as "friendly souls with skins of every shade and hue," slept in the spaces between boxes, bags and slabs of deteriorating beef. At the bow was tied a huge land turtle, nicknamed Lizzie. Miller had caught it and hoped to see it live long enough to reach the Bronx Zoo in New York. At mealtime, some of the men would use its hard carapace as a seat.[76]

The heavily laden launch with its bulky side cargo made no better than a mile an hour against the strong current of the Sepotuba. "The swells are bad, & so is the heat," noted Kermit, but "fortunately the mosquitoes are few."[77] On the third day, rapids began forming, and the launch seemed at times to stand still as the engine shuddered to make headway. The crew and passengers pitched in by poling and grabbing at overhanging tree branches, all aware that the boat had cracked its propeller on a rock on the first trip up and could lose it at any moment.[78]

During the quieter stretches of the voyage to Tapirapuan, the officials in the party brought their journals up-to-date; chatted in a bedlam of English, Portuguese, French, and German; and read. Rondon prepared himself mentally for the river survey ahead by studying a textbook on applied geographical astronomy; Father Zahm, queasy and irritable from the heat and rough water, glanced at an Italian novel; Roosevelt ranged between Gibbon's Roman history, Scott's *Quentin Durward*, and the *Chason de Roland*; and Kermit read Bate's classic, *Naturalist on the Amazon*.

Shortly before noon, on January 16, the overcrowded launch reached Tapirapuan. "So far there have been no hardships on this trip," the Colonel wrote Quentin after arriving, "although of course there has been some fatigue and some discomfort." Ahead lay a four-hundred-mile journey on muleback across the Brazilian plateau to the headwaters of the unknown river, where the real adventure would begin. "This is the last letter you will receive from me," he told his youngest son, "for I think it will take six weeks to two months in getting to you, and I hope that not long after that I will be able to send a telegram to Mother announcing that I have gotten out of the wilderness and am about to sail for home."[79]

NOTES

1. T. R. to Eleanor Butler Roosevelt, 12-10-13, *KRP.* 2. Kermit Roosevelt to Belle Willard, 2-8-13, *KRP.* 3. T. R. to Ethel Roosevelt Derby, 12-10-13, *TRC.* 4. T. R., *Brazilian Wild.*, pp. 38–39. 5. Ibid., pp. 42–43. 6. Rondon, *Lectures*, p. 16. 7. Ibid., p. 18. 8. T. R., *Brazilian Wild.*, pp. 51–52. 9. Ibid., pp. 49–50. 10. Worcester, *Makers of Latin America*, p. 72. 11. T. R., *Brazilian Wild.*, p. 154. 12. Ibid., pp. 154–55. 13. Magalhães, *Ao Candido Mariano.* 14. Bodard, *Green Hell*, p. 13. 15. Rondon to T. R., 5-18-15 (as quoted in *Bulletin of the American Geographical Society*, n.d.). 16. Rondon, *Lectures*, p. 63. 17. T. R. to Henry Cabot Lodge, 12-12-13, *Letters*, Vol. 7, #5878, p. 756. 18. T. R., *Brazilian Wild.*, p. 183. 19. Zahm, J. A., to Albert Zahm, 12-12-13, *CAZA.* 20. T. R., *Brazilian Wild.*, p. 58. 21. Cherrie, *Diary*, 11-18-13. 22. Zahm, *South America's Southland*, p. 424. 23. T. R., *Excelsior Diary*, 12-13-13, *TRC;* T. R., *Brazilian Wild.*, pp. 58, 64–65. 24. Zahm, *South America's Southland*, p. 424; Miller, *In the Wilds*, pp. 221–222. 25. Kermit Roosevelt to Belle Willard, 12-15-13, *KRP.* 26. Cherrie, *Diary* 11-23-13. 27. Miller, *In the Wilds*, pp. 209, 212, 214. 28. Cherrie, *Diary*, 11-26-13 and 12-6-13. 29. Ibid., 11-25-13. 30. Ibid., 12-15-13. 31. Dyott, *Man-Hunting*, p. 40; T. R., *Brazilian Wild.*, p. 60. 32. Waldon, "Making Exploring Safe," *Saturday Evening Post.* 33. T. R. to Robert Bridges, 12-15-13, *CWBL;* Robert Bridges to Frank M. Chapman, 3-18-14, *SCRIB.* 34. T. R., *Brazilian Wild.*, p. 155. 35. Miller, *In the Wilds*, p. 215. 36. T. R., *Brazilian Wild.*, p. 64. 37. Miller, *In the Wilds*, p. 216. 38. Roosevelt, Kermit, *Diary*, 12-17-13. 39. Miller, *In the Wilds*, p. 217. 40. T. R., *Brazilian Wild*, pp. 70–71. 41. Ibid., p. 77. 42. Ibid., p. 78. 43. Roosevelt, Kermit, *Diary*, 12-21-13. 44. T. R., *Brazilian Wild.*, p. 79. 45. Ibid. 46. Roosevelt, Kermit, *Diary*, 12-22-13. 47. T. R., *Brazilian Wild.*, p. 90. 48. Leo E. Miller to Frank M. Chapman, 12-24-13, *AMNH.* 49. Ibid. 50. Kermit Roosevelt to Belle Willard, 12-24-13, *KRP.* 51. T. R. to Edith Kermit Roosevelt, 12-24-13, *KRP.* 52. Cherrie, *Diary*, 12-24-13. 53. *New York Times*, 5-2-14 (quoting Anthony Fiala's diary entry for 12-25-13). 54. Cherrie, *Diary*, 12-25-13. 55. T. R., *Brazilian Wild.*, pp. 102, 109. 56. Roosevelt, Kermit, *Happy Hunting Grounds*, p. 40. 57. T. R., *Brazilian Wild.*, p. 106. 58. Wagenknecht, *Seven Worlds*, p. 19. 59. T. R., *Brazilian Wild.*, p. 114. 60. Miller, *In the Wilds*, p. 220; *New York Times*, 5-2-14 (Anthony Fiala quoted); Fiala, *T. R., Memorial Meeting*, p. 16; Wiley, *T. R.'s America*, p. 309 (Miller quoted). 61. Wiley, *T. R.'s America* (Leo Miller quoted), p. 309. 62. Kermit Roosevelt to Edith Kermit Roosevelt, 1-3-14, *KRP.* 63. Magalhães, *Impressões.* 64. J. A. Zahm to Albert Zahm, 1-5-14, *CAZA.* 65. Leo E. Miller to Frank M. Chapman, 1-1-14 and 4-11-14, *AMNH.* 66. Cherrie, *Diary*, 1-2-14. 67. Cherrie, speech found in his River of Doubt diary, dated 5-26-27. 68. Kermit Roosevelt to Belle Willard, 1-5-14, *KRP.* 69. *New York Times*, 1-10-14. 70. "T. R., Patron of the American Museum," *American Museum Journal.* 71. Magalhães, *Impressões.* 72. Zahm, *South America's Southland*, p. 462. 73. T. R., *Brazilian Wild.*, p. 140. 74. Roosevelt, Kermit, *Diary*, 1-11-14 & 1-12-14. 75. T. R. to Quentin Roosevelt, 1-16-14, *Letters*, Vol. 7, #5879, p. 757. 76. T. R., *Brazilian Wild.*, pp. 155–56. 77. Roosevelt, Kermit, *Diary*, 1-14-14. 78. Kermit Roosevelt to Belle Willard, 1-12-14, *KRP.* 79. T. R. to Quentin Roosevelt, 1-15-14, *Letters*, Vol. 7, #5879, p. 757.

VII

We Have Weeded Out Everyone
Unfit for Exploration

Tapirapuan, at the head of the Rio Sepotuba, was the last outpost of civilization before the Amazon Valley a thousand miles to the north. Here in 1908 Rondon had carved a port out of the jungle through which to funnel reels of zinc wire, crates of china insulators, tools, and food to his telegraph construction crews as they slowly worked their way across the bleak, windswept expanse of the *chapadão*—the high plains of central Brazil. With the line nearing completion in 1914, Tapirapuan had lost its importance, but what remained of its population put on a good show for Roosevelt's arrival. Strings of colorful pennants and Chinese lanterns adorned the row of one-story mud-walled houses that made up the Telegraph Commission headquarters. Nearby, in a grassy central square, the flags of Brazil and the United States were flanked by the national colors of the other twelve South American republics. Miller recalled that the raising and lowering of the flags "were always impressive ceremonies," and accompanied by military band music.[1]

But there was no hiding the chaos that existed off the parade ground. Scores of oxen and mules, requisitioned from neighboring ranches, roamed freely, digging in their hooves when the muleteers and packers tried to drag them back to the corrals to be loaded. Little had been done before the expedition's arrival to sort out two warehouses full of equipment donated by the Brazilian government. All this was in addition to what the launches had brought up. It took six days of sweating labor and bad tempers to finally organize a pack train.

While waiting, the members of the expedition had a last fling with the pampered life they had enjoyed for so many weeks coming up the

98

Paraguay. A nearby cattle ranch provided beef, chickens, and plenty of fresh milk. It was hot, between 91 and 104 degrees, but the Colonel reported few mosquitoes and as usual pronounced himself "very comfortable."[2] After being seasick all the way up the Sepotuba, Father Zahm had something good to say about this camp when he wrote his brother: "T. R. and I are everywhere the recipients of special attention, & nothing is too good for us. We now occupy adjoining rooms in the best house in this place & have several men detailed to look after our every want."[3] Even Cherrie and Miller rated a valet—a young soldier sent over from Captain Amilcar's command.

The two naturalists got in some last-minute collecting at Tapirapuan. Large mammals were scarce, but Miller trapped a rich harvest of rodents from the cultivated fields. Cherrie acquired over a hundred more birds, all the while battling the numbing pain of a palm thorn that had pierced his leg and partially paralyzed the muscles in his foot.

The skinning work took place in a shed made of corrugated iron, with Miller's pet owl, Moses, looking down on the proceedings from his perch. Kermit, still flushed with fever, helped the naturalists skin and pack the accumulated specimens. He also hunted untiringly but brought in only a few monkeys and an armadillo for his efforts. The dangerous and much-sought-after peccaries eluded him, for which he blamed his timid hounds. "Found fresh pig tracks," he noted in disappointment one day, "but the dogs wouldn't follow."[4]

Roosevelt brought Frank Chapman up-to-date on the expedition's progress at this time: "We have done well since I wrote you" [October 15]. Cherrie's bird count exceeded 1,000 already, and Miller so far had collected almost 250 mammals, including jaguar, anteaters, tapir, and various species of deer. From now on, though, Roosevelt doubted that they would have the time to collect any more big mammals. In four to six weeks, they would start descending the unknown river. "It is not possible to give a forecast as to the time that will be required . . . If, as I expect, everything comes out all right I shall have much to tell you when in May or thereabouts I turn up in New York."[5]

Roosevelt remained dubious about the success of his *Scribner's* articles. Enclosing chapter V ("Up the River of Tapirs") to Robert Bridges, T. R. brooded that "perhaps none of them are really good—it is impossible for me to tell, because here on the ground I may think the experience and observations interesting when they are really uninteresting." He hoped to send off the next installment in a fortnight. The final two or three articles would reach *Scribner's* about the same time that he did, and he was more hopeful about public acceptance for these latter ones, since "there ought to be a certain interest in our experiences in going down a river that no civilized man has ever seen."[6]

Frank Harper was the first casualty of the increasing physical demands being placed on the party. The tropics did not suit the Colonel's city-bred secretary. Coming up from Porto do Campo, he had contracted malaria, and now he lay in his hammock weak and miserable.[7] Roosevelt suggested that it would be a good idea for him to return home. He left on Sunday afternoon, January 18, on the launch that would take him down to Cáceres to wait for a steamer south. In saying good-bye to him, Cherrie noticed how eager Harper was "to get away in [the] direction of civilization and its comforts and conveniences."[8]

With Harper went five crates of bird and animal skins the naturalists had collected. A much bigger crate was hammered together to hold Miller's giant live turtle, Lizzie. Thinking of the long voyage it would face, Miller dropped pieces of sliced melon and other fruits through the bars of the crate. One of the camaradas stood watching and finally shook his head at the waste of food. "Don't give her all that," he advised Miller. "A turtle is just like a camel and the elephant; it can go six months without eating." Miller later learned that Lizzie survived the trip and proved to be the largest of her species in the Bronx Zoo's collection.[9]

The men needed by the expedition as drovers, camp helpers, guards, and paddlers were drawn from a contingent of the Thirty-eighth Infantry Battalion stationed at Tapirapuan and also mustered from what were called "regional volunteers"—local cowboys and rivermen. Dr. Cajazeira examined them and was appalled at their poor physical condition, finding "three soldiers whose chronic malarial status was something fearful" and many others with enlarged spleens, a sign of malarial infection. Altogether, 148 men were chosen, an indication of how large the expedition had grown by this time.[10] Perhaps the most eager of the volunteers was Julio de Lima, a muscle-bound ox of a man from the Atlantic coastal town of Bahia, who bragged of his strength and practically begged Rondon to take him along.

Loading the pack animals proved more difficult than anyone bargained for. The oxen were for the most part fresh from the range and unused to being harnessed. The gauchos had to blindfold them before attempting to put a load on their backs. When the eye patches were removed, the animals panicked, bucking across the corral in clouds of dust and scattering saddles and bundles. The time lost to breaking them in infuriated Kermit, who counted every day until he could join his fiancée. "I have been ready to kill the whole lot and all the members of the expedition," he wrote savagely to Belle, after witnessing the fiasco. People used to get angry at him for being so unconcerned about delays, he recalled; "They wouldn't now though, if they knew how delays make me feel." But he had to keep his fury silent, because it would upset his father if he was heard complaining.[11]

Roosevelt could see by the sheer amount of baggage on hand—more than 360 crates and bundles—that the expedition was overburdened. He had to use all his tact to persuade Rondon to leave behind half of the pavilion-sized tents the government had furnished. Rondon did so reluctantly, heartbroken at the thought that someone of T.R.'s stature should travel across Brazil in anything less than first-class style.[12]

Faced with more loads than animals to carry them, Captain Amilcar, the transport chief, began making reductions on the spot. First to go were crates of candy the government had purchased from Colombo's Confectioners Shop. This brought immediate howls of protest from the expedition's cinematographer, Lieutenant Reis, he who had so artfully penned Christmas cards on the *Nyoac*. Amilcar chastised the young officer for putting his sweet tooth ahead of the welfare of the mules, but then relented and let Reis pick out a few of the choicer containers. Afterward, Amilcar took a piece of chalk and marked the boxes with a cross, muttering to an assistant not to let this "contraband" go through until last.[13]

The expedition's baggage train, numbering some 250 mules and oxen, was too big to move as a single unit. Rondon accordingly divided it into two *turmas*, or groups. The larger of these, under Amilcar's command, departed from Tapirapuan on January 19, taking with it 150 pack animals, Fiala's Canadian canoes, and all the food and equipment needed for the Dúvida and Gy-Paraná descents. A smaller detachment, led by Roosevelt and Rondon, marched out two days later, with 98 mules, 9 hunting horses, and enough food to last them for the month-long trek across the *chapadão*. Fiala rode on ahead with his motion-picture camera to record the procession on film.[14]

Rondon's marching orders called for Roosevelt's column to follow the telegraph road to the Falls of Utiarity on the Rio Papagaio, some 175 miles north of Tapirapuan. From there they would turn west and follow the telegraph wire another 200 miles to the station at José Bonifácio, not far from the headwaters of the unknown river. Amilcar's pack train was to stay a day or more ahead of them and clear the trail if necessary.

The first day's march, on January 21, proved to be a short one. The mounted members of Roosevelt's detachment set off at a steady jogging trot, following the telegraph road north along the right bank of the Rio Sepotuba. The mule train was soon left behind. Cherrie rode an obliging little hunting mule named Angel Falls but admitted that after covering seventeen miles in four and a half hours, there "were none of our party that was not ready to quit for the day!" They crossed the river on a primitive ferry made of rough planks laid over several dugouts and found a ready-made camp of palm-thatched huts waiting for them at the rapids called Salto da Felicidade. The Brazilian and American flags were tied together and hoisted on a pole in front of Roosevelt's shelter.[15]

The pack mules lagged so far behind that it was 10:00 P.M. before the cook could concoct a dinner of beef, pork, rice, and underdone black beans for the saddlesore riders. The food was laid out on two rawhide skins, around which everyone squatted or sat cross-legged. A stickler about protocol, Rondon produced two folding canvas chairs for Roosevelt and Father Zahm. The Colonel noticed that Rondon did not have a chair and refused to sit down in his until Rondon found one too, declaring that he wanted no special favors while in the wilderness.[16]

The mules were left free to graze all night, and not until 9:00 the next morning were the last stragglers brought in and loaded. As camp broke up, Sigg informed the doctor that Father Zahm had become nauseous during the preceding day's short ride. Worried that the priest's advanced age and lack of horsemanship could lead to an accident, Cajazeira rode by his side all day.[17]

The trail now turned west from the Sepotuba into thick tropical forest, where sunlight filtered palely through canopies of arching palm fronds and the foliage of lofty trees. The woods sang with bird calls. Roosevelt's keen ear picked out the loud, three-time whistle of "gorgeous red-and-green trogons, with long tails, perched motionless on the lower branches" and the call of the false bell-bird, "which is gray instead of white like the true bell-birds; it keeps among the very topmost branches."[18]

When not studying bird songs, Roosevelt passed the long hours in the saddle by reciting aloud such favorite poems as "The Saga of King Olaf" and the works of Kipling, Shelley, and Keats. He had only to read a poem several times to be able to later recall it exactly. Kermit, riding alongside, would match his father stanza for stanza, carrying on a family tradition.[19]

The forest gradually thinned to sandy open country, sparsely covered with stunted gray-barked trees and scruffy grass. By 4:00 P.M., without having stopped once, Rondon finally called a halt at a clearing, the site of an abandoned telegraph construction camp. Weeds flourished in the fields where rice, manioc, and corn had once grown. Called Kilometer 50, it was exactly that distance from Tapirapuan. Heavy rain began falling as the men erected the tents, but three hours later, Cherrie noted, "the sky was aglitter with stars."[20]

By 7:00 the following morning, January 23, the first of the mules and their drovers were filing out of Camp Kilometer 50. The road immediately began climbing the foothills of the Serra dos Parecis, the mountain range that rises over two thousand feet in places to form the southern rim of the great central plateau covering half of Brazil. As they gained the heights, Roosevelt and his companions stopped for a backward glance at the vast Paraguayan marshes shimmering in the morning haze. Far behind them, the pack mules struggled up the steep slopes.

The sky turned overcast, and cool winds swept across the empty plains. After weeks of being cooped up on a crowded river steamer, Roosevelt exulted in the sense of energy and freedom of the wide open spaces.[21] Cherrie, riding behind him, felt the same exhilaration: "All day we travel over a high open plateau—a rolling country—at the top of every ridge one has a magnificent view for miles in every direction."[22] The shadeless, sandy vistas reminded Father Zahm of the Arizona desert: "During our first day in this arid land we did not find a drop of water for a stretch of twenty miles." At intervals along the trail lay the sun-bleached bones of pack animals abandoned at earlier times by Rondon's construction crews. More ominous to Zahm was the sight of scattered wooden crates stenciled "Roosevelt South American Expedition," thrown off by some of Amilcar's unruly oxen several days before. They had to leave these discarded boxes behind, as the overloaded mules could carry no more weight.[23]

By forced marching, Roosevelt's detachment reached the next camp-site, Aldeia Queimada, at midday. The name meant "burnt village" and marked the site of a former Parecis Indian settlement burned to the ground by soldiers led by a brother of Gov. Costa Marques, whose family had entertained Roosevelt so lavishly. Rondon had since been able to pacify the Parecis through peaceful persuasion and got many of them to work for his Telegraph Commission.[24]

At this camp, Rondon received word of a temporary breakdown in Amilcar's detachment. While making a nighttime crossing of the Rio Sepotuba, Amilcar had lost control of his pack animals, and a full day had been spent tracking down runaway mules. He also reported that many of his oxen were limping from exhaustion. The debacle caused three members of his command—Dr. Soledade, the botanist Hoehne, and Lieutenant Reis—to resign their commissions, all convinced the expedition would never make it to Bonifácio station. Rondon accepted the discharges, happy to be rid of malcontents, and commended Amilcar on his diligence.[25]

Kermit sought his own form of escape from the tedium of the marches by spending the days hunting on his big, white mule, accompanied by his dog Trigueiro and a wrinkled old camarada. His absence gave the Colonel added cause to worry, but T. R. recognized his son's need for solitude. By late afternoon, sometimes empty-handed, at other times with a pair of slender pampas deer roped behind his saddle, Kermit would return to the old camp and collect his personal belongings. Then he would start out for the new campsite, "first through the sunset," as he wrote Belle, "then the twilight, & then the night; hearing the birds singing away, & then gradually becoming hushed as night fell."[26]

A sixteen-mile march on January 24 brought Roosevelt's party up over the divide separating the watersheds of the Paraguay on the south and the streams flowing northward to the Amazon. Rondon chose the banks of the Rio Perdiz, a small tributary of the Tapajós, as a campsite. The advance party waited in the rain all afternoon for the pack train to arrive. "My poncho N.G. [no good] and I got soaked," Cherrie grumbled later in his diary. When the mule train stumbled in long after dark, he, Miller, and Fiala spread their bedding side by side beneath a single fly tent, glad to have any kind of shelter. By 10:00, in a miracle of improvisation, the cook was able to ladle out dinner to men who had not eaten for fourteen hours.[27]

Such miserable camping conditions only worsened Father Zahm's attitude. This was not the pleasure cruise down easy-flowing rivers that he had described to Roosevelt the previous summer. Exhausted from the marches and disillusioned with the way his cherished expedition had changed, Zahm had turned into a chronic complainer. He depended constantly on Sigg for assistance. When it was suggested that Sigg be sent on ahead for a few days to help prepare a camp, Zahm protested so strongly that the idea was dropped.[28]

Roosevelt, on the other hand, took a boyish delight in every aspect of the march across the Brazilian plains. He found it "a picturesque sight" each morning as the packers brought in the scattered mules and the big tents were lowered and folded up. Breakfast was necessarily a bountiful meal, as there was no stopping for lunch. The traditional beans and rice were augmented by crackers, canned corned beef and salmon, coffee, English tea, and *matté*—the powerfully stimulative South American tea, which Roosevelt for some reason declined to try. Afterward, while the pack animals were being loaded, he would set up his portable writing table to forge ahead on his *Scribner's* article, stopping now and then to sharpen his pencil with a penknife.[29] Kermit recalled that his father was "invariably good-humored" about doing his daily stint of words—"he was paying for his fun."[30] But writing never came easily for Roosevelt, especially in the field. He weighed every word, revising and correcting so much that some of his pages became almost indecipherable. In South America, as in Africa, he was dogged by a sense of having failed as a journalist. Sometimes, after a long day in the saddle, he refused to write a word and instead picked up a book and read for several hours until he was in the mood.[31]

T. R., with his insatiable curiosity about the natural world, found ample subjects to study at each camp. While waiting for the mule train to arrive, the former president recorded details about anthills as tall as men, red grasshoppers as big as sparrows, and "an extraordinary colony of spiders."

> It was among some dwarf trees, standing a few yards apart from one another by the water. When we reached the camping-place, early in the afternoon . . . just ahead of the rain—no spiders were out. They were under the leaves of the trees. Their webs were tenantless, and indeed for the most part were broken down. But at dusk they came out from their hiding-places, two or three hundred of them in all, and at once began to repair the old and spin new webs. Each spun his own circular web, and sat in the middle; and each web was connected on several sides with other webs, while those nearest the tree were hung to them by spun ropes, so to speak. The result was a kind of sheet of web consisting of scores of wheels, in each of which the owner and proprietor sat . . . The webs could hardly be seen; and the effect was of scores of big, formidable-looking spiders poised in midair, equidistant from one another, between each pair of trees. When darkness and rain fell they were still out, fixing

their webs, and pouncing on the occasional insects that
blundered into the webs.[32]

In the evening, sitting around a campfire, the members of the
expedition shared episodes from their pasts. Kermit took charge of
translating from Portuguese to English and back again. Rondon and
Lyra had grim memories of being the first explorers in the very country
they were now passing through and of living for weeks on nothing
more than fruit, nuts, and honey stolen from beehives. Fiala spoke of
being marooned in the Arctic and hunting polar bears, and Cherrie
revealed incidents from his younger days as a part-time insurrectionist
with a band of Venezuelan rebels. But Roosevelt topped them all as a
raconteur. "No one could tell a better story," Kermit recalled of his
father.[33] His repertoire ranged from tales of cowboy life in the Dakota
Badlands, to hunting lions in East Africa, to wrangling with politicians
as president. Rondon had never met a man who could talk so much.
"He would talk all of the time . . . and on all conceivable subjects." To
the Brazilians, Roosevelt was a *pandego*—the life of the party.[34]

When not trading reminiscences, the explorers speculated endlessly
on where the River of Doubt flowed. Unlike other great river explorations,
this search was not for the river's source, which Rondon had already
found, but for its mouth. The area of the search was enormous—a roughly
wedge-shaped region nine hundred miles long and four hundred miles
broad, lying half in the Mato Grosso and half in Amazonas state, and
bounded on the east by the Tapajós, on the west by the Madeira, and
on the southwest by the Rio Gy-Paraná. At the north end, the point of
the wedge touched the mighty Amazon itself. Unless the Dúvida ended
up dissolving into some great interior lake or swamp, it had to come out
into one of these boundary rivers. The question was which one.

The best maps of 1914 were of no help in solving this geographical
puzzle. Much of central Brazil was then still designated as "unexplored
territory," although piecemeal attempts had been made over the centuries to chart its maze of rivers. The Tapajós had been discovered in
1726 and used since as a trade route from southern Mato Grosso to the
Amazon. At the end of the eighteenth century, the great Portuguese
explorer-geographer Ricardo Franco had surveyed the Amazon and
Madeira and recorded the locations of all tributaries entering these two
great rivers. During the ensuing hundred years, few of these affluents
were officially explored very far up from their mouths. Their upper
courses were known only to Indians and to wandering *seringueiros*, the

rubber hunters who prowled the backlands. As a result, cartographers were dependent on guesswork—and imagination—to fill in the blank spaces between the Madeira and the Tapajós. When Rondon began his own surveying work in 1907, he found that the existing maps contained "so many great errors and numberless omissions" as to be useless. In one instance, he found the Rio Gy-Paraná wrongly placed on the old charts by as much as two degrees of longitude.[35]

There was sharp disagreement among the Brazilian officers as to the Dúvida's probable course. Amilcar thought it turned east at some point and joined the Tapajós. From the beginning, Lyra believed it would prove to be a tributary of the Gy-Paraná, the nearest of the boundary rivers. In that event, Roosevelt's exploring adventure would take less than a week to accomplish, after which the party would march back to descend the Ananás, the other mystery river Rondon had discovered on his 1909 expedition. The Colonel was willing to explore both streams, but would allow his name to be given only to a really important river.[36]

The Gy-Paraná connection seemed plausible to Rondon as well until 1913, when his exploring teams found no evidence that the Dúvida formed one of its headwaters. From that moment, Rondon became convinced that his so-called River of Doubt "could only be the upper part of some river whose mouth on the Madeira was already known."[37] His first choice was a river long known to the rubber gatherers as the Madeira's largest tributary—the Rio Aripuanã. This name did not appear on any standard map of Brazil, including the one the American Museum of Natural History had furnished Roosevelt. The mouth of the Aripuanã was situated very far down on the Madeira's right bank, at about 5 degrees south latitude. If the Dúvida was the Aripuanã's unexplored upper course, the combined length of the two rivers could be as much as a thousand miles.

Rubbermen whom Rondon had met told him how they had traveled far up the Aripuanã and encountered rapids, above which the river was joined by another big river coming in from the west. Hostile Indians had kept them from going farther up either stream. Rondon was also aware that in 1909, officials of the Amazonas State Boundary Commission had gone up the right, or eastern, branch of the Aripuanã as far as 8 degrees 48 minutes south in order to mark the border with Mato Grosso. It was possible that the Dúvida was one of these two branches, but Rondon could not be sure whether it would prove to be the eastern or the western branch, if either. To help solve this mystery, he had directed another assistant, Lieutenant Pyrenius, to travel up the Aripuanã to the first fork he found and wait there to see if Roosevelt's party came out one branch or the other.

By January 26, five days after leaving Tapirapuan, the Colonel's pack train was still a hundred miles from Utiarity, creeping along at no better than three miles an hour. Weakened from lack of grass, the mules were gradually giving out. At each camp, one or more of them were cut loose to wander off. In the early days of building the telegraph line, Rondon had lost so many animals on this barren route that he had been forced to import big motorvans from France to transport his supplies. Three of the machines were still operating and were now pressed into service. "It was a strange sight to see them racing across the uninhabited *chapadão* at a speed of thirty miles an hour," Miller recalled. The wheels on both sides of the vehicle—a forerunner of the World War I tank—were fitted with an endless belt of slats, which enabled the trucks to charge through mud holes and streams without bogging down.[38] Cherrie and Miller took advantage of this speed, hitching a ride to Utiarity and gaining a few days for collecting before the rest of the party arrived. Father Zahm saw an opportunity to avoid riding a mule any further and got Rondon's permission to go in one of the trucks with Sigg.

Grinding gears and backfiring, the motorvans departed the next morning for what Rondon promised would be a one-day journey. It took the better part of three to reach Utiarity. The Indian driver in Miller and Cherrie's truck was a genius at coaxing the engine to life when it stalled and at building ramps of stones and branches when the slatted treads mired in deep sand and mud.[39] Father Zahm fared less well in the choice of a chauffeur, finding himself wedged in the front seat between Sigg and "an ignorant and careless negro" who showed "his incompetence in many ways." Zahm never forgave Rondon for what he thought was a calculated slight and remembered the episode as an example of how much he suffered on the trip.[40]

Meanwhile, the long file of mules continued to lumber on toward Utiarity. In the daytime, swarms of piums—tiny blood-sucking sand flies—followed the travelers like clouds of smoke and forced them to wear head nets and gauntlet gloves. The bite of a pium barely left a mark on the skin but itched maddeningly for weeks.[41] At dusk, mosquitoes fanned out over the campsite and crept into tents and under the folds of the most carefully tucked-in netting. In preparing for the trip, Roosevelt had taken along some bottles of "fly dope," a primitive insect repellent that his personal physician, Dr. Lambert, had used in the North

Woods and swore by. T. R. disliked using the greasy ointment, which soon washed off with perspiration, but there were times when the only way he could get a few hours of sleep was to smear it liberally over his face and neck.[42]

Crawling insects were just as much of a psychological and physical torment as the winged species. Many of the campsites en route to the River of Doubt were plagued by armies of leaf-carrying ants. Called *carregadores*, meaning "porters," by the Brazilians, these swarming ants would cut up and carry off anything made of cloth or leather left on the ground. There were also invasions by armies of termites, which did not bite, and by what T. R. described as "huge black ants," measuring an inch and a quarter long, "which were very vicious" and bit painfully.[43]

On January 28, the telegraph line came into sight, running west from the Mato Grosso capital of Cuiabá to the Madeira. For the first time, the Colonel's party heard the wind humming in the wires, a sound that would be part of every campsite until they reached the unknown river, when another and more disturbing sound would fill their ears.[44]

The next day, a six-hour march brought them to the banks of the Rio Sacre, where the supply road ended. The mules were unloaded and ferried across in small groups on a hand-pulled pontoon made from planks and dugouts. Rondon had sent word with the motorvans for the operator of the telegraph station on the western side of the river to prepare a camp for the party. A row of tents stood pitched beneath the flags of Brazil and the United States, facing the huts of a Parecis Indian village and within sight and sound of the thunderous falls known as Salto Bello.

On an earlier visit, Rondon had installed some wooden benches overlooking the falls. From this spectacular vantage point, the Colonel gazed out over a wall of green water that plunged 150 feet into a wooded ravine, sending up a perpetual veil of mist. Lyra's chance remark that Salto Bello could produce thirty-six thousand horsepower of electricity if harnessed to generators set the ever-optimistic Roosevelt to envisioning an industrial civilization—towns, factories, and trolley lines—sprouting up some distant day on these desolate plains.[45]

Of more immediate interest to the Colonel were the Parecis Indians at this settlement. He described them as "an unusually cheerful, good-humored, pleasant-natured people," still living in a half-wild state but grown tame through Rondon's frequent gifts of fresh beef, blankets, and tools. Short and sturdily built, the Parecis had light brown skin, tangled black hair, and handsome features—except when they opened their mouths. Adults and children alike suffered from rotted teeth, perhaps because of their steady diet of manioc, maize, and sweet potatoes. Many of the men had adopted trousers, shirts, and sandals and were employed by the Telegraph Commission as guards and repair workers. The women went naked except for loincloths. They breast-fed their chubby babies while holding them on their hips in cloth slings. Polygamy was common, but Roosevelt, whose moral code was as strict as Queen Victoria's, took a broad-minded view of the Parecis's communal life. "The women seemed to be well treated," he was relieved to find, and "the children were loved by every one . . ."[46]

Roosevelt was fascinated by the Parecis's favorite sport, a game similar to soccer that he dubbed "head ball" because only the player's head was allowed to touch the ball. The object was to keep the ball—an eight-inch-diameter hollow blob of latex tapped from a rubber tree—passing in the air between two opposing teams. If the ball landed, one of the participants would have to get it airborne again by dropping to the ground and butting it with his head. "Why they do not grind off their noses I cannot imagine," wrote T. R. "Some of the players hardly ever failed to catch and return the ball if it came in their neighborhood, and with such a vigorous toss of the head that it often flew in a great curve for a really astonishing distance."[47]

Kermit endured some anxious hours at the Rio Sacre campsite, when the mule carrying his belongings failed to arrive. Its saddle bag contained all the letters he had written to Belle since leaving Tapirapuan, and which he expected to send back from Utiariy. When the missing mules finally did show up, he was relieved to find his baggage intact. Wisely, he had kept Belle's photograph and her letters safely buttoned up in his shirt pocket. "I have got wet through so many times that they're becoming very worn even inside their cases," he confessed, "but they're such a comfort to me, Belle. I don't know what I'd have done if they had got lost."[48]

Only eight miles of westward march separated the Rio Sacre from the wider Rio Papagaio, tributary of the Juruena and site of the Falls of Utiariy, one of the great natural wonders of South America. Rondon had discovered the cataract in 1907 during his first exploring expedition. He never forgot "the deafening roar of this furious mass of water," taller than Niagara and twice the width of the waterfall of Salto Bello.[49] The name Utiariy honored the sacred falcon of the Parecis people, whose homeland the Papagaio bordered. Half a mile upstream from the falls, where Roosevelt's pack train was ferried across, a telegraph station had been operating since 1910. A large settlement of Parecis Indians had developed around it. The station master and his brown-skinned wife doubled as schoolteachers to the Indian children, who were already speaking Portuguese and learning to read.[50]

The Colonel rode in side by side on muleback with Rondon and was welcomed by the Parecis headman, who paraded proudly in the uniform of a Brazilian army major. The chief's two wives and the rest of the villagers crowded close to stare with friendly curiosity at the khaki-clad strangers whom Rondon had brought with him. Seeing an American ex-president for the first time caused a stir, but there was no denying the affection the Indians held for Rondon. The children took turns being cuddled in his arms. "Out here he is a real king," Kermit informed Belle. After failing to persuade Brazilians to work in the wilderness, Rondon had organized the Indians to guard the hundred-mile stretches between telegraph stations. He had even gone so far as to send his best native workers to Rio de Janeiro to learn telegraphy.[51]

Sad news awaited the Colonel at Utiarity. A telegram announced the death of his young niece, Margaret Roosevelt, Edith's traveling companion during the tour of the South American capitals. Margaret had fallen ill with typhoid soon after reaching New York and died a few days later. Out of respect, Rondon canceled the festivities the Indians had planned for Roosevelt.

Father Zahm's usefulness to the expedition he had organized came to an end at Utiarity. While waiting for Roosevelt to arrive with the pack train, Zahm had made inquiries with the telegraph employees as to whether he could obtain a chair fastened to two long poles and supported by four men. This would save him from the dizzying discomfort of riding a mule for several hundred more miles. When Rondon informed him that the Parecis Indians would never submit to carrying anyone across the wilderness in this way, Zahm pointed out that he had used just this sort of transportation on his earlier travels through Peru, where the natives were taught that it was a honor to carry a representative of the Church.[52] That might be true in Peru, Rondon replied, but except for sickness or disablement, "no one in Brazil could obtain such a mode of conveyance"—it went against their democratic ideals.[53]

Roosevelt had no choice but to side with Rondon in this dispute. He summoned Zahm to his tent. As painful as it was for him to say to his old colleague, it came down to this: If Zahm could no longer ride a mule, he must return to Tapirapuan. The expedition could not keep anyone who was not physically fit, and Zahm was only endangering his life by going on any farther. It was arranged that Zahm would remain at Utiarity for a few more days and then go back with the motorvans.

"Father Zahm is being sent back from here," Kermit informed Belle afterwards. "He showed him[self] so completely incompetent & selfish that he got on everyone's nerves, and then he did a couple of things that made it easy to send him back . . . fortunately Father has managed it without any real bad feeling."[54]

In spite of his removal, Zahm still talked about going on into Venezuela as originally planned, and alone if necessary, "in the interest of the expedition." The Colonel wired the Booth Steamship Company agent at Manáos to release to Zahm the food cache that had been shipped there for the journey up the Rio Negro. He also handed Zahm a letter addressed to the Venezuelan consul at Manáos, expressing his regrets to the president of Venezuela at not being able to visit that country.[55]

Neither Roosevelt nor Zahm made any mention of this episode in their memoirs of the trip. Leaving the expedition he had put so much care into creating was a bitter experience for Zahm—"the greatest disappointment of my life," he later told T. R.[56] In the end, Zahm would give up trying to complete his northward journey and instead, as soon as he reached Buenos Aires, sailed for Europe to recover his health.

On February 1, the day after removing Zahm, Roosevelt wrote out a pencil memorandum to justify his action:

> Every member of the expedition has told me that in his
> opinion it is essential to the success and well being of
> the expedition that Father Zahm should at once leave
> it and return to the settled country.

One after another, all ten of the American and Brazilian members of the party—including Sigg—signed their names to this document.[57]

The poor condition of the pack animals made a rest of several days at Utiarity imperative. After two weeks of stumbling through deep sand drifts and mud-choked trails, the mules looked even bonier than they had at Tapirapuan. The grass along the way had been so sparse and thin that it was only a matter of time before many of the animals collapsed from hunger.

Rain now fell so constantly that even Father Zahm, who had once dismissed the idea of a rainy season as exaggerated, had to admit it was a reality.[58] Blankets and clothing hung limp and offered no warmth in the sopping humidity. Overnight, rifles and iron camp fittings turned scratchy with rust. Green and white mold spores bloomed on leather harnesses, boots, and binocular cases. The perpetual dampness even held surprises for sleepers, as Kermit found out one night when his hammock rotted through, dumping him to the ground and "causing lots of bad languages" to come out of his mouth.[59]

The Colonel finished his sixth *Scribner's* article at this camp. He entrusted one carbon copy to Rondon's Indian runner, the other set to Father Zahm. The photographs tucked away in the envelopes looked "pretty good," T. R. wrote Robert Bridges, but he could not shake off his pessimism about the writing. "I have'n't [sic] the least idea whether any of these chapters are what you wish, or whether they are worth anything." As a title for the future book version of his articles, he suggested *Through the Brazilian Wilderness.** He had toyed with the word "Hinterland" but thought it might sound "too . . . Dutch."[60]

When not hunched over his writing table, T. R. spent hours looking down at the Falls of Utiarity. Under cloudy skies, the deep greens and pure whites of the thundering water took on shimmering, pearlescent tones. Wrapped in the ceaseless roar, he had time to think about Edith and how lonely she must be at snowbound Sagamore Hill, of the new grandchildren waiting for him in the spring, and of Kermit's wedding, to be held in Spain or Virginia, wherever their womenfolk decided.

By February 3 the rain had held off long enough for Rondon to decide that the march could resume again. The next objective was the telegraph station on the Rio Juruena—the name given the upper course of the Tapajós—some sixty miles west of Utiarity.

In the final hours at Utiarity, Cherrie and Miller packed up the bigger animal pelts and saw them loaded on the trucks. Miller had added a soft-shelled armadillo—shot by T. R.—to his list of mammals, but rain had kept Cherrie from acquiring many more birds.

"As usual we did not leave camp . . . until late (1:15 P.M.)," Cherrie wrote of the February 3 departure, "and of course [we] rode through the hottest part of the day."[61] Rondon planned a short march so as not to strain the pack animals; a week of grazing had not restored their strength. The drovers had to prod the mules' flanks to keep up the pace. Behind them, teams of grunting, emaciated oxen pulled two high-wheeled

---

*This turned out to be the eventual title. The book was published in 1914 by Charles Scribner's Sons.

carts piled up with freight. A separate herd of oxen, not carrying loads, brought up the rear of the column. These beasts were doomed to be gradually slaughtered to provide fresh meat for the expedition. To save weight, Roosevelt had reluctantly agreed to leave the Canadian canoes and the outboard motor at Utiarity. He had wanted to try them out on the unknown river, but with a two-hundred-mile march still ahead, it was essential to cut down all unnecessary baggage.

Also left behind at Utiarity were Father Zahm, Sigg, and two disabled camaradas whom Dr. Cajazeira had pulled out of the expedition, one half dead with malaria. The motorvans were to take them all to Tapirapuan the following morning. Roosevelt had asked Sigg to accompany Zahm at least as far as the Paraguay River and see him safely put on a steamer. Although Sigg's nursing skills and handiness had proven valuable up to this point, T. R. decided that his services were not essential for the river exploration. Sigg took his dismissal hard, ashamed at what his newfound friends in Paraguay would say when he turned up unexpectedly.[62]

Everyone in the party was glad to be free of Zahm's incessant complaining, and apparently no one more so than Roosevelt himself. Cherrie observed that "Zahm had gotten much on T. R.'s nerves!"[63]

The pack train was predictably hours late in arriving at the new campsite, located by a swampy creek. Darkness had fallen by the time the first *tropa* of mules and their footsore attendants trudged in. Rondon was not with them; he had been detained farther back on the trail in his efforts to keep some semblance of order in a transport system that was slowly disintegrating. By this time, some of the mules could barely walk, even without loads. As soon as the muleteers untied the girdle ropes and heaved off the packing boxes, the animals stumbled away in a desperate search for grass and water. The men pitched the tents in the wavering light of the campfire, and the cook heated up a late supper of beef, rice, and black beans.

Before crawling into his tent, the Colonel sat up with the naturalists to listen to the night sounds. Mosquitoes hummed around their head nets. From the swamp, they could hear the strange, shoutlike croakings of the bullfrogs. This reminded Miller of the curious tree frog he had observed in Colombia, which swelled itself with air to near bursting, then brayed like a donkey. Cherrie spoke of an encounter with a monster frog in British Guiana, which evacuated air in short, roaring bursts.[64]

Later in the night, the mosquitoes grew so aggressive that Cherrie was forced out of his netting-draped hammock and into the tent he shared with Miller. He lay on the floor, sweating freely, and listened to the whine of insects just outside.[65]

The rain held off long enough the next day, February 4, for the pack train to reach the banks of the Burity River, where the Telegraph Commission employed several Parecis families to operate a ferry service. The strong, clean current of the Burity provided a community bathtub for the expedition, whose members scrubbed off several days of sweat and grime and inspected their numerous insect bites. At this encampment, biting flies—from sand flies to big blood-sucking boroshuda flies—proved to be as tormenting as the mosquitoes. There were also small, nonsting-ing bees, which caused a slight tickling sensation as they crawled over hands and faces and tried to creep behind the lenses of eyeglasses. The Brazilian name for them was *lambe-olho*, or "eye lickers," after their predilection for the liquid of human eyes.[66]

By this time, Roosevelt had decided that another member of the party would have to be sent back. At the Burity camp, he told a crestfallen Anthony Fiala that he would not be able to take him down the River of Doubt. He suggested that Fiala return to Utiariy and join one of Rondon's assistants, Lieutenant Lauriodó; descend the Rio Papagaio, the as-yet-unexplored tributary of the Juruena; and from there go down the Tapajós to the Amazon.[67] Officially, Rondon wanted the Papagaio mapped to its junction with the Juruena, but the offer also represented a face-saving gesture for Fiala, who had not measured up to the harsher standards of personal efficiency now being demanded of everyone in the expedition.

Fiala's experience in the Arctic did not serve him well in South America. "[He] was quite incompetent to do a single thing," Miller con-fided to Frank Chapman. "Most of his equipment was useless, or as it has been appropriately termed, 'doodle-dabs.'"*[68] The paper dials on the compasses he had brought from New York wilted in the tropical humidity. Fiala had taught himself how to use a naval sextant on the voyage down to Brazil but discovered that it could not measure the extreme high angle of the sun while the party crossed the Parecis Plateau.[69] He tried to devise an observation instrument from bent wire, but the leaders of the expedition came to depend on Lyra's accurate theodolite to determine their latitude and longitude.

Fiala was also unfairly blamed for the collapse of the mule train. Every previous expedition across the bleak *chapadão* had suffered severe losses in pack animals, mainly because of the lack of adequate grass. If Fiala was guilty of anything, it was having listened to Zahm and

---

* This term was probably coined by Cherrie, who had a wry wit and referred to Fiala behind his back as "Thermos" for his obsession with fancy camp equipment.

placed too much emphasis on luxuries when he drew up the list of provisions in New York. His comrades would later find whole cases of olive oil, dried mustard, malted milk, stuffed olives, prunes, applesauce, and Rhine wine—"all nice enough in their place," Miller remarked to Chapman, "but certainly not worth lugging along on such a tremendous journey."[70]

Fiala accepted the Colonel's decision like a good soldier, but Cherrie described him as almost in tears when he left the Burity camp at 10:00 that night.[71] A dozen years earlier, Fiala had been cheated by circumstances from reaching the North Pole long before Robert E. Peary got there. Now another—and his last—chance to make geographical history had escaped his grasp. Fiala never wrote of his experiences in South America, other than a few public reminiscences and a brief technical appendix for T. R.'s book about the expedition.

"I think his going had a saddening effect on all of us," Cherrie recorded late that night, as sheets of rain beat against the tent walls. "Of the North Americans only four of our original party are left!"[72]

Roosevelt had no second thoughts about paring down the size of party. Three weeks later, on the eve of starting down the Dúvida, he wrote Robert Bridges: "We have weeded out everyone unfit for exploration."[73]

NOTES

1. Miller, *In the Wilds*, p. 223. **2.** T. R., *Brazilian Wild.*, p. 165. **3.** J. A. Zahm to Albert Zahm, 1-18-14, *CAZA*. **4.** Roosevelt, Kermit, *Diary*, 1-19-14 & 1-20-14. **5.** T. R. to Frank M. Chapman, 1-16-14, *Letters*, Vol. 7, #5880, p. 758. **6.** T. R. to Robert Bridges, 1-18-14, *CWBL*. **7.** Harper, Troman, reply to author's questionnaire. **8.** Cherrie, *Diary*, 1-8-14; Harper, Troman, reply to author's questionnaire. **9.** Miller, *In the Wilds*, p. 224. **10.** Cajazeira, *Relatorio Apresentado*. **11.** Kermit Roosevelt to Belle Willard, 1-20-14, *KRP*. **12.** T. R. to John Scott Keltie, 2-25-15, *Letters*, Vol. 8, #5975, p. 905. **13.** Magalhães, *Relatorio Apresentado*. **14.** Miller, *In the Wilds*, p. 226. **15.** Cherrie, *Diary*, 1-21-14. **16.** Rondon, *Lectures*, p. 39. **17.** Cajazeira, *Relatorio Apresentado*. **18.** T. R., *Brazilian Wild.*, p. 174. **19.** Roosevelt, Kermit, *Happy Hunting Grounds*, p. 32. **20.** Cherrie, *Diary*, 1-22-14. **21.** T. R., *Brazilian Wild.*, p. 175. **22.** Cherrie, *Diary*, 1-23-14. **23.** Zahm, *South America's Southland*, pp. 479–80. **24.** Cherrie, *Diary*, 1-23-14. **25.** Magalhães, *Relatorio Apresentado*. **26.** Kermit Roosevelt to Belle Willard, 1-23-14, *KRP*. **27.** Cherrie, *Diary*, 1-24-14. **28.** Kermit Roosevelt to Edith Kermit Roosevelt, 2-8-14, *KRP*. **29.** T. R., *Brazilian Wild.*, p. 181. **30.** Roosevelt, Kermit, *Happy Hunting Grounds*, p. 44. **31.** T. R. to Corinne Roosevelt Robinson, 6-21-09, *Letters*, Vol. 7, #5219, p. 17. **32.** T. R., *Brazilian Wild.*, p. 178. **33.** Roosevelt, Kermit, *Happy Hunting Grounds*, p. 38. **34.** Rondon, "Col. Roosevelt as His Guide Remembers Him," *New York Times*. **35.** Rondon, *Lectures*, p. 61. **36.** Ibid., p. 69. **37.** Ibid., p. 65. **38.** Miller, *In the Wilds*, p. 227. **39.** Ibid., pp. 227–28. **40.** J. A. Zahm to T. R., 3-14-14, *PPS*. **41.** Nash, Roy, *Conquest of Brazil*, p. 82. **42.** T. R., *Brazilian Wild.*, p. 253. **43.** Ibid., p. 186. **44.** Roosevelt, Kermit, *Diary*, 1-29-14. **45.** T. R., *Brazilian Wild.*, p. 189. **46.** T. R.,

Brazilian Wild., p. 191; Miller, *In the Wilds*, pp. 228–29. **47.** T. R., *Brazilian Wild.*, p. 193. **48.** Roosevelt, Kermit, *Diary,* 1-29-14; Kermit Roosevelt to Belle Willard, 1-31-14, *KRP.* **49.** Rondon, *Lectures,* p. 44. **50.** Oliveira, *Expedicão Scientifica.* **51.** Kermit Roosevelt to Belle Willard, 1-31-14, *KRP.* **52.** Viveiros, *Rondon,* p. 385. **53.** Rondon, *Lectures,* p. 46. **54.** Kermit Roosevelt to Belle Willard, 1-31-14, *KRP.* **55.** T. R. to Agent, Booth Steamship Co., 2-3-14, *JAZP;* Carroll, "Mind in Action," *The Ava Maria* (6-1-46), chapter XI, p. 689. **56.** J. A. Zahm to T. R., 3-14-14, *PPS.* **57.** T. R.'s handwritten note, 2-1-14, signed by all members of the expedition, *KRP.* **58.** Cherrie, *Diary,* 2-1-14. **59.** Roosevelt, Kermit, *Diary,* 2-1-14. **60.** T. R. to Robert Bridges, 2-1-14, *CWBL.* **61.** Cherrie, *Diary,* 2-3-14. **62.** Jacob Sigg to T. R., 5-5-14, *PPS.* **63.** Cherrie, *Diary,* 2-3-14. **64.** T. R., *Brazilian Wild.*, p. 205. **65.** Cherrie, *Diary,* 2-4-14. **66.** Cajazeira, *Relatorio Apresentado.* **67.** Cherrie, *Diary,* 2-4-14. **68.** Leo Miller to Frank M. Chapman, 2-25-14, *AMNH.* **69.** Fiala, Anthony, appendix to *Brazilian Wild.*, pp. 389–90. **70.** Leo Miller to Frank M. Chapman, 2-25-14, *AMNH.* **71.** Cherrie, *Diary,* 2-4-14. **72.** Ibid., 2-14-14. **73.** T. R. to Robert Bridges, 2-25-14, *CWBL.*

VIII
A Chance of Disaster

By February 6 the loss of pack animals reached the crisis stage. Of the ninety-eight mules Roosevelt's detachment had started out with three weeks before, only forty-two were left, and ten of these were too weak and unsteady to walk, let alone carry a load. Nine had been abandoned in the three days since leaving Utiarity. The draft oxen had given out and could no longer pull the carts through the mud and sand.[1]

The Colonel and Kermit walked back to the fog-shrouded Burity ferry to persuade Rondon "to discard all luxuries" right there.[2] Everyone was forced to cut his baggage in half. More of the big army tents were thrown away, and the two ox carts were abandoned with their cargoes. Cherrie and Miller had to make do with several hundred shotgun shells and a dozen animal traps, throwing away much of their taxidermy equipment. The naturalists found it hardest to part with two trunks of specimens, but Rondon promised that these would be taken back to Tapirapuan when the packers returned.

Not content just to see the loads reduced, Roosevelt proceeded to interrogate Rondon as to whether the Brazilian had enough food for his own men when they started down the Dúvida. If there weren't enough mules to carry the essential supplies, T. R. told him, they should turn their saddle mules into pack animals and walk the rest of the way. This was too much for Rondon's pride to bear. He repeatedly assured Roosevelt that he had everything necessary for the paddlers and that fresh mules would be found at the outlying telegraph stations. Roosevelt took him at his word.[3]

"We've been going through a regular course of shedding men and provisions," Kermit wrote Belle after arriving at the February 6 camp. The American contingent had decreased to half its original number, and consisted of the two Roosevelts, Cherrie, and Miller. The Brazilian side had shrunk even more, from nine officers at the start to just three: Rondon, Lyra, and Dr. Cajazeira.[4]

With fewer mouths to feed, the Colonel's detachment pushed on to the telegraph station on the Rio Juruena, two days' march to the northwest. There they hoped to rendezvous with Captain Amilcar's pack train.

By now the daily marches had settled into a regular pattern. The sleeping camp woke to the short blasts of a bugle and cups of steaming coffee brought to each of the tents by a camarada orderly. Breakfast spread out over two hours, after which Rondon read his Order of the Day, giving the length of march for that day and the number of the telegraph pole where the next campsite would be located. The poles, tree trunks stripped of bark, were set three hundred feet apart and stenciled with large numerals consecutively, like house numbers. This made it easy for stragglers to find the new camp, even in the dark.[5]

While the mules were being gathered up, the Colonel worked on his *Scribner's* articles or read. Books were in short supply on this expedition. T. R., whose taste in literature ran to the serious and uplifting, had brought with him several volumes of the Everyman's edition of Gibbon's *Decline and Fall of the Roman Empire*. He freely lent these out to Cherrie and Miller when they wanted something to read.[6] Sometimes Roosevelt would bend a little and borrow one of Kermit's few books—the adventures of the French detective Arsène Lupin, perhaps, or the Oxford editions of English and French poetry. Kermit realized how hard up his father was when he asked for the French poems, which T. R. didn't generally care for. After listening to his father criticize the Gallic verse, Kermit would threaten to take the book away if he didn't stop.[7]

Rondon held the daily marches down to a dozen miles a day in order to preserve the strength of the remaining mules. On arriving at the new campsite late in the afternoon, Cherrie and Miller would use the few remaining hours of daylight to collect, but the lack of birds and animals on the wide plains, plus the frequent rain, worked against their efforts. Nights in camp were the best time, according to Miller, who remembered with pleasure the male camaraderie. After supper, the explorers would sit around the leaping flames of a huge bonfire, listening to Roosevelt recount his hunting adventures in the American West and in Africa. The stories were told in such a vivid way, Miller recalled, "that we . . . could visualize pronghorn, cougar, bear, and lion, as well as their actions in their native wilderness." On rainy nights, he and Cherrie crowded into the Colonel's tent to discuss history, literature, and science. The visit would usually end with one of T. R.'s blood-chilling ghost stories, full of gore, werewolves, and vampires, and brought to a climax when Roosevelt grabbed the nearest listener's shoulder just as the "haunt" seized his victim.[8]

On February 8, after marching some 230 miles in nineteen days and losing half of their pack animals, Roosevelt's party reached the banks of the Rio Juruena and rested. Only 150 miles now separated them from the headwaters of the unknown river.

The name Juruena was given by mapmakers to the upper course of the Tapajós, one of the Amazon's five great tributaries. At the point where the Telegraph Commission's pontoon ferry crossed it, the Juruena was already three hundred feet wide, a deep, rushing stream of clear water bordered by white sand beaches and filling the cleft of a forested valley.[9]

As Roosevelt's detachment unhitched its loads and began crossing over, the explorers could see the last teams of Captain Amilcar's oxen climbing the green slopes on the opposite shore. Amilcar himself had only left the Juruena that morning.

At the telegraph station on the western side, Roosevelt learned that Fiala's descent of the Rio Papagaio had started off with a near-fatal accident. Soon after leaving Utiarity, his canoe had been swamped in the dangerous Rapids of the Devil. "We were simply sucked in," Fiala later wrote.[10] Caught in the undertow, he was saved from drowning when a strong-armed paddler pulled him to shore. The canoes were retrieved and the trip begun again, but Fiala lost his cameras and most of the motion-picture film he had taken of the expedition's progress through Brazil. The loss of the films was the final blow for the unlucky Fiala, who had hoped to show them on a joint lecture tour with Father Zahm.[11]

Since leaving Tapirapuan, the explorers had lived on two meals a day; often a dozen hours would separate breakfast from dinner, depending on how late the mule train straggled in. The enforced diet proved to be a hardship for everyone except the Colonel, whose waistline, for the first time in years, had begun to shrink appreciably. Then Rondon decided to restore the midday meal during the two days at Juruena station. "[And] what did I [hear]," Kermit wrote Edith Roosevelt in mock indignation, "but bad old Father telling them not to do so! I had to discipline him by telling him that just [because] he wanted [only two meals a day] there was no reason why he should force fasting upon the rest of us."[12]

A far more warlike race of Indians than the Parecis inhabited the lands bordering the Juruena—the naked Nhambiquaras. Word of Rondon's arrival brought a group of these nomadic hunters to the telegraph station. In obedience to his long-standing order, they left their palmwood bows and six-foot-long bamboo arrows a mile outside the settlement.

Rondon had achieved only partial success in subduing this tribe. During the first surveying expedition in 1907, his small party had been continually harassed by Nhambiquara warriors. They killed his pack animals, stole his equipment, and frightened his men so badly that they refused to light cooking fires at night, to avoid becoming targets. On subsequent expeditions, with a larger force, he found the situation reversed, as the Nhambiquaras abandoned their villages and fled before his advancing column. Nevertheless, the idealistic Rondon felt that he was an intruder, writing in his diary at the time: "We must do everything possible to show them . . . that we have no other intention than of protecting them." He forbade his soldiers to ever shoot an Indian, regardless of the provocation. When gifts of food, ax heads, and glass beads failed to attract the Indians, he tried music. He cranked up an old Victrola after dark and played recordings of Italian grand opera. Hearing Puccini for the first time, the Nhambiquaras could not contain their curiosity and wandered into Rondon's camp.[13]

Nowhere in his African travels had Roosevelt seen "wilder or more absolutely primitive savages" than the Nhambiquaras: "The men wore a string around the waist. Most of them wore nothing else, but a few had loosely hanging from this string in front a scanty tuft of dried grass, or a small piece of cloth . . . The women did not wear a stitch of any kind anywhere on their bodies." Rondon's kindly treatment had made the Indians boldly familiar, and they crowded into the mud and wattle hut where Roosevelt sat writing, surrounding him so closely that he had to push them gently away.[14] Kermit had a sympathy for primitive people and found the Nhambiquaras "a very pleasant set [who] . . . didn't look at all as if they had given Rondon all the trouble they have." He noted that they had "small hands & feet, and really nice faces," and grew sad at the thought of how they would change "when civilization comes here."[15]

Rondon ordered one of the loose steers slaughtered and turned an entire quarter of beef over to the visiting Indians, whose usual diet consisted of ants, snakes, and deer. The Nhambiquaras tore the meat apart and threw the chunks into the fire, raking them out a short time later with a stick. The cooking went on for hours, until every last scrap of meat was eaten. Miller noticed how several of the hungry children, after accidentally spilling a beaker of honey on the ground, scooped up handfuls of the honeysoaked sand to eat until a large hole remained. When moonlight flooded the camp, the Indians danced and sang until early morning, and then made off with two of the expedition's hunting dogs.[16]

The next day, February 10, the march was delayed while Rondon, intent on upholding the law, wasted several hours in a search for the dog-nappers. Miller for one wished that the departing Nhambiquaras had taken all the dogs, describing them as "a mongrel, worthless lot," useless for hunting or guarding camp, and full of fleas and ticks.[17]

West of the Juruena, many more rain-flooded rivers stood in the expedition's path. The pack train forded those that were shallow enough and crossed the larger streams by bridge or ferry. When swamps bordered the river or the current was very swift, the men spent long hours getting the frightened mules and oxen across. On one occasion, a ferryload of irreplaceable provisions tipped over into the rushing water.

"We keep crawling along, gradually cutting down the distance to the Dúvida, but oh so slowly," Kermit complained to Belle at this time. He admitted that his heart was not really in this trip. "I'm afraid I'm not very much of an explorer at present. All the rest are hoping that the river may be a long and important [one] . . . whereas all I ask of the river is that it may be as short and easy to travel. . . as possible."[18]

Kermit's impatience for the trip to be over and done with may have been partly because of his acute physical discomfort. While at Juruena, he had had a relapse of fever, and boils broke out on his legs, including one "in a very bad place for riding." The boils hurt so much that he couldn't sleep at night, and during the day he rode his mule "standing in stirrups most of [the] time."[19]

Late on the tenth the expedition reached the Rio Formiga, after a fifteen-mile march in chilling rain. Amilcar turned up at this camp. Roosevelt and Rondon had not seen him for three weeks, although they had exchanged telegrams. The three men stood ankle-deep in mud and water, comparing notes. Roosevelt admired this "cool, competent officer who was doing a difficult job with such workmanlike efficiency." Rain streamed down Amilcar's bare head, but he was too busy seeing after the rear guard of his pack train to care. He reported losing a number of mules so far, but only three of his oxen had had to be abandoned.[20]

It soon became apparent that not all the Nhambiquaras had made peace with Rondon's Telegraph Commission. On February 11, at the Rio Juina, the Colonel's party rode past a deserted guard post and the fresh graves of two Brazilian soldiers and their officer. Nhambiquaras had killed them and buried them standing up, with their heads and shoulders exposed, as a warning to other intruders. The victims had since been decently buried. The next day, camped by the Rio Primavera, the explorers found the graves of two more telegraph workers who had been killed as they slept in their hammocks. In some instances, the attacks had been brought on by soldiers raping Nhambiquara women.

Bones of long-perished mules and oxen were now seen more frequently on the trail. In some places, still-living mules abandoned by Amilcar's detachment stood motionless in the sun, waiting for death. At each camp, Rondon pulled one or more of his own mules out of the line as "debilitated." As the animals wandered in search of food and grass, they made easy targets for the Nhambiquara hunters. One of the camaradas told Rondon of seeing a group of Indians feasting on the raw flesh of a mule they had just killed.[21]

On February 15, Roosevelt's detachment came to the settlement of Campo Novos. This had been the third telegraph station west of the Juruena, until the line was relocated several miles away. The Colonel described this region as "utterly unlike the country we had been traversing."[22] The travelers were now on the edge of the Cerro do Norte, a vast tract of grassy hills, forested valleys, and numerous brooks and streams. Luxuriant pastures around Campo Novos made it possible for a small cattle ranch to exist there.

Freed of their burdens, the pack mules chewed their way up the surrounding green hills. The camaradas set up two kitchens, one in the open, and the other under a canopy of ox hides. Chicken, pigs, and goats were put to the cleaver and roasted on spits. The cook sweated over a pot of *canja*, Roosevelt's favorite soup, which contained a turkey-sized currasow Kermit had shot with his Luger automatic. There were pails of fresh, unpasteurized milk to drink, Roosevelt's favorite beverage next to coffee. At supper, Cherrie cracked a molar on a small stone hidden in the cooked rice on his plate.[23]

From Campo Novos, Roosevelt sent his editor a batch of forty-five photographs to illustrate his magazine articles. These included a number of shots of Nhambiquara Indian life in its "Adam & Eve" state. "Kermit, Cherrie and Miller want their negatives back when you have finished with them," T. R. informed Robert Bridges, but the pictures were all being offered free of charge to *Scribner's*. "I am going to give Cherrie & Miller a thousand each out of what you give me, as a nest egg for a further South American trip for each; & Kermit is in my employ!"[24]

Roosevelt still debated the wisdom of taking his son into the wilderness. Twice during the march from Tapirapuan he suggested to Kermit that he "go straight on out" instead of accompanying him down the Dúvida. "I have hated this trip, and felt miserable enough at being so far from you," Kermit wrote Belle after one of these talks. But to turn back now, he thought, "would be far far worse than never to have come at all."[25]

On February 18, two days after leaving Campo Novos, the party reached the telegraph station at Vilhena. More than eight hundred feet above sea level, it marked the watershed between those streams running into the Tapajós on the east and the Madeira on the west. Beyond Vilhena, the landscape changed again. "Our road from here on to the Rio Dúvida is over [a] nearly level, treeless plateau," Cherrie noted at this camp. "I say treeless, but here and there it is dotted with clumps of heavy timber and tangled undergrowth that mark the source of some stream."[26] Miller wrote of how, for many square kilometers, all other vegetation gave way to millions of wild pineapple plants, just beginning to ripen and sweeten the air.[27]

Grass again grew scarce. "The mules strayed far last night in search of food," Kermit recorded on February 20, after reaching the new camp by the Rio Amarante. "We didn't get off until noon; making the arrival time [here] very late." Six more mules had to be abandoned, and Rondon sent an urgent message to Amilcar to send back oxen to take up the loads.[28]

Bands of hungry, curious Nhambiquaras came daily to the camps to squat in the sand and stare at the expedition's mules, food, and equipment. On the marches, there were encounters out of the Stone Age: Naked Indian families walked in single file, the women draped with baskets, gourds, and small clinging children, and the men, silent and wary, walking before and behind them carrying their long bows. To all these groups, Rondon played the part of a Brazilian Father Christmas, dispensing handfuls of colored glass beads, hatchets, "and other odds and ends" and in return accepting skull caps made from tawny jaguar skins, pottery, and feathered nose ornaments.[29]

While hunting on February 21, Kermit came upon a trail made by Nhambiquara hunters and followed it to their encampment. He advanced while calling out and gesturing broadly in the old Anglo-Saxon way of showing peaceful intentions. Using improvised sign language, Kermit won over the undoubtedly surprised Indians, drank some of their potent pineapple wine, and then led half a dozen men and boys back to the expedition's campsite. After feasting on roast steer, the Indians began a slow dance around the fire, singing what Kermit described as "a solemn, rather monotonous though pretty melody." The entertainment grew livelier when he, Cherrie, Miller, and the younger Brazilians joined in, while Roosevelt and Rondon clapped in time.[30]

When more Indians, including women and children, drifted over the next morning at sunrise, the explorers had to keep an eye on their possessions. Roosevelt watched, amused, as one Nhambiquara woman stole a fork, buried it in the loose sand, and sat on it, only to meekly reach under and give it up when confronted by the owner.[31]

On this same day, February 22, the party arrived at the telegraph station at Três Burity, where the government operated a cattle ranch. The manager of the ranch turned out to be Rondon's uncle, seventy-six-year-old Miguel Evangelista. Barefoot and wearing a straw hat, Uncle Miguel still drove cattle from horseback with the energy of a young man. In the past year he had killed three jaguar with a spear. Dr. Cajazeira examined the old gentleman and was surprised to find that "his organs appear ageless."[32]

Eight fresh mules were picked up at this station. The travelers also ate well for the last time. The Colonel drank his fill of fresh milk and took second helpings of creamy chicken *canja*, beef roasted on an open spit, and juicy watermelon—this last grown from seeds left by American railroad engineers who had passed through some years earlier.

Twelve miles farther west lay the telegraph station at José Bonifácio. Cherrie could not restrain his delight when he wrote in his journal after arriving there on February 23:

> At last we have arrived at the end, or rather the virtual end, of our long overland journey. Thirty three days in the saddle since leaving Tapirapuan. We now have only *two* short marches of 7 or 8 miles each to the banks of the Dúvida, where we begin the canoe journey down its unknown length.[33]

Bonifácio was the place Kermit had been longing to see since leaving Rio de Janeiro five months before. "It's a great relief," he wrote Belle, "to . . . be starting on the last part of the trip; I have continually been afraid that the pack train might give out completely, or at any rate enough to cause some very long delay; but now we're here and ready to start down the river; and each day brings me nearer to you, my own dearest dearest Belle."[34]

The Colonel's letters to Edith Roosevelt from this time have not survived, but Kermit's letter to her may well reflect his father's uncertainty about the journey still ahead:

> Here we are ready to start down the Dúvida, all well and cheerful. No one has an idea, or at least every body has half a dozen,—which comes to the same thing—, as to where the Dúvida goes. I think the chances are that it eventually becomes the [Aripuanã], which is the largest tributary of the Madeira and enters it near its junction with the Amazon. It's almost impossible even to guess at the amount of time it will take to go down it. If things go in the best way possible I think we may be in Manáos in a month and a half; two months is really the most probable, tho three or four is possible.

Kermit was glad that the party had been cut down so drastically since leaving Tapirapuan. Father Zahm would never have survived the journey, he told his mother. If Harper, Sigg, and Fiala had not been sent back, the strain of carrying their baggage and feeding them "would have caused serious trouble if not disaster for we have just got through as it was."[35]

While at Bonifácio, Miller made a rare catch of a ratlike gopher, the cururú, which the Indians said never emerged from its burrow but instead tunneled through the pastures a foot below the surface, living on grass pulled in by its roots. When Miller's traps failed to catch the rodents, he enlisted the help of several Nhambiquaras and a soldier with a hoe. They spent half a day excavating one of the gopher galleries. Caked in mud and sand, the Indians dug feverishly with pointed sticks and their bare hands, yelling continually as they worked. Finally, one of them thrust an arm deep into an exposed side tunnel, pulled out a squirming gopher, and threw it down on the ground, where it stumbled around in bewilderment until captured. "Col. Roosevelt was *greatly* pleased with it," Miller wrote Frank Chapman, "and says it's the best thing in the whole collection so far."[36]

The number of mammals collected now stood at 316; Miller hoped to top 400 by the time he reached Manáos. Cherrie's bird count had also surged ahead during the preceding weeks and was nearing 1,500. These are remarkable achievements considering the short period of time involved—less than three months—and the fact that the expedition was constantly on the move. By comparison, the Brazilian naturalists, who had started later than their North American colleagues, had collected only 300 birds and 17 mammals.[37]

On February 24 Roosevelt and company departed Bonifácio and followed the humming telegraph wire another seven miles over a shrub-covered prairie to camp by a stream that Rondon knew fed into the River of Doubt. Here they were reunited with Amilcar's command, which had arrived the day before. The work of dividing the expedition into two exploring teams and apportioning the food now began.

In the absence of Father Zahm, Amilcar took charge of the Gy-Paraná group, to be assisted by Miller, transport officer Lieutenant Mello, the geologist Oliveira, and Reinisch, the taxidermist. Thirty camaradas were to accompany them, some to serve as paddlers, the rest to handle the mules and oxen for the five-day journey west to the headwaters of the Gy. Miller was excited at the prospect of finding new species of birds and animals along its course; no naturalists had gone down it before.[38]

Twenty-two men were chosen to descend the River of Doubt: T. R. and Rondon, Kermit, Cherrie, Lyra, and Dr. Cajazeira, together with sixteen camaradas as paddlers and steersmen. They would take two dogs, Kermit's faithful Trigueiro and Rondon's pet, Lobo. Should the Dúvida's course prove to be a short one, the party would return and go down Rondon's other unknown river, the Ananás.

To provide for a possible voyage down the Ananás, two weeks' rations were left under guard at Bonifácio station. Forty of the ninety food containers so carefully packed in New York were earmarked for the Amilcar-Miller party; the remaining fifty cans, plus the U.S. Army emergency rations, would feed the six officials of Roosevelt's Dúvida team. Rondon was responsible for providing food for the sixteen camaradas.

It was while counting out the rations that a serious shortage was discovered. In spite of his assurances to Roosevelt, Rondon had somehow allowed several mule loads of provisions for his men to be left behind when the pack train was reorganized at the Burity River. As a result, there was not enough bread now for the sixteen paddlers, or enough sugar, an energy food and morale booster for wilderness work. It was too late to go back for the lost loads, and there was no time to wait for another mule train to arrive. Within weeks the rainy season would begin to taper off, and the explorers could find themselves stranded on a river too low to navigate.

All Roosevelt could do at this point was to cut his own group's rations in half to share with the camaradas and hope that the difference could be made up by hunting and fishing. He realized that they faced "a chance of disaster" because of Rondon's "rather absurd lack of forethought," but he had come too far now to give up the trip. Nor did he see any point in quarreling with Rondon about the situation—that would not bring the food back, and a falling-out among the chiefs would doom the expedition. Instead, he "simply took charge of things" from that moment, working through Kermit to keep tabs on everything that was done, while remaining polite and friendly with the Brazilians, whom he regarded as "really very fine fellows," even if they were poor organizers.[39]

Everything not essential for exploration was now discarded. Two large tents were kept to shelter the six-member official party, while the camaradas slept in the open in hammocks. Rondon's surveying instruments were spared, as was Dr. Cajazeira's medicine chest with its all-important supply of quinine salts. Cherrie packed away some boxes of light-gauge shotgun shells for bird collecting and three bottles of scotch, carefully wrapped in a blanket, for himself and Kermit.

There was room in each man's duffel bag for some books. The titles reflected the high literary tastes shared by the explorers. Lyra, who had studied astronomy in Germany, carried some pocket editions of the poems of Schiller and Goethe. Kermit took along some Portuguese novels and his indispensable Oxford poetry anthologies. For Rondon, mental relaxation meant grappling with a translation of Thomas à Kempis's work, *The Imitation of Christ*. Roosevelt's selections were the most diversified, including Gibbon's Roman history, some Greek plays by Sophocles, Sir Thomas More's *Utopia*, and small, red-leather-bound editions of the writings of Marcus Aurelius and Epictetus, these last two a gift from Major Shipton at the conclusion of the Argentine tour.

At this last telegraph station, the Colonel dispatched a confident message to Foreign Minister Müller in Rio de Janéiro. Released to the press, the communiqué sped along seventy-five hundred miles of undersea cables to appear on the front page of the *New York Times* for February 28, 1914, under the headline "Roosevelt Finds a River." It reported that "no great difficulties were encountered" en route to the Dúvida and that the exploring party's health was excellent.[40] This would be the last news of Roosevelt's expedition until, with any luck, it emerged at Manáos in April.

The Colonel sent a brief, hopeful message to Edith, something for her to hang on to while enduring the silent months at Sagamore Hill. Kermit's cable to Belle Willard first crossed the Atlantic Ocean to the offices of the Direct Spanish Telegraph Company in Madrid. A puzzled operator there read it and then redirected it to the Hotel Ritz in London, where the daughter of the United States Ambassador to Spain was staying:

> Just received from town of jose bonifacion [sic] which we do not find on map the following telegram starting duvida father sends best love all well Kermit[41]

Through Miller, who was chosen as the expedition's postman, T. R. sent *Scribner's* his seventh article and an appendix for the eventual book edition of the magazine pieces. He hoped that Bridges had received his earlier chapters. "I am as unable as ever to tell whether they are of interest, but the trip itself is certainly of interest. No men except these pioneers who now accompany us have been over the ground before. No civilized man has ever been down the Dúvida, the descent of which shall begin in a couple of days. Anything may then happen."[42]

There was one final matter to attend to. Poised on the edge of the unknown, Roosevelt decided he could use a haircut. With the nearest barber a thousand miles away, Cherrie was summoned to do the honors. He hacked away at the former President's locks with a pair of surgical scissors fished out of his skinning tray. "I did the job," wrote Cherrie, "but the Colonel refused to let me take his picture after I had finished!"[43]

By evening on February 25, Roosevelt and Rondon had moved their camp six miles farther west to the banks of the Dúvida. Several weeks earlier, Rondon's construction crews had come this way, cutting a wide swath through the forest to protect the telegraph wire from falling timber. They had built a rough wooden bridge to span the river's sixty-five-foot width. The bridge would serve as the starting point for Rondon's survey.

On the north side of the bridge, Lieutenant Mello supervised a work party busy caulking seams in a collection of dugouts drawn up on the muddy bank. Two more dugouts had filled with rain and had sunk during the night, still tied to their mooring ropes. Kermit stripped off his clothes and helped the camaradas raise the sunken canoes, nearly losing both of them to the strong pull of the current. A swarm of vicious maribundi wasps stung the men repeatedly as they struggled in the water. It was a foretaste of what lay in store for the expedition.[44]

NOTES

1. Roosevelt, Kermit, *Diary*, 2-6-14. 2. T. R. to John Scott Keltie, 2-25-15, *Letters*, Vol. 7, #5975, p. 905. 3. Ibid. 4. Kermit Roosevelt to Belle Willard, 2-6-14, *KRP.* 5. Miller, *In the Wilds*, p. 230. 6. T. R., *Brazilian Wild.*, p. 223. 7. Roosevelt, Kermit, *Happy Hunting Grounds*, pp. 30–31. 8. Miller, *In the Wilds*, p. 231; Wagenknecht, *Seven Worlds*, pp. 73–74. 9. Cajazeira, *Relatorio Apresentado.* 10. Fiala, "With Roosevelt in the Jungle," *Literary Digest.* 11. Fiala, quoted in *The RoPeCo Magazine.* 12. Kermit Roosevelt to Edith K. Roosevelt, 2-8-14, *KRP.* 13. Elliot, C. Elwyn, "The Rondon Mission," *Pan American Magazine.* 14. T. R., *Brazilian Wild.*, pp. 217–18. 15. Kermit Roosevelt to Belle Willard, 2-8-14, *KRP.* 16. Miller, *In the Wilds*, p. 233. 17. Ibid., p. 234. 18. Kermit Roosevelt to Belle Willard, 2-10-14, *KRP.* 19. Roosevelt, Kermit, *Diary*, 2-7-14, 2-8-14, & 2-10-14. 20. T. R., *Brazilian Wild.*, p. 221. 21. Leo E. Miller to Frank M. Chapman, 2-25-14, *AMNH.* 22. T. R., *Brazilian Wild.*, p. 227. 23. Cherrie, *Diary*, 2-15-14. 24. T. R. to Robert Bridges, 2-15-14, *TRC.* 25. Kermit Roosevelt to Belle Willard, 2-14-14, *KRP.* 26. Cherrie, *Diary*, 2-18-14. 27. Miller, *In the Wilds*, p. 237. 28. Roosevelt, Kermit, *Diary*, 2-20-14. 29. Rondon, *Lecture*, p. 54. 30. Kermit Roosevelt to Belle Willard, 2-22-14, *KRP.* 31. T. R., *Brazilian Wild.*, pp. 235–36. 32. Cajazeira, *Relatorio Apresentado.* 33. Cherrie, *Diary*, 2-23-14. 34. Kermit Roosevelt to Belle Willard, 2-24-14, *KRP.* 35. Kermit Roosevelt to Edith K. Roosevelt, 2-24-14, *KRP.* 36. Leo E. Miller to Frank M. Chapman, 2-15-14, *AMNH.* 37. Miller, *In the Wilds*, p. 242. 38. Ibid. 39. T. R. to John Scott Keltie, 2-25-15, *Letters*, Vol. 8, #5975, p. 905. 40. *New York Times*, 2-28-14. 41. Telegram, Kermit Roosevelt to Belle Willard, 2-24-14, *KRP.* 42. T. R. to Robert Bridges, 2-15-14, *CWBC.* 43. Cherrie, *Diary*, 2-25-14. 44. Roosevelt, Kermit, *Diary*, 2-25-14.

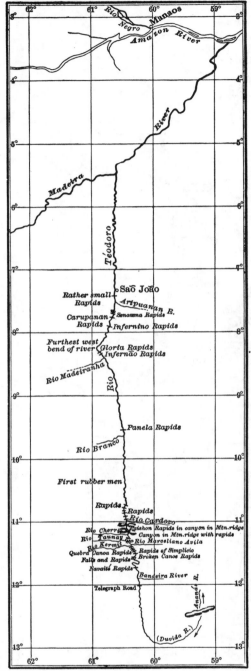

Manaos
62° 61° 60° 59°
Rio Negro
Amazon River
River
Madeira
Téodoro
Rather small Rapids
Saõ Joaõ
Aripuanan R.
Senauma Rapids
Carupanan Rapids
Infernino Rapids
Furthest west bend of river
Gloria Rapids
Infernão Rapids
Rio Madeiranha
Rio
Panela Rapids
Rio Branco
First rubber men
Rapids
Rapids
Rio Cardozo
Bishop Rapids in canyon in Mtn. ridge
Rio Cherri
Rio Taunay
Canyon in Mtn. ridge with rapids
Rio Kermit
Rio Marceliano Avila
Quebra Canoa Rapids
Rapids of Simplicio
Falls and Rapids
Broken Canoe Rapids
Navaité Rapids
Bandeira River
Telegraph Road
Ananá R.
(Duvida R.)

When the official map from Brazil failed to arrive in time, T. R. drew this sketch map of the River of Doubt for inclusion in his book, Through the Brazilian Wilderness, *which Charles Scribner's Sons published in September 1914. Roosevelt preferred the name Rio Téodoro, as did the Brazilians, who found it easier to pronounce than Roosevelt.*

Inside the map:

CARIBBEAN SEA

Cartagena · La Guaira
CARACAS · GEORGETOWN · PARAMARIBO
VENEZUELA · GUIANA · CAYENNE
Orinoco R.
BOGOTA
COLOMBIA
Buenaventura
EQUATOR
QUITO
ECUADOR
Guayaquil · Negro R. · Manaos · Amazon · Para
Paranahiba
Yapura R.
Putumayo
Maranon R.
Napo R. · B · R · Purus · Madeira · Tapajos · Xingu R. · Tocantins · Araguaya · San Francisco
Juruá · A · Z · Parahiba · Pernambuco
LIMA · Callao · Cuzco · Utiarity · Bahia
Jose Bonifacio · Porto Tapirapuan
S. Luiz de Caceres · Cuyabá
Arequipa · La Paz · BOLIVIA
SUCRE · Corumbá · Coimbra
Potosi · Porto Murtinho · Taquary
Iquique
TROPIC OF CAPRICORN
Concepcion · RIO DE JANEIRO
PARAGUAY · São Paulo
ASUNCION · Santos
Tucuman · Corrientes
Salado R. · Porto Alegre
Valparaiso · Mendoza · Parana · URUGUAY · Rio Grande do Sul
SANTIAGO · Rosario · MONTEVIDEO
Concepcion · BUENOS AIRES · Rio de la Plata
Colorado
Valdivia · Negro R.
ARGENTINA
PACIFIC OCEAN
ATLANTIC OCEAN
FALKLAND IS.

L.L. POATES CO., N.Y.

Col. Roosevelt's trip is shown with an unbroken
line thus, ▬▬▬▬ save on the Unknown River
which is shown by broken line thus, ▬ ▬ ▬ ▬
Fiala's trip down the Papagaio (never before descended) and the Tapajos is shown thus, ✕✕✕✕
Miller's trip down the Gy-Parana and the
Madeira is shown thus, ● ● ● ● ●

*This map traces T. R.'s entire South American journey, which lasted for eight months—from
October 1913 to May 1914. The routes of the three separate exploring teams are indicated.*

1. *"I'm feeling like a bull moose!" T. R. in his prime, accompanied by Edith Roosevelt during the 1912 campaign.*

2. *"Reading with me is a disease,"* T. R. *cheerfully admitted, as here in 1912, while crossing the North River on a ferryboat. Roosevelt's interest in books and the Bible led to his friendship with Father Zahm.*

3. *Father John Augustine Zahm in 1913. His love of the tropics sparked in Roosevelt a similar interest, and the South American expedition followed.*

4. *Kermit Roosevelt in 1913. A year earlier, he had graduated from Harvard University and accepted a job with the Brazil Railway Company. "He would not have been happy in ordinary work at home," T. R. wrote a family friend after Kermit's departure. In the photo at the right, Kermit is shown with his younger brother Archie (to his right) in the summer of 1912.*

5. Gold braid and epaulets—Colonel Candido Mariano da Silva Rondon in the uniform of the Fifth Engineers Battalion, a few years before he met Theodore Roosevelt.

6. *George K. Cherrie later in life, looking more like a college professor than a man who had spent four decades bird-hunting in the tropics. He was probably the most prolific bird collector ever employed by the American Museum of Natural History. In forty expeditions to South America, he collected 120,000 specimens.*

8. Dr. Frank M. Chapman, the "bird man" of the American Museum of Natural History and dean of American ornithologists. He secured museum sponsorship for Roosevelt's South American expedition.

7. Leo E. Miller, the young, Indiana-born mammalogist assigned to the Roosevelt expedition. In 1913, Miller's monthly salary as a naturalist amounted to $75— half of what Cherrie, the senior man, earned. Eventually, the low pay and arduous conditions of field work led Miller to switch to a business career.

9. *Anthony Fiala, former Arctic explorer, photographer, and cartoonist for the* Brooklyn Daily Eagle. *He had the unenviable job of coping with the massive amount of equipment and supplies the expedition took down to Brazil.*

10. *Frank Harper, T. R.'s British-born private secretary. He caught malaria soon after the expedition entered the wilderness and had to be sent home.*

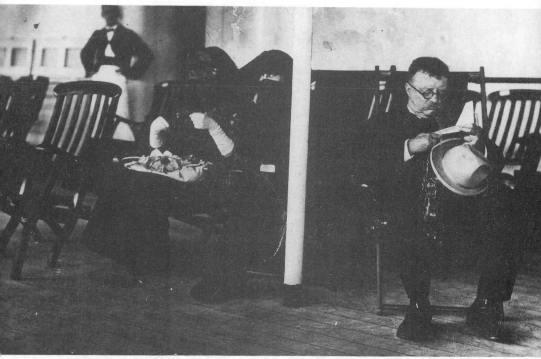

11. T. R. on board the Vandyck, *en route to South America. He combated the boredom of the long voyage by reading two or three books a day and dancing the Virginia Reel at night in the ship's ballroom. Edith and Margaret, veiled to protect their complexions from the sun, sit nearby.*

12. *The North American members of the expedition at Bahia, Brazil, October 18, 1913. From the left: Anthony Fiala, George Cherrie, Father Zahm, T. R., Kermit Roosevelt, Frank Harper, and Leo Miller.*

13. *The invitation that Roosevelt at first turned down, for fear of looking "as though I was advertising myself" after the election. The importance of coffee in Brazil's trade with the United States is clearly evident in this cartoon by the* Chicago Tribune's *famed artist John T. McCutcheon.*

14. On the steps of the Guanabara Palace at Rio de Janeiro, October 21, 1913.
An obviously pleased Roosevelt poses with Zahm, Fiala, and Brazilian
officials. For some reason, Edith and Margaret Roosevelt, George Cherrie,
and Leo Miller are not present.

15. Roosevelt and
Brazilian foreign
minister Dr. Lauro
Müller outside the
Itamaraty Palace.
Father Zahm stands
at T. R.'s right.
Fiala, touching his
hat brim, is directly
behind Müller.

16. *U.S. ambassador Edwin V. Morgan greets Edith Roosevelt on her arrival at Rio de Janeiro.*

17. *Receptions, banquets, and tours of military institutions, such as this one at the Brazilian Naval College, filled T. R.'s days in Rio de Janeiro. Edith stayed in bed until noon each day, conserving her strength for the evening entertainments.*

19. *T. R. with military aides at the U.S. legation in Buenos Aires.*

18. *"I have been received with immense enthusiasm." T. R.'s automobile arriving at the government palace in Buenos Aires, Argentina, November 5, 1913. At one point his motorcade was mobbed by hundreds of friendly Argentines eager to catch a glimpse of him.*

20. *In Buenos Aires, as everywhere in South America, the Boy Scouts paraded for T. R.*

CARLOS C. WIEDNER
in
"Sucesos"
Valparaiso, Chili.

THE GREAT THEODORE AND THE SOUTH AMERICAN REPUBLICS

Theodore—"They just seem to take the words out of my mouth—and I thought I would conquer them by my eloquence."

21. How the cigar got into the nonsmoking Colonel's hand in this cartoon is a mystery, but there was no question about his popularity with South Americans in general.

CESARE in NEW YORK SUN
The Lawgiver of the Andes
One Party, One Law, One Roosevelt

22. *For many conservatives back home, Roosevelt's first speech at Buenos Aires, in which he advocated repeal of unpopular judicial decisions, was nothing less than an assault on the U.S. Constitution. Here the perennially critical* New York Sun *depicts T. R. as a defiant demagogue, brandishing the "Big Stick" and trampling on a statute book.*

23. *Somewhere in South America. T. R. and an unidentified man are too busy talking to notice the camera. A bowler-hatted Harper walks ahead of them.*

24. *Crossing the Andes from Chile into Argentina, November 29–30, 1913. Roosevelt considered these two days the happiest of his South American trip—because he was left alone to enjoy the outdoors without a hand to shake or a speech to make. Riding with him are two members of the Argentine reception committee.*

25. *The* Adolfo Riquelmo, *the gunboat-yacht of the president of Paraguay. Awnings fore and aft protected Roosevelt's party from the torrid sun on the voyage from Asunción to Corumbá.*

26. *"It was evident that he knew his business thoroughly . . ." T. R. meets Colonel Rondon at the Brazilian border, December 12, 1913. When Kermit was not around to translate from English to Portuguese, the two leaders of the expedition could communicate with each other only in bad French.*

27. The side-wheeler Nyoac *was the expedition's home on the upper Paraguay.*

28. A field naturalist's work is never done . . . George Cherrie prepares a bird skin on the afterdeck of the Nyoac *while T. R. and Frank Harper (in white shirt) look on.*

29. *"A very pretty and graceful creature" was how T. R. described the bush deer he killed on the Rio Sepotuba on January 9, 1914. Rondon posed with him for the ritual hunter's photograph as the animal hung from a tree. Afterward, Leo Miller had the job of skinning it as a museum specimen.*

30. *Lunching in the jungle . . . As Rondon looks on, Kermit's favorite dog, sleek-coated Trigueiro, eats out of T. R.'s hand.*

From a sketch by Anthony Fiala.

31. *The strenuous jaguar hunt of New Year's Day 1914, in Anthony Fiala's pen-and-ink sketch. T. R. and Kermit are seen wading across a bayou choked with water lilies and teeming with piranha.*

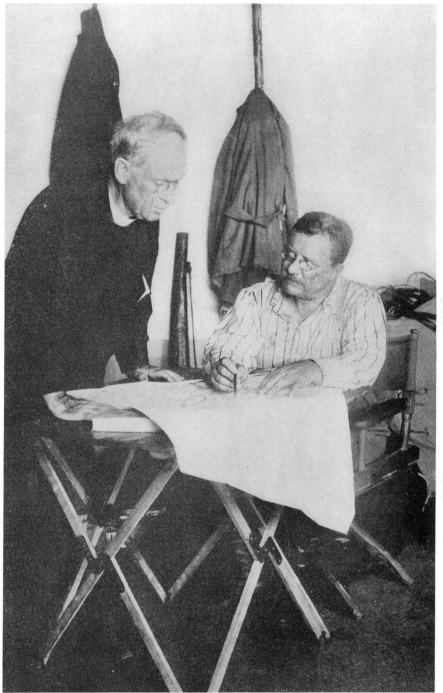

32. *Father Zahm conferring with T. R. over a map at Tapirapuan, where the party stopped in mid-January 1914. Two weeks later, sickly and unable to ride a mule, the priest-explorer would find himself ousted from the expedition he had conceived.*

33. *The two colonels at Tapirapuan, mid-January 1914. Roosevelt was only five feet, eight inches tall, but here he seems to tower over the bantam-sized Rondon.*

34. *The corral at Tapirapuan. From this point, the expedition started out on a month-long journey across the barren, wind-swept* chapadão *to the River of Doubt. Many of the mules seen here would never make it, victims of exhaustion, lack of water, and poor grass.*

35. *At Tapirapuan. Cherrie about to mount his little mule, Angel Falls.*

36. ". . . *the exceedingly movable evening meal* . . ." *Supper on the overland march. Seated from left to right: Zahm, Rondon, Kermit (on the ground), Cherrie and Miller, some of the Brazilians, T. R. and Fiala.*

37. As Roosevelt looks on, Kermit (white helmet) and Miller (center) examine
a freshly killed animal. The man in the black hat with his face turned toward
T. R. is probably Fiala.

38. Rondon holds open the jaws of a jaguar shot by T. R.

39. Cherrie poses with a Parecis Indian woman and her chubby, grimy baby at the Rio Sacre camp, January 27, 1914.

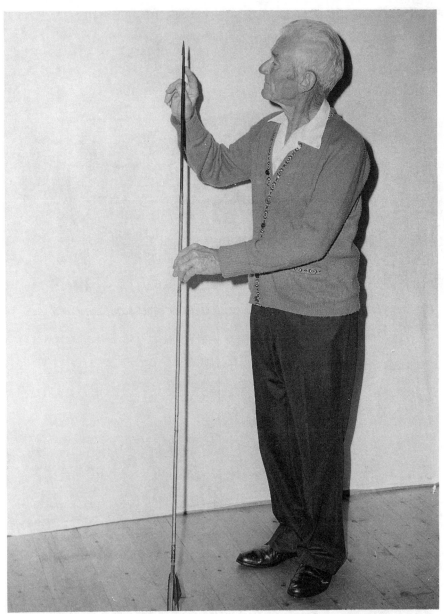

40. *Hubert Cherrie, one of George's sons, examines a Nhambiquara arrow in 1976, sixty-two years after his father brought it back from Brazil. It is a beautiful, if lethal, piece of workmanship, measuring seventy and one-half inches long and made of slender bamboo, with an ebony upper section and a carved rosewood tip. Before a hunt, the tip would be dipped in curare poison and protected from rain with a small bamboo cap. At the bottom of the shaft are three dark blue feathers, probably plucked from a macaw. The eight-inch-long feathers were curved slightly inward to give a twirl to the arrow in flight and make it more accurate.*

41. Lieutenant João Salustiano Lyra, Rondon's right-hand man and the expedition's astronomer.

42. "I must make good to Scribner's . . ." *Insects whine and buzz around him as T. R., attired in head net and gauntlets, works on his magazine pieces. He wrote practically every day while in South America and in seven months turned out the equivalent of a 120,000-word book.*

43. *The north side of the telegraph bridge, Friday morning, February 27, 1914. The river was sixty-five feet wide at this point and would soon broaden. One of the telegraph poles can be seen in the center background.*

44. *Cherrie (back to camera) steps aboard Roosevelt's dugout. The canoe in the foreground is full of surveying instruments.*

45. *The sixteen paddlers—the camaradas—reminded Roosevelt of pirates in a Howard Pyle book illustration: "One or two of them were pirates, and one worse than a pirate; but most of them were hard-working, willing and cheerful."*

46. *Rondon balances himself skillfully as he directs some last-minute loading of the canoes. The bundles of branches tied along the sides helped improve buoyancy.*

47. *The start. Leo Miller took this photograph from the telegraph bridge as the last of the seven dugouts disappeared down the unknown river.*

48. *"The lofty and matted forest rose like a green wall on either hand." The first days on the River of Doubt were idyllic, free from the rapids that would soon turn the journey into a nightmare of exhaustion and disappointment. T. R. is in the center of the picture looking at the camera; Cherrie is at the far right.*

49. *This strange rock formation, which reminded Roosevelt of "an old-fashioned beaver hat up-side down," was encountered on March 2, when for the first time, rapids blocked the party's path. It proved a good spot for T. R. and Rondon to have their picture taken by Cherrie.*

50. *At Navaitê, the river squeezed itself into a gorge so narrow that Cherrie was able to touch the other side with the barrel of his shotgun.*

51. *Rapids of the Dúvida. The noise came first—a dull, insistent roaring that gradually grew in intensity. Then the current began to race, and white water rose ahead of the dugouts. The rapids often extended for more than a mile, requiring long portages to get around them.*

52. *Portaging around rapids was a brutal job that called for every man to lend a hand. On some days, three or more rapids had to be gotten around by dragging the canoes overland or letting them down the side of steep falls with ropes.*

53. *It is difficult to appreciate the tremendous labor involved in portaging. First a pathway had to be cleared through the forest, then hundreds of six-foot-long log rollers, on which to heave the heavy canoes forward, had to be cut and laid down at two-foot intervals.*

54. *Building a new dugout at Camp Duas Canôas, March 19–21, 1914. The camaradas worked far into the evening by candlelight to hollow out the huge log. Mosquitoes and ants bit savagely at their bare feet and ankles as they worked.*

55. *While the boat builders chop away, T. R. and Cherrie cool off in the river, even though piranha had been caught in it. When Kermit appeared with his camera, the bathers ducked down in sudden modesty.*

56. *Rapids like these claimed one man's life and wrecked five of the seven canoes the expedition had started out with.*

57. *The view from the first of two mountain ranges the party had to struggle through at the end of March and the first week of April. Cherrie felt his heart "sink with dread" when he saw how the river rushed "like an arrow of light" into the next chain of hills, where more waterfalls awaited.*

58. *Nature seems to be in control of this scene in which Roosevelt, still looking healthy, stands bareheaded at the foot of a group of graceful pacova palms. After he injured his leg and began to lose a drastic amount of weight because of stomach trouble, he forbade any picture to be taken of him.*

59. *One of the few quiet stretches of the River of Doubt. Cherrie (fifth from the left) rides in a dugout with a group of camaradas. The glare of the sun and the tropical heat can almost be felt in this photograph.*

60. *Like Cherrie, Kermit let his beard grow during the descent of the river. His skill at rope handling made all the difference during the portages.*

61. *Sick with malaria and crippled by a leg injury, Roosevelt spent the last weeks on the river as an invalid, barely able to see out from under the canvas tent rigged over his canoe.*

62. *The real heroes of the expedition—the camaradas—gather around the wooden plaque officially marking the former River of Doubt as the Rio Roosevelt. The ceremony took place on April 27, 1914, exactly sixty days after the descent began. T. R. was too sick and ashamed of his shrunken appearance to join his companions in this photograph.*

63. "I am worth more than several dead men yet." T. R. as he appeared after arriving in New York on May 19, 1914. Compare this photo with photo 1, taken during the 1912 campaign.

64. Roosevelt was not the first explorer to return home to find his discoveries challenged by the experts. In this New York Sun *cartoon, T. R. confronts his critics head-on, waving the map of South America and knocking over the busts of famous earlier explorers in his eagerness to set the story straight.*

65. At the dinner preceding T. R.'s speech before the National Geographic Society in Washington, D.C., on May 26, 1914. Roosevelt, still thin in the face and deeply tanned, talks with a fellow guest. The man with the huge walrus mustache behind them is another famous explorer, Robert E. Peary of Arctic fame.

66. T. R. visiting the Cherrie family in Newfane, Vermont, in August 1914. Ten-year-old Hubert (fourth from left) was so excited at meeting this great man that he extended his left hand by mistake to the Colonel, who pumped it up and down with a burst of laughter.

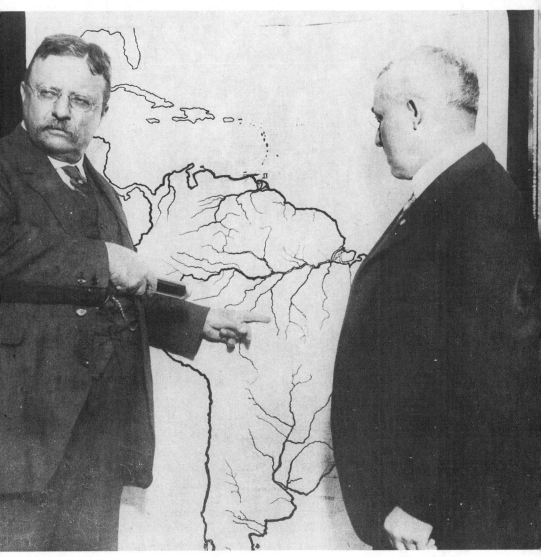

67. *A year after returning from South America, Roosevelt was still explaining where his river ran. He points to it on a large-scale map in the home of J. Paul Goode, a University of Chicago professor. Goode later wrote an article praising T. R. for giving "the world a new great river."*

68. *In 1927, British explorer George M. Dyott made the first successful retracing of Roosevelt's 1914 voyage down the River of Doubt. One of Dyott's men stands next to a huge post erected by the Brazilian government at the telegraph bridge to commemorate the naming of the Rio Roosevelt. Missing is the original varnished plaque—probably stolen by Indians.*

IX
A Land of Unknown Possibilities

On Friday, February 27, 1914, Theodore Roosevelt, his son Kermit, and twenty other Americans and Brazilians started down the River of Doubt with no clear idea where it would take them. "We were quite uncertain," T. R. wrote at the time, "whether after a week we should find ourselves in the Gy-Paraná, or after six weeks in the Madeira, or after three months we knew not where."[1] Their objectives were to map the river and if possible collect birds and animals along the way. Exactly how the exploration should be conducted was a matter of dispute between the two expedition chiefs.

Rondon had waited for this day ever since July 1909, when he had first cupped his hands to drink from the Dúvida's swiftly flowing waters and wondered about its ultimate union with a greater river. This was to be Rondon's last expedition, bringing to a close seven years' work mapping northwestern Mato Grosso state and building the telegraph line. He intended to make a detailed survey of this "doubtful" river, convinced that out of it would come the key to understanding the relationships of numerous rivers flowing in the wide basin between the Madeira and the Tapajós.

For Roosevelt, the overriding issue was to get down the river as quickly as possible. Though he recognized the geographical importance of what they were undertaking, the fact remained that the party could not survive a protracted journey. Unless game and fish were found in sufficient quantities en route, they could face the prospect of starvation. If they were lucky, they would find Lieutenant Pyrenius waiting for them somewhere lower down long before that. But in the meantime, it was

prudent to move quickly, even if it meant producing only a sketch map
on this first descent of the river. Always in the back of his mind was
concern for Kermit's safety.

The condition of the seven dugouts tied up at the river bank did
not ease Roosevelt's anxiety: "One was small, one was cranky, and two
were old, waterlogged, and leaky," he wrote. "The other three were good."
The biggest of these, more than twenty-five-feet long, was assigned to
him, Dr. Cajazeira, Cherrie, and three paddlers. Rondon and Lyra chose
the next largest from which to conduct the river survey. The smallest
and most maneuverable dugout went to Kermit, who, with two helpers,
was to act as scout for the surveyors. The other four less seaworthy canoes
were strapped into pairs as narrow rafts to hold cargo and the eight
remaining boatmen.[2]

Crammed with duffel bags, tents, coils of rope, surveying instruments, and rations, the canoes rode dangerously low in the water. Great
care was needed in getting in and out of them. To improve buoyancy,
the boatmen tied bundles of long, green burity palm branches along
the sides.[3] Even with such an improvement, dugouts were the worst
possible choice for a river that was certain to contain many falls in ele-
vation. Extraordinarily heavy, weighing between 900 and 2,500 pounds
empty, dugouts capsized easily and were mules to steer. By contrast,
the roomy Canadian canoes Roosevelt had been forced to leave behind
weighed only 160 pounds, carried a ton of freight, and darted through
rapids like minnows.[4]

Of the sixteen paddlers—the camaradas—assigned to the expedition,
Roosevelt had nothing but praise. "[They] were a strapping set," he wrote,
". . . lithe as panthers and brawny as bears." Their faces mirrored the
racial melting pot of Brazil: Indians, negroes, olive-skinned Portuguese,
and various strains in between.[5] Many of them, such as Paixão, a giant
of a black soldier and a natural leader, had served with Rondon before.
Paixão had proven he could manage men, and Rondon made him sergeant
over the paddlers.[6] As hunters, the crack shots were Antonio the Parecis,
a full-blooded Indian with a kindly, slow-witted nature, and Antonio
Correa, whom Roosevelt described as "an intelligent, daredevil mulatto,
probably with also a dash of Indian blood" in his veins.[7] The overworked
cook, Franca, earned his place by learning how to make *canja* with all
kinds of feathered substitutes for chicken.

Before departing, Roosevelt had a chance to say good-bye to Miller,
who stopped on his way west with Amilcar's detachment to descend
the Rio Gy-Paraná. There was a final round of picture taking and hand-

shakes in the rain between the two exploring parties. "Wait for me at Manáos," Roosevelt said to Miller, who expected to reach the rubber capital weeks before his chief did. Miller asked if anyone had mail to entrust to his care. At the last minute, the Colonel realized he had run out of money with which to purchase food and new canoes if they should find the rubber camps lower down the river. He borrowed $500 from Miller's museum expense money, promising to pay him back when they met up again.[8]

Then it was time to go. A little after midday, Kermit and Rondon whistled for their dogs to jump on board. The Colonel wedged his bulk into a space between the bundles in his dugout. He was dressed for exploring in sun helmet, neckerchief, long-sleeved shirt, suspenders, and hobnailed boots. Rondon, soberly uniformed in an army field tunic and helmet, waited for Roosevelt's nod to start. Then he signaled Kermit's little canoe to take the lead. One by one, the dugouts swung out into the stream and were carried along by the pull of the current. The figures on the bridge raised their hands and called out, "Good luck!" Within minutes the last canoe disappeared around a forested bend in the river.

On the telegraph bridge, Miller stopped waving and stared for a while at the dark mass of trees screening the departed canoes. He felt a chill of fear for the safety of Roosevelt's party and wondered if they would all reach Manáos alive. Then he shook it off and ran to catch up with Amilcar.[9]

Now entirely on their own, Roosevelt's party found themselves descending a wild, timber-choked mountain stream that had overflowed its banks after weeks of torrential rains. The surrounding forest stood drowned in a network of lagoons and channels extending far inland. Scores of palm trees, uprooted by the scouring current, lay strewn like matchsticks along the shoreline. In some places, a dead tree sagged far enough across the narrow river to force the boatmen to make a frantic detour around the huge trunk. It was then, T. R. wrote, that "the muscles stood out on the backs and arms of the paddlers as stroke on stroke they urged us away from and past the obstacle."[10]

The river appeared to flow generally north toward the Amazon but changed direction every few hundred meters, making it impossible for the explorers to guess where they were going. In the space of a few hours they would find themselves heading toward every point on the compass.[11] At the bends, the boatmen stabbed the water with their paddles to keep from slamming into the piled-up trunks and branches jutting out from the shore.[12]

Rondon faced a formidable task in surveying a river as puzzling as the Dúvida. The expedition had started from a known location at the telegraph bridge: 12 degrees 1 minute south latitude and 60 degrees 15 minutes west longitude. Beyond that, nothing was known about the river or the land through which it flowed. If the Dúvida turned west to join the Gy-Paraná or swung east to the Tapajós, the exploration would be a short one, ending up on rivers already well known. But if the Dúvida turned out to be a tributary of the Madeira, as Rondon suspected, or the Amazon, he would have between eight hundred and a thousand miles of river to chart. In the days before aerial mapping, the only accurate way to do this was to laboriously measure each change in angle of the river's course by compass, and then correct the work by frequent solar observations.

The success of this so-called "fixed station" survey depended on the endurance of the sighting scout—in this case, Kermit Roosevelt. While Rondon and Lyra held their canoe back, Kermit ranged ahead in the smallest canoe, searching for places that offered a clear view upstream. When he found one, his paddlers, Henrique and Simplicio, steered for it and hung on to shoreline branches while Kermit leapt ashore. With his machete, he chopped away the undergrowth to clear a space for the red-and-white sighting pole. Streaming with sweat and cursing at the ants and wasps that stung his face and neck, Kermit waited long enough for Rondon and Lyra to measure the angle and distance, then climbed back into the dugout. Rondon's concern for accuracy was such that during that first afternoon of charting the Dúvida, Kermit landed 114 times in six miles to plant the sighting rod.[13]

Leaving the surveyors to their work, T. R. let his dugout glide on, propelled by the relentless current and the surge of the boatmen's paddles. It was interesting work to explore a tropical wilderness never before seen by civilized men:

> The lofty and matted forest rose like a green wall on either hand. The trees were stately and beautiful. The looped and twisted vines hung from them like great ropes. Masses of epiphytes* grew both on the dead trees and the living; some had huge leaves like elephants' ears. Now and then fragrant scents were blown to us from flowers on the banks.[14]

---

* Nonparasitical plants living on plants and taking their nourishment from dust and rain, air ferns being one example.

Everyone in the party was struck by the absence of animal life on-shore. Few birds were seen or heard, which added to the peculiar sense of isolation. The flooding of the forest along the river had driven game to seek higher ground—an ominous sign for a riverborne expedition that had hoped to stretch its inadequate food supply by hunting. It also meant that Cherrie would have less chance to add to his collection of specimens.

The light was fading when the weary, famished surveyors turned up. The Colonel was relieved to see his son return from his first day as Rondon's scout apparently unscathed, except for the red bumps of wasp and ant stings dotting his face, hands, and legs. Kermit relaxed by taking a few healthy swigs from a bottle of scotch that Cherrie had pulled from his duffel bag. On such occasions, Cherrie recalled, "We felt the need of spiritual help . . ."[15]

To gain a head start the next morning, the surveyors pushed off in their dugouts directly after breakfast. Before they left, though, Rondon performed two rituals that reminded everyone that this was a military as well as a scientific expedition. The twenty-two Americans and Brazilians lined up at attention while Rondon read his Order of the Day, which detailed work assignments and the objectives to be accomplished. He also set up the first of the hardwood posts that were to mark every camp on the unknown river. On the raw squared face of the post, Rondon chiseled the letters "R–R" (for Roosevelt and Rondon), the camp number, date, and the estimated distance in meters from the telegraph bridge.[16]

An hour after the surveyors left, the two pairs of lashed dugouts carrying the kitchen gear and heavier cargo started downstream. Roosevelt held his own dugout back at the now-deserted camp to give Cherrie time to search for birds, whose calls had awakened him at dawn.

Cherrie made good use of his time and brought back half a dozen rainbow-colored specimens, including a large woodpecker with a black and cinnamon body and a bright red neck. These were the first birds to be captured by a naturalist on the River of Doubt. It was an important enough event for Roosevelt to wait while the catch was skinned and rolled up into tubes of magazine pages for safe keeping. Not until noon did he and Cherrie climb into their dugout and push off to join the others.

There were few birds to be seen or caught the second afternoon on the river. The travelers again were surprised by the lack of wildlife on the swiftly passing shoreline. They heard briefly the screaming chatter of howler monkeys echoing deep in the forest and watched a solitary otter swimming lazily downstream. But for the most part, Roosevelt and his canoe companions gazed upon a lifeless landscape of singular beauty.

> As we drifted and paddled down the swirling brown current, through the vivid rain-drenched green of the tropic forest, the trees leaned over the river from both banks. When those that had fallen in the river at some narrow point were very tall, or where . . . two fell opposite each other, they formed barriers which the men in the leading canoes cleared with their axes . . . In places the palms stood close together, towering and slender, their stems a stately colonnade, their fronds an arched fretwork against the sky. Butterflies of many hues fluttered over the river. The day was overcast, with showers of rain. When the sun broke through rifts in the clouds, his shafts turned the forest to gold.[17]

The same afternoon brought the discovery of a good-sized stream entering the Dúvida from the right. This caused great rejoicing among the explorers, because it raised the probability that they were descending an important river that had so far escaped the attention of geographers.[18] Rondon was sure this first tributary was the Festa da Bandeira (Flag Day River), which the expedition had crossed ten days earlier on the march to the telegraph station at José Bonifácio. With the added volume of water, the Dúvida swelled to greater breadth, engulfing the shoreline forest and leaving only the high ground dry. To reach the night's camp, a mile below the Bandeira, the boatmen had to hack their way for hundreds of feet through the branches of submerged trees.

March 1, the third day of the Dúvida descent, began with a predawn swimming bath. The Colonel, an early riser, was always the first man in the water. The sight of the portly, stark-naked former president of the United States bobbing up and down and merrily humming snatches of old hymns and cowboy ballads amused his fellow explorers. "He was a big man," Rondon remembered, "and when he floated on his back, he looked like some sort of a great, fat fish which had come to the surface."[19]

By now, the mapping of the Dúvida's corkscrew course was proceeding so slowly that the main party had to wait in camp until late morning to give the surveyors time to do their work. The delay provided Cherrie with a few precious hours to add birds to his collection and hunt for food. By 11:00 A.M., as heavy rain fell, the Colonel's dugout started downstream with the two cargo rafts trailing behind. For much of the twelve-mile run that day, his boatmen bailed their way through showers that were more like "vertical sheets of water."[20]

There was ample evidence that Indians, perhaps migrating bands of Nhambiquaras, had once lived on this river and fished its waters. At the mouth of a small tributary entering from the right, Rondon reached out from his canoe to touch a row of sticks standing upright in the water—the remnants of a primitive fish trap. Farther downstream, the explorers ducked their heads when the dugouts swept beneath a drooping rope of dried-out vines flung across the river. It was one of the spans of a native footbridge that the high water had torn away.

Trees had to be cut down on a piece of high ground for the camp of March 1. While working, one of the barefoot axmen noticed a deadly coral snake and tried to strike it with his axe. When he missed, the three-foot-long snake slithered over to where Roosevelt stood. According to Cherrie, T. R. did a much livelier dance than even his shipboard horn-pipe in order to crush the serpent with his boot.[21] When it was dead, he got down on his hands and knees and noted the "distinctly revealing" contrast of the snake's brightly colored skin against the matted brown leaves. He had heard it said that the coral snake's brilliant coloring enabled it to escape detection from predators, but here was evidence to the contrary.[22]

Roosevelt often recorded such scientific discoveries the same day he witnessed them. Rondon recalled that he "wrote every day, never neglecting his literary work, even when heroic effort was required." As soon as a campsite was chosen and the tents were erected, T. R. would set up his portable table, arrange sheets of foolscap and carbon paper, and begin writing, sometimes until 9:00 P.M.[23] The finished pages were added to the growing pile inside the black leather bag that never left his sight.

Rondon also liked to observe the former president when he was deep in thought:

> I used to love to watch him think. A person could watch Roosevelt think! It was a very amusing sight, for he always gesticulated. He would be alone, not saying a word, yet his hands would be moving, and he would be waving his arms and nodding his head with the greatest determination, as though arguing with somebody.[24]

Before reaching this camp, Cherrie had managed to shoot a potbellied gray monkey. He skinned it and turned it over to the cook. Roosevelt was hungry enough to pronounce his first taste of roast monkey meat "very good eating,"[25] but it was to be a rare treat in the days that followed. The hunters often found tapir trails in the woods around the camps but rarely saw a target to shoot at. Their hope that they could augment their short rations was already dimming. Roosevelt shared half of the official party's daily issue of bread and hardtack with the paddlers to give them some bulk in their diet. He also made the hours between breakfast and supper seem shorter by passing out bits of chocolate to them each noon, as long as the supply lasted. Rondon the purist looked down on this strange treat, but Roosevelt endeared himself to the men by such thoughtfulness.[26]

The next day, March 2, the surveying party's patience was again put to the test in mapping twelve more miles of the Dúvida. To Cherrie, riding in Roosevelt's canoe, it seemed almost incredible how many times the river twisted and turned and doubled back on itself. Equally remarkable was the river's width at this point. For miles the high water flowed sluggishly through standing trees and around isolated clumps of land. In the glare of the tropical sun, the travelers imagined themselves to be floating on a great inland lake or marsh.[27]

The dreamlike quality of this day's passage ended abruptly in the late afternoon when the current began unaccountably to race. Within minutes, the startled explorers were bouncing through a short stretch of rapids, luckily without harm. Then, instead of slowing down again, the current grew even more turbulent, racing at breakneck speed. The men in the dugouts heard a sound that was to haunt them in the weeks ahead—the steady drumming of falling water that pounded their eardrums like uninterrupted thunder. When the paddlers saw a barrier of foaming water ahead, they steered at once for the right bank and tied the canoes to trees standing in the water. Leaving the camaradas to set up a campsite, the officials of the party cut their way through tangled growth along the bank to explore the river ahead.

They found a serious obstacle confronting them. For half a mile, the river descended through a long stretch of rapids that included two falls, each the height of a man. Just below these rapids, the river suddenly converged into a narrow sandstone gorge whose jagged walls in places were less than six feet apart. No canoe could survive the whirlpools that roared through it. Kermit took a photograph of Cherrie kneeling on one ledge of this strange chasm and touching the other side with the tip of his shotgun barrel. "It seemed extraordinary, almost impossible," wrote T. R., "that so broad a river could in so short a space of time contract its dimensions to the width of the strangled channel through which it now poured its entire volume."[28]

A simple footbridge of three logs laid side by side spanned the sandstone gorge at one point, suggesting that this was an Indian crossing place. The explorers found well-beaten trails running through the woods for the length of the rapids. On one of these trails, Kermit knelt down and examined a fresh trail marker on the ground. It consisted of two short branches, each with eight leaves, laid crosswise to each other to signify some message. The branches were recently cut, which awakened a fear among Roosevelt's party that they might be attacked by natives who had never seen white men before. Now no one stepped away from camp without picking up a rifle.[29]

On the other side of the river, Rondon poked about the burnt-out remains of palm huts of an abandoned Indian village. He speculated that the absent owners were the Navaitê people, a subgroup of the Nhambiquaras. Appropriately, Rondon named the rapids Navaitê. Roosevelt, on his own map of South America, chose to pencil the more descriptive words "Bridge Rapids" in the blue space representing the Atlantic Ocean, adding below that their exact position, based on Lyra's theodolite readings: 11 degrees 44 minutes south, 60 degrees 18 minutes west.[30] In four days, the expedition had progressed only twenty miles in straight-line distance down the River of Doubt.

The explorers now had come upon the first important obstacle to their progress down the Dúvida. The portage around Navaitê Falls extracted two and a half days of what T. R. called "severe and incessant labor" from men already short on food.[31] This setback came as a shock, but it was merely the first of a series of disasters that were soon to overtake Roosevelt's expedition.

March 3 . . . The day was spent transferring the camp from above Navaitê Rapids to a point below the gorge where the dugouts could be safely relaunched. The camaradas made repeated treks along the uneven forest trail, balancing duffel bags and food crates on their bent backs like foraging ants. Rondon put everyone in the party to work, except for the cook, a boatman down with fever, and Kermit, who again had painful boils on his thighs. The pain was so great that he could do nothing but lie facedown on his hammock under mosquito netting. He passed the time reading the Oxford Editions of French and English poetry and slapped at white termites that were "attacking everything" in sight.[32]

March 4 . . . By dawn, Lyra's ax-swinging crews were already widening one of the Indian trails into a portage route. Following a technique as old as Egypt, the men cut several hundred log rollers and laid them down at two-foot intervals, forming a skidway over which to drag the canoes. Another work party hoisted each of the dugouts out of the water and up to higher ground. From there, two camaradas yoked themselves to the drag rope at the front and another man pushed and pried from behind with a pole, and the canoe bumped and slid over the uneven log carpet. As the canoes descended the downhill slope to the launching place, several of them rammed into sharp sandstone ledges. One canoe, Roosevelt's, split so badly that it was questionable how long it would last even after being patched. Still another dugout broke free of its ropes as it was being lowered into the water. It plunged to the bottom and enormous effort was required to raise it.[33]

By all the explorers' accounts, the profusion of insects at Navaitê Rapids made the three-day encampment there an experiment in torture. Roosevelt spoke of horseflies as big as bumblebees and of small stinging bees that mixed in with swarms of nonstinging bees and took their human victims by surprise. He and Cherrie awoke on March 4 to discover that the tent they shared was alive with termites. The Colonel put on his spectacles and leaned over the edge of his cot to see a line of tiny fragments of red cloth helmet liner streaming out under the tent flap. Examining his spare clothing, he found that the insects had eaten all but one leg of a pair of underdrawers. He was not amused when Kermit and Cherrie laughed out loud at the sight.[34]

As always, the mystery of the River of Doubt dominated the party's campfire discussions. "We were still wholly unable to tell where we were going or what lay ahead of us," Roosevelt found after six days of exploration. Lyra clung adamantly to his theory that the Dúvida fed into the Gy-Paraná. If so, they should meet Miller and Amilcar coming down that river, but time was proving this less and less likely. Each day the surveyors found more tributaries, thereby strengthening Rondon's argument that so big a river must surely flow directly into the Madeira or the Amazon.

But who could say for sure? The river might fool them all and end in some dismal swamp, thus stranding the party. Roosevelt summed up the terrible dilemma his expedition faced:

> We did not know whether we had one hundred or eight
> hundred kilometers to go, whether the stream would be
> fairly smooth or whether we would encounter waterfalls,

> or rapids, . . . [or] meet hostile Indians . . . We had no idea
> how much time the trip would take. We had entered a
> land of unknown possibilities.[35]

March 5 . . . At noon, the explorers climbed into the dugouts, relieved to be moving on the water again where bees, flies, and wasps could not get at them in large numbers. Their ears, faces, and hands itched and burned like fire. Many of the shoeless camaradas hobbled painfully on feet swollen and inflamed from innumerable bites and stings.

Below Navaitê Rapids, the Dúvida broadened once more. There were no further rapids, and the surveyors recorded a gain of eight miles this day. The river wound back and forth in dizzying S curves, heading by turns east or north through dense stands of trees. Roosevelt found it all beautiful to look upon but unnerving: "We never could tell what might appear around any curve."[36]

March 6 . . . By now, eight days after leaving the telegraph bridge, it was obvious that Rondon's use of the fixed-station method of mapping the Dúvida was becoming impractical. The surveyors were averaging as many as ninety sightings a day to record the river's erratic course. In the last two days alone, Rondon had recorded eighteen streams and five tributaries entering the Dúvida.[37] As discoverer, he had the privilege of naming them for Brazilian national heroes, officers of the Telegraph Commission, and his fellow explorers. Modestly, he refrained from naming any for himself. But the time needed to conduct such a meticulous survey delayed the progress of the expedition and ate into rations that could not be replaced by hunting. The appearance of more rapids, late on this day, served only to compound the problems of feeding twenty-two men from an ever-shrinking food supply.

Near 3:00 P.M. Roosevelt had let his canoe drift far below the surveying party, when he felt the current accelerate. "We passed over one or two decided ripples, and then heard the roar of the rapids ahead, while the stream began to race."[38] His paddlers pulled at once for shore, and the Colonel got out to have a closer look. About a quarter mile down, the river dashed against glistening boulders and foamed over ledges of red porphyritic rock, ruling out any passage by the canoes.

On closer inspection, Rondon found that dangerous rapids extended for at least a mile and included two steep falls three hundred feet apart. There was no way to avoid another long portage.

March 7 . . . Lyra's men needed all of this day to chop a five-hundred-yard-long road through the virgin forest. When it was finally opened, the camaradas carried the baggage down below the last rapids to a picturesque bay where the river curved past a beach of clean, firm sand. Three tall burity palms stood like sentinels in the water, shading the tents with their fronds. Masses of white and lilac orchids grew on the rocks and trees by the riverbank. The boatmen fashioned shelters for themselves from branches, roofed with twelve-foot-long banana tree leaves, and hung their hammocks underneath.

While Lyra's tireless axmen felled trees, the hunters in the party fanned out to forage for food. Cherrie bagged several birds, bringing his Dúvida collection to sixty birds, including some he thought new to science. After skinning them, he donated the flesh to the camp soup pot. The Colonel found some solitude by following the river for several miles, wearing head net and gauntlets against the insects and carrying a volume of poetry in his pocket for company. He was alone on these excursions and usually returned empty-handed. In the dense tropical forest, his weak eyesight kept him from seeing an animal from far enough away before it heard his footsteps and fled.[39]

Kermit was more successful at hunting than his father. On his feet again after the doctor had treated his boils, the younger Roosevelt hunted and explored far downstream with Antonio the Parecis and the two dogs. They nearly cornered a tapir, which bounded across the rapids to safety, and then shot a monkey and a jacu, a sort of small turkey. That night, the hard-working camaradas tasted fresh meat, but the pleasure of full stomachs was ruined when Kermit spoke of more rapids that he had seen several miles below their present camp—rapids that would require still another portage.[40]

March 8 . . . "At work till after nightfall hauling canoes out of the water & up the hill," Kermit wrote wearily of the start of the second major portage in less than a week. His rope-handling skills—learned from building steel bridges—proved invaluable on this occasion, as did his command of Portuguese. He and Lyra jointly supervised the camaradas. The combined strength of all the men was needed to drag the dugouts three hundred yards over uneven ground. When darkness fell, they had relaunched one boat below the falls, while the others sat beached at different points on the portage.[41]

March 9 . . . Using shoulders, hands, and bare chests straining against drag ropes, the camaradas managed to haul the remaining six canoes through the forest to the foot of the second falls. In the water again, the boats were reloaded and made ready to run through the last of the "6th of March Rapids," as they were now officially called. Then Rondon suddenly turned cautious and decided that only the two largest canoes could be trusted to get through the rapids safely. He directed Lyra to cut another two-hundred-yard-long trail and bring the other five canoes around by land. Doing so cost a day's advance and a day's rations, neither of which the party could afford to lose.

This delay angered Roosevelt, who saw his hopes for getting home in a reasonable period of time thwarted by an unpredictable river. In his frustration, he began to repeatedly question Rondon on the details of his Orders of the Day, ready to seize upon any unnecessary delay. He made note of the distance traveled each day and the altitude of each camp, as measured by Lyra's aneroid barometer, and put his faith in the knowledge that a river's descent is usually steepest in its upper course.[42] As they had come down more than three hundred feet in altitude already, the rapids must surely end soon.

March 10 . . . Half of this day was gone before the explorers re-embarked, only to have to scurry to shore three times during the afternoon when they came upon the new series of rapids Kermit had seen earlier while hunting. On two occasions, the canoes had to be emptied and the loads carried around on a hastily slashed trail. Meanwhile, teams of naked paddlers guided the dugouts on a hair-raising zigzag ride through the white water. Watching these men skillfully dodge boulders and sudden whirlpools was exciting for onlookers like Cherrie, but the chance for a deadly accident was always present.[43]

One of the clumsy pairs of tied-together canoes quickly filled with water as the paddlers took them through the roughest rapids. The dugouts would have been pounded to splinters if the paddlers on board had not leapt out and dragged the sunken hulls to land. In doing so, one of the men lost his footing and sliced his face open against a sharp-edged rock.

Rather than risk another mishap, Kermit and Lyra decided to pass the other double canoe down the edge of the rapids with ropes. If these rafts were lost, there would be no way to carry the party's rations. All social distinctions were set aside as Kermit, an American ex-president's son, worked side by side in the river with Lyra and the camaradas. Except for his boots, Kermit was as naked as they were and too busy and excited to be stopped by the savage bites of giant ants that dropped onto his back from drooping branches. By the time he crawled out of the water, his body was covered with bite marks and blisters.

When the canoes were safely moored late that afternoon, the party made camp in a pesthole of ants, bees, and bloodsucking flies. Rondon's survey indicated that the party was no more than a mile below the 6th of March Rapids. After twelve days on the river, they had come down only seventy-five miles from the telegraph bridge, for an average of just over six miles a day.[44]

March 11 . . . The explorers awoke to confront a serious misfortune. During the night, heavy rain had caused the river to rise. The larger pair of cargo canoes, leaky from the start, had broken free of their moorings and been carried away by the surging current. A search was made to find them but was called off when large chunks of the hulls were found floating in the shallows downstream. By a miracle of luck, the food crates in them had been brought to shore the night before, but the remaining double canoe was not big enough to carry the additional loads.

Roosevelt did not like the idea of stopping for several days and seeing the party's food dwindle further. But he saw there was no alternative. "We had to build either one big canoe or two small ones."[45]

Rondon set out in the rain to search for a suitable tree. By evening, after rejecting several candidates that were found to be rotten, he chose a huge tatajuba tree, fully five feet thick at the base. The axmen quickly sank their blades into the dense, yellowish wood.[46] Once they felled the tree, they marked off the trunk at twenty-five feet and began the work of hollowing and shaping.

March 12–13 . . . For two days, the thudding of axes and adzes resounded in the woods surrounding Broken Canoe Rapids, as Rondon aptly chose to call this camp. Stripped to the waist, pairs of camaradas stood astride the giant log, gradually burrowing into its side, which would become its top when rolled over. Rondon never left the scene and kept his men working as late as 11:00 P.M.[47] When the light faded, the boat builders continued chopping by candlelight.

During the canoe-building halt, Cherrie's efforts to add to his collection of bird life were hampered by rain and insects. He tramped the forest for hours in sodden clothing, always alert for a flash of color or movement in the branches, but was lucky to bring back a single bird in his bag. On one occasion, he shot what looked like a new species of toucan, only to see it fall onto a boulder and smash its bill, thereby ruining its value as a specimen. His hands were swollen from mosquito and fly bites, making it difficult to perform the delicate surgical cuts required in skinning his catches. He was also disheartened to find that his light-gauge shotgun shells were moldering in the intense humidity. Without them, he would not be able to bring down a bird without damaging its skin and plumage.[48]

The party's fear of running out of food intensified during the boat-building halt. They had reached the stage where, as the Colonel wrote, "we were endeavoring in all ways to economize our food supply."[49] The camaradas had by now turned to eating palmitos—palm hearts—which grew abundantly. The bland, celerylike vegetable was low in nutrition but filled their stomachs. Everyone searched in vain for the normally plentiful, protein-rich Brazil nut. Unknown to Roosevelt's party, 1914 was one of the years the nut crop failed on this part of the river. To make up for this, Kermit hunted with fanatical energy, despite being wet through as always and continually bitten by insects. He returned to camp at times holding up a pair of dead monkeys by their tails or draping the limp form of an eight-foot-long water snake around his neck.[50]

While waiting for the dugout to be finished, the Colonel and Cherrie took an inventory of the party's food supply. Cherrie recorded some sobering arithmetic:

> We went over our provisions today. The men have suf-
> ficient for *thirty-five* days and we have enough for about
> fifty days. It is estimated that we have about 600 kilo-
> meters [375 miles] to go [to reach Lieutenant Pyrenius's
> camp on the lower Aripuanã]. During the past 15 days
> since starting, we have averaged about 7 *kilometers!* (Due
> north we have only averaged about 2½ miles out of a
> possible 400.) At that rate, we will be shy about 35 days
> food! There may be very serious times ahead of us.[51]

Roosevelt did not record his private thoughts about their growing predicament. His articles for *Scribner's Magazine*, which formed a daily journal of his experiences on the River of Doubt, spoke of privations but not of the despair that was slowly enveloping his expedition. It was Cherrie, the veteran naturalist and plainspoken farmer, who confided to his diary what he and his companions were feeling at this time:

> There isn't anyone of our party that will not be very
> thankful when this trip draws to a close. There are *too*
> many uncertainties and possibilities to face to make it a
> thing to anticipate with gusto.[52]

March 14 . . . By noon the newly finished dugout, which Rondon christened *Aripuanã*, was dragged down to the river and successfully launched. Seeing it ride easily in the water lifted everyone's morale.[53] Within an hour, the expedition had started downstream again.

Below Broken Canoe Rapids, the Dúvida fell measurably, plunging headlong through half a dozen rapids. There was no talk of portaging this day—too much time had already been lost—and the explorers now took their chances, even though the heavily loaded canoes rode only a few inches out of the water. "The two biggest rapids we only just made," the Colonel recorded, "and after each we had hastily to push ashore in order to bail."[54] At one point, his canoe was caught up in the suction of a shifting whirlpool and took on water. Cherrie and stout old Dr. Cajazeira jumped overboard in order to lighten the load so that the paddlers could fight their way clear.

For now, with so few stretches of smooth water, Rondon had to temporarily give up surveying by fixed stations. He resorted instead to the less-accurate method of sighting on Kermit's small canoe as it skimmed on ahead without stopping. This put the Colonel's son in greater danger as he and his paddlers fought to avoid being sucked into the next rapids while keeping in sight of Rondon's canoe. By using this "rapid survey" method, the surveyors charted ten more miles of the river before darkness set in—a good day's run. That night in camp, the air turned fresh and cool. The men crawled into their hammocks and for once slept well.

March 15 . . . The Ides of March, the party's seventeenth day on the unknown river, began under strangely good auspices. The Dúvida turned briefly benign, enough so that Rondon resumed his fixed station survey. For almost four miles there were no rapids, and the paddlers stroked easily, letting the swiftly flowing current carry the dugouts along. For a few peaceful hours, Roosevelt and his fellow explorers had time to admire the stately palms and towering Brazil nut trees that flanked the shoreline in a symphony of vivid greens.

Then boulder-strewn hills began rising on either bank and the travelers heard a by now familiar sound, faint at first but gradually growing in stomach-wrenching intensity. As Roosevelt's canoe rounded a bend in the river, he saw a broad swath of white water with an island in the middle filling the distance. It was here, he later recorded, that "grave misfortune befell us, and graver misfortune was narrowly escaped."[55]

Rondon's experienced eyes and ears told him that dugouts could not run through these rapids, which were split by the island into two dangerously rough channels. He signaled Kermit's scout canoe to return. Rondon then landed on the left bank with Lyra to explore a possible portage route, leaving orders with his canoemen that when Kermit arrived, he should wait there. On hearing of Rondon's order, however, Kermit chose to ignore it and to see for himself if the channel on the right side could be navigated. He told his paddlers, João and young Simplicio, to pull across to the island.

What happened next is not clear. As T. R. told the story, Kermit and his paddlers had gone up to the edge of the rapids in the right channel and were on their way back upstream when the accident occurred.

> Before they had gone a dozen yards . . . one of the shifting whirlpools . . . came down-stream, whirled them around, and swept them so close to the rapids that no human power could avoid going over them. As they were drifting into them broadside on, Kermit yelled to the steersman to turn her head, so as to take them in the only way that offered any chance whatever of safety. The water came aboard, wave after wave, as they raced down. They reached the bottom with the canoe upright, but so full as barely to float, and the paddlers urged her toward the shore. They had nearly reached the bank when another whirlpool or whirling eddy tore them away and hurried them back to midstream, where the dugout filled and turned over.

The steersman, João, grabbed at the tow rope and began swimming to shore but lost hold of the rope before he reached land. Simplicio was thrown from his seat in the bow and disappeared beneath the water. Kermit, still clutching his Winchester rifle, managed to climb onto the upturned keel of the capsized canoe. He rode through a second set of rapids until he was thrown off, losing his rifle as he fell. Again in the words of T. R.:

> The water beat his helmet down over his head and face and drove him beneath the surface; and when he rose at last he was almost drowned, his breath and strength almost spent. He was in swift but quiet water, and swam toward an overhanging branch. His jacket hindered him but he knew he was too nearly gone to be able to get it off, and, thinking with the curious calm one feels when death is but a moment away, he realized that the utmost his failing strength could do was to reach the branch.

He reached, and clutched it, and then almost lacked
strength to haul himself out.[56]

Trigueiro survived as well, swimming alongside his master. The dog
clawed his way up the muddy bank, shook out his coat, and trotted
down the trail when Rondon and Lyra appeared. Unaware of what had
happened, Rondon looked at Kermit's wet clothes and dripping beard
and smiled, "Well, you have had a splendid bath, eh?" Then, stunned,
he heard Kermit describe how he had just escaped from drowning after
his canoe had been carried over the falls by a whirlpool and that his two
assistants had probably swum to the other bank.[57]

One of the missing paddlers, João, turned up a short time later,
after swimming across the river. He told Rondon a different version of
what took place. After drifting up to the edge of the rapids, Kermit had
decided to try running them. He ordered his paddlers to start down,
and when they told him it was too dangerous, he repeated his order.
The two camaradas felt they had to obey him.[58]

Simplicio's body was not found, nor was any wreckage of the canoe.
Kermit searched along the river for several miles on his own and swam
out to retrieve an oar and a food crate floating in midstream.

The Colonel was deeply affected by his son's brush with death.
"Kermit was a great comfort and help to me," he wrote, "but the fear of
some fatal accident befalling him was always a nightmare to me." The
fact that Kermit was to be married when they got out made it all the
more poignant—"It did not seem to me that I could bear to bring bad
tidings to his betrothed and to his mother."[59]

There was no time to mourn for Simplicio. Roosevelt saw his death
as "one of the accidents that may at any time occur" on a wilderness expedition. It must not be allowed to hold up their progress.[60] One afternoon's mischance had cost the party a life, one of the dugouts, adzes
needed for boat building, and most critical of all, ten days' provisions
that could not be replaced.

An atmosphere of deep depression hung over the portage of March 15.[61]
It was necessary to cut a long trail around the rapids, over which the
dejected camaradas carried the loads. Afterward, the saddened company
heard Rondon honor the drowned boy. On one face of the camp marker
post, he inscribed in Portuguese: "In These Rapids Died Poor Simplicio."[62]

The "camp of misfortune," as Roosevelt called it, was abandoned the
next morning in the rainy, early-morning darkness.[63] There were now
only five canoes for twenty-one men and none of them light enough for

use in surveying by fixed stations. Rondon reverted once again to the survey in motion, training his compass on Kermit's helmeted figure in the dugout far ahead.

The mapping was soon called off, however, as the canoes reached more rapids. Rondon and Lyra crossed to the right side of the river and found a side channel long enough to let down the empty canoes by ropes. The camaradas immediately began unloading the dugouts.

Satisfied that his subordinates could handle matters, Rondon struck out along the left side of the river with Lobo to hunt and look for edible nuts. He had gone about a kilometer when he heard what sounded like the scream of a spider monkey, the largest simian of the Amazon and an excellent source of meat. Creeping along as quietly as he could, Rondon studied the upper branches of the trees for movement. Lobo ran ahead, sniffing at the ground. Minutes later, Rondon heard the dog yelp in pain. Its cries grew louder, then ceased. He first thought the dog had stumbled into a jaguar or a peccary, until he heard human voices—"short exclamations, energetic, and repeated in a kind of chorus with a certain cadence peculiar to Indians who . . . are ready [to] commence the attack." Resisting an urge to help his mascot, he instead fired a round into the air and ran back to the camp.[64]

He reached the foot of the rapids out of breath and found the portage half completed. But Rondon's immediate concerns were Indians and "my poor wounded and abandoned dog." He asked Roosevelt to guard the lower end of the portage route and sent Cherrie racing back to protect the boatmen at the head of the rapids. Then Rondon picked up some ax heads, filled his pockets with colored beads as gifts, and led an armed escort consisting of Lyra, Kermit, and Antonio the Parecis back to find Lobo.

At the end of a bloodstained trail lay the dog's body, pierced by two arrows, one of which had ripped through the stomach. In tears, Rondon examined the arrowhead, made of bamboo and shaped into a barbed lance. The Nhambiquaras did not make such heads, so the Indians who had attacked Lobo were from some other, unknown tribe. Nearby, Rondon picked up a long pole tied to a woven basket stuffed with animal intestines, evidently used as bait for bow-and-arrow fishing. The Indians, probably two or three in number, had been frightened by the gunshot. After burying Lobo in a shallow grave, Rondon arranged the axes and glass beads around the fishing basket in a show of friendship.[65]

Meanwhile, by the river, a greater loss than Rondon's dog had taken place. Four of the dugouts had been successfully passed down the rapids by ropes. But as the newly built *Aripuanã* was being let down, the rope broke. One of the boatmen nearly drowned as the big canoe slid beneath the surface and was swept away in a tangle of ropes and pulleys.

"It was a very bad thing to lose the canoe," the Colonel wrote of this latest disaster, "but it was even worse to lose the rope and pulleys."[66] Without them, there was no way to hoist the dugouts up even small hills during portages. The danger of Indian attack ruled out staying at this camp to build a new boat, but the four remaining canoes could not carry all the men and their equipment, however much they might cut down baggage.

That night at Broken Rope Rapids, the leaders of the expedition held a council on the best way to proceed. Afterward, Cherrie recorded their decision:

> Late this evening, after a long discussion of ways and means, we have determined to try for a day or two fastening our four canoes together as two balsas [rafts]. Loading our baggage and supplies into them, manning each with three paddlers and with Col. Roosevelt and the Doctor in charge. The remaining thirteen of us will walk along the shore.[67]

Space on the two rafts would be so limited that each man was allowed to take only one trunk or duffel bag of personal effects. Roosevelt kept a small tent to put his cot in, while the other five officials would share a single large tent. Rondon gave up a box of surveying instruments.[68]

The implications behind these sacrifices made even an old campaigner like Cherrie edgy:

> Our position is really a very serious one. Provisions are every day decreasing. It is impossible to go back. The journey ahead is undoubtedly a *very long* one. The difficulties to overcome can only be judged by what we have passed through!

He ended his entry for March 16 with a gloomy prediction: "It is very doubtful if all our party ever reaches Manáos."[69]

NOTES

1. T. R., *Brazilian Wild.*, p. 243. 2. Ibid., pp. 243–44. 3. Ibid., p. 267. 4. Ibid., p. 355. 5. Ibid., p. 244. 6. Rondon, *Lectures*, p. 107. 7. T. R., *Book Lover's Holiday*, p. 162. 8. Leo Miller to Frank M. Chapman, 2-25-14, *AMNH*. 9. Miller, *In the Wilds*, p. 242. 10. T. R., *Brazilian Wild.*, p. 245. 11. T. R. "The Unknown River," *Scribner's Magazine*. 12. Cherrie, *Diary*, 2-27-14. 13. Rondon, *Lectures*, p. 71. 14. T. R., *Brazilian Wild.*, pp. 245–46. 15. Cherrie, *T. R., Memorial Meeting*, p. 27. 16. Cherrie, *Diary*, 2-28-14. 17. T. R., *Brazilian Wild.*, p. 247. 18. Roosevelt, Kermit, *Diary*, 2-28-14. 19. Rondon, "Col. Roosevelt as His Guide Remembers Him," *New York Times*. 20. T. R., *Brazilian Wild.*, p. 248. 21. Cherrie, *Dark Trails*, p. 281. 22. T. R., *Brazilian Wild.*, p. 249. 23. Rondon, "Col. Roosevelt as His Guide Remembers Him," *New York Times*. 24. Ibid. 25. T. R., *Brazilian Wild.*, p. 249. 26. Rondon, "Col. Roosevelt as His Guide Remembers Him," *New York Times*. 27. Cherrie, *Diary*, 3-2-14. 28. T. R., *Brazilian Wild.*, pp. 251–52. 29. Roosevelt, Kermit, *Diary*, 3-2-14. 30. Pencil notes on T. R.'s own map of South America, *TRC*. 31. T. R., *Brazilian Wild.*, p. 255. 32. Roosevelt, Kermit, *Diary*, 3-4-14. 33. T. R., *Brazilian Wild.*, p. 255. 34. Cherrie, *Dark Trails*, p. 284. 35. T. R., *Brazilian Wild.*, p. 255. 36. Ibid., p. 256. 37. Rondon, *Lectures*, p. 76. 38. T. R., *Brazilian Wild.*, p. 258. 39. Rondon, *Lectures*, p. 77. 40. T. R., *Brazilian Wild.*, p. 259. 41. Roosevelt, Kermit, *Diary*, 3-8-14. 42. Rondon, *Lectures*, p. 77. 43. Cherrie, *Diary*, 3-10-14. 44. T. R., *Brazilian Wild.*, p. 261. 45. Ibid., p. 262. 46. Rondon, *Lectures*, p. 79. 47. Cherrie, *Diary*, 3-12-14 & 3-13-14. 48. Cherrie, *Diary*, 3-11-14 & 3-12-14. 49. T. R., *Brazilian Wild.*, p. 265. 50. Roosevelt, Kermit, *Diary*, 3-11-14 & 3-13-14. 51. Cherrie, *Diary*, 3-13-14. 52. Ibid., 3-12-14. 53. Ibid., 3-14-14. 54. T. R., *Brazilian Wild.*, p 267. 55. T. R., *Brazilian Wild.*, p. 268. 56. Ibid., pp. 268–70. 57. Rondon, *Lectures*, p. 81. 58. Ibid., p. 82. 59. T. R., *Brazilian Wild.*, p. 270. 60. Ibid. 61. Cherrie, *Dark Trails*, p. 290. 62. T. R., *Brazilian Wild.*, p. 270. 63. Ibid., p. 271. 64. Rondon, *Lectures*, p. 84. 65. Ibid., p. 85. 66. T. R., *Brazilian Wild.*, p. 273. 67. Cherrie, *Diary*, 3-16-14. 68. T. R., *Brazilian Wild.*, p. 274. 69. Cherrie, *Diary*, 3-16-14.

X
We Do Not Know What the Morrow Will Bring Forth

March 17 . . . Soon after sunrise, thirteen able-bodied members of the expedition began making their way single file along the riverbank. They were preceded by several sweating camaradas who used their machetes to cut a path through the maze of vines and bushes. On the river, the Colonel and Dr. Cajazeira followed them in the double canoes with six boatmen. The strong pull of the current made it difficult for the two groups to keep in sight of each other. Roosevelt had to repeatedly motion his paddlers to pull to shore in order to let the walkers catch up.

Forty minutes after starting out, those in the dugouts were blocked by rapids. These turned out to be rather shallow falls, which the canoes ran through so uneventfully that Rondon christened them Bôa Passagem— Good Passage Rapids. An hour and a half later, the two detachments got under way again.

After an hour's smooth paddling, swirls began forming again on the water's surface. The river at this point threaded through a cluster of seven islands, making the passage even more dangerous, as there was little room to maneuver. In the lead, Roosevelt's heavily loaded raft got caught in the first stretch of rapids and had to run them, nearly sinking when a vicious crosscurrent slammed the craft against some boulders.[1]

Coming up from behind, the paddlers on Dr. Cajazeira's double canoe had witnessed Roosevelt's brush with disaster and chose a different channel; they got through unscathed.

At the foot of these Rapids of the Seven Islands, Rondon and Kermit found a narrow but very deep river pouring into the Dúvida from the left, or western, side. After measuring its width and depth, Rondon judged it to be the biggest tributary they had so far encountered. He named it for Kermit.

Finding this tributary ended all speculation that Rondon's so-called River of Doubt was somehow tied to the Rio Gy-Paraná. Lyra finally had to concede defeat.[2] He knew as well as Rondon that the Gy received no feeder stream the size of the newly found Rio Kermit, let alone a river as broad as the Dúvida.

"There was no longer any question that the Dúvida was a big river, a river of real importance," the Colonel wrote proudly of this occasion. But at the same time, he and his companions remained "still wholly in the dark as to where it came out."[3] There was a small chance that it turned eastward at some point to join the Juruena-Tapajós; the greater likelihood was that it entered the Madeira, several hundred miles below their present position.

Equally heartening to the explorers was an unexpected increase in their food supply at this camp. Earlier, Kermit had stumbled across two more food crates washed ashore from the wreck of the canoe in which Simplicio had drowned.[4] Then, in the evening, for the first time, Lyra's patient attempts at fishing paid off when he pulled in two fat-bellied pacu, a sweet-tasting fish that fed on fruit. Antonio the Parecis declared that pacu were never known to swim up steep falls.[5] This led the entire company to assume that they had seen the last of the bad rapids and that fish would be plentiful from now on. As the men's spirits rose, Cherrie reflected on "how little it took to cheer us!"[6]

March 18 . . . Before breaking camp this morning, Rondon had the bugler summon the whole company to hear him read a special Order of the Day. He announced to the Brazilian and American contingents that the tributary discovered the day before was to be named in honor of the Colonel's son. He unwrapped a highly varnished oval plaque, obviously prepared long in advance, bearing the words "Rio Kermit." After nailing it to the camp marker post, Rondon went on to declare that on behalf of the government of Brazil, the river "which we had since 1909 called 'Dúvida' would henceforth be known as the 'Roosevelt.'"[7] He called for three cheers for the United States of America, for the honorable Theodore Roosevelt, and for Kermit. The Colonel pretended to be surprised at the honor, even though he had known since leaving Rio de Janeiro that this was to happen if the river proved to be significant. Not to be outdone, he led a hat-waving chorus of "hip, hip, hurrahs" for Brazil, Rondon and his Telegraph Commission, the doctor, Lyra, and all the boatmen.

Lyra had kept track of who got cheered and said that they had forgotten Cherrie. So they gave three cheers for Cherrie and broke camp on a
lighthearted note.[8]

In the same order as the previous day, the walking party picked up
their rifles and machetes and started north again along the left bank. This
time they had a well-marked trail to follow, made by Indians who fished
in the Rio Roosevelt. From time to time, the Colonel and Dr. Cajazeira
held their rafts back to let the men onshore gain some distance.

Evidence mounted that the explorers were not alone in the spookily
silent forest. Several times during the morning they found Indian fishing villages, some newly constructed. One of these consisted of three low,
palm-thatched huts, each with a small opening to crawl through. The
occupants apparently had just fled, scared off by Trigueiro's furious
barking. Footprints outside the huts led away into the forest. As a goodwill gesture, Rondon left an ax, a knife, and strings of red glass beads
inside one of the huts. Moving on, the marchers heard voices several
more times but saw no one.[9]

Toward noon, Rondon found another tributary entering the Rio
Roosevelt from the right over six-foot-high falls of foaming green water.
While his fellow explorers rested and admired the scenery, Rondon
measured the stream and noted its southeasterly angle of entrance. He
speculated that it was the lower course of the river he had explored in
the highlands and named the Marciano Avila. He was all set to make a
short side trip to confirm his theory, but Roosevelt insisted they keep
moving.[10]

Five miles farther down, the explorers found more rapids requiring
the canoes to be unloaded. By the time they completed the portage,
too little daylight remained to go on, and Rondon chose a campsite
where the river made a sharp right bend and opened into a broad bay.
Tall specimens of the araputanga tree grew there, a soft, easily worked
wood that would make a more buoyant dugout than the short-lived
Aripuanã had proven to be. Roosevelt objected to stopping to build
new canoes while surrounded by Indians, but Rondon argued that they
could not afford to pass up good boat-building timber.[11]

March 19–20 . . . Rondon gave the name Duas Canôas to this, their
fourteenth, campsite on the river, but it would have been more appropriately called Camp Calamity. His axmen misjudged the direction of
fall of the first lofty araputanga and sent it crashing into the kitchen along
with smaller trees, scattering pots and pans and the terrified cook. The
huge trunk turned out to be rotten, and more trees had to be found. At

night, streams of leaf-bearing *carregadores* ants sneaked into the tents and silently carried away sections of socks and undershirts. The explorers tried burning the marauders out of their nests, only to find themselves confronted by a formidable column of foraging ants that could be held back only by fire. To cool off, the Colonel and Cherrie stripped naked and waded out into the river for a swim, ignoring the fact that piranha had been caught in it. When Kermit appeared unexpectedly with his camera, the two older men ducked down in sudden modesty, leaving only their grizzled heads above water.

The woodsmen found two sound trees and began work on a pair of dugouts. Concern about an Indian attack prompted Rondon to post guards for the first time at night. He got up at 2:00 each morning to make sure they were still awake.[12]

By the twentieth, one canoe was finished and the boat builders had started on the second, after what Kermit called "encouragement on our part."[13] The three North Americans expected to be back on the river, as a united expedition, by noon the next day.

Their anxiety to be moving again increased when they discovered that someone had broken into the expedition's emergency rations. Fifteen of the seventy-five boxes were missing,[14] suggesting that more than one of the camaradas may have been involved. The likeliest suspect was Julio, the braggart who had been so eager to come on the expedition. For a time he served as bowsman in the Colonel's dugout, but the stress of descending an unknown river had brought out the worst in him. When asked to lift a paddle or a bundle, he snarled at his superiors, and then begged shamelessly for favors. He could not be trusted to cut down palm hearts or gather nuts because he would stay out after the others had gone back and eat what he had collected. Of the entire company, Julio was the only one who had not lost weight in the past three weeks.[15]

Rondon did not immediately accuse Julio of stealing the rations, apparently wanting to catch him in the act. Rondon would then have to decide whether to abandon Julio in the forest or take him along as a manacled prisoner. For time being he ordered Sergeant Paixão to keep an eye on Julio, and put a close guard over the food crates.

March 21 . . . The expedition did not depart at noon after all. Cherrie returned from a hurried morning of bird collecting to find the second dugout still unfinished. Under vigorous questioning by the Colonel and Kermit, Rondon finally admitted that he had wanted Lyra to shoot the noon sun again to accurately establish the latitude of the Marciano Avila tributary. To conceal his purpose, Rondon had quietly ordered his men to slow down work on the dugouts.[16] The two Roosevelts and Cherrie could only throw up their hands and wait.

When Lyra had worked out the latitude satisfactorily, Rondon moved a pair of dividers over his map and made some calculations. He had good news for his North American colleagues. The Rio Aripuanã, he informed them, had been explored as far as the Amazonas–Mato Grosso line. He believed the expedition was descending one of two branches that formed the Aripuanã and estimated that they were roughly 280 miles from the junction of the two rivers—where Lieutenant Pyrenius was waiting.

"This means we have a much lesser distance to go than we expected," Cherrie recorded afterward.[17] The only question was how long it would take to get there.

March 22 . . . "Off with a good many delays," Kermit wrote of their 8:30 A.M. departure from Two Canoes Camp.[18] The entire company was once again united on the water. There were now six dugouts—four of the original fleet doubled up into rafts, and the two new canoes. To these Rondon, in his precise way, gave names suggesting their appearance: *Esbelta* meaning slender, and *Chanfrada,* beveled. With them, he now had the means to reinstitute the fixed station survey. Once again Kermit began working his way downstream to implant the red-and-white sighting rod every few hundred yards, just as he had last done the day Simplicio drowned.

But after only twenty minutes of surveying, the party came to the rim of more rapids. Everyone climbed out except three of the best paddlers, who took the loaded canoes down one after another in an hour. In that brief time, however, another catastrophe was barely avoided. While descending, one of the rafts began filling with water. The paddlers scrambled overboard and grabbed the sides of the double hulls to keep them from being washed away. Had it not been for the quick action of another boat crew, a good portion of the provisions would have been carried away.

By noon the explorers had gotten no farther than six miles from the previous camp when, incredibly, they again struck rapids, this time extending for almost a mile. The grueling portage took six hours, during which all the canoes were nearly wrecked on the rocks. With no intended irony, Rondon named the rapids the Falls of Good Fortune.

To add to their anxiety, the explorers found another deserted Indian settlement, consisting of some empty thatched huts and small fields where corn and beans were grown during the dry season. The tree stumps around the clearing bore the sharp, clean marks of axes and knives.

Once again, there were fresh footprints in the mud on the riverbank. But never once did Roosevelt's party see an Indian. Cherrie was later to recall that "the footprints, the abandoned camps, and the voices of unseen people became uncanny."[19]

Real or not, the threat of an Indian attack brought about a confrontation between Roosevelt and Rondon on how the expedition should be managed. That night, after the tents had been pitched, the Colonel informed Rondon that the fixed station method of surveying the river had to end. It was a luxury they could no longer afford. Kermit had barely escaped drowning in the accident that killed Simplicio, and now he faced a greater danger. "I cannot accept the prospect of having my son's life threatened constantly by the presence of Indians, more than the life of any other member of the expedition, whenever his canoe goes out in front." From this point on, they should record only the main features of the river and let other explorers, better equipped than they were, fill in the details.

Rondon considered the survey by fixed stations indispensable; without it, he said, the expedition would be completely useless. But he was there to serve as Roosevelt's guide through the wilderness and would accede to his wishes. "Senhor Kermit will no longer proceed in front." Satisfied, T. R. tried to patch things up between them by telling Rondon, "In my life I have known two great colonels: the one who [built] the Panama Canal . . . and . . . Rondon."[20]

There would have been no exploration at all if he had not "taken hold of the thing," T. R. told a British geographer, Sir John Keltie, a year after this exchange with Rondon.

> There would have been no observations worth anything
> if I had not insisted upon their being taken in practical
> shape . . . the minute they got away from me, my beloved
> companions proceeded to do their work in such fashion
> as to make it valueless . . . they did an extraordinary
> amount of work; but they would leave out certain essen-
> tial things. This was characteristic of everything they did.
> Their short-comings in preparation were astonishing.[21]

Rondon saw the incident in a different light. The American ex-president had been in a hurry to get home to his family and political duties; he was tired of exploring. "For this reason, the topographical survey proceeded without our being able to obtain all the benefit of the technical resources which we had at our disposal and with which we had carried out a sufficiently exact and correct work."[22]

March 23 . . . Early-morning fog enveloped the river below Good Fortune Falls as the canoes set out again. Within an hour, the rising sun burned through, revealing a landscape of supernal clarity that roused the poet in Roosevelt:

> In the dazzling light, under the brilliant blue of the sky, every detail of the magnificent forest was vivid to the eye: the great trees, the network of bush ropes, the caverns of greenery, where thick-leaved vines covered all things else. Wherever there was a hidden boulder the surface of the current was broken by waves. In one place, in midstream, a pyramidal rock thrust itself six feet above the surface of the river."[23]

Then the current grew more turbulent. New rapids appeared and led through a low canyon littered with boulders. Rondon and Lyra had difficulty picking a route through the wild disorder of rocks. When they saw Indian palm huts on the left bank, they quickly crossed to the other side, where they found a channel passable for the dugouts.

It took seven hours for the camaradas to carry the baggage over the portage. Roosevelt and Cherrie sat on the rocks at the lower end, watching the boatmen ride the emptied canoes through the rough water. They chatted about Cherrie's Vermont farm and how spring must be breaking through the last crusts of snow in the fields back home. There were potatoes to get into the ground soon and twelve hundred maple trees in the woodlot to be tapped for syrup. "It's a busy time now for Fred Rice," Cherrie remarked, thinking of the hired man who managed Rocky Dell Farm during his absence.[24]

Kermit was not content to sit with his elders and talk about farming. With an afternoon on his hands, he ranged through the forest with Trigueiro and found still-green Indian shelters whose curiously hooded tops reminded him of jack-in-the-pulpits. He sampled some strange tree-borne fruits: the jaracatia, a yellow, cucumber-shaped fruit with a seedy pulp, and later on a sipotá, hard shelled with a large stone surrounded by a sweet, slippery substance. Twice he saw monkeys capering in the high branches but missed when he shot at them.[25]

After reloading the canoes, the explorers made another four miles before dark, for a total of eight that day. Had it not been for the rapids,

Rondon figured, they could have made three times that distance.[26] At the campsite that night the sound of roaring water filled the air—there were big rapids ahead.

March 24 . . . The routine of breaking camp was interrupted when a tapir was spotted paddling across the river. The hunters raced to get their rifles, but the men's excited shouts scared the hoglike animal to the opposite shore before anyone could take aim. "An ample supply of tapir beef would have meant much to us," the Colonel noted in disappointment. For more than three weeks, the only fresh meat the explorers had tasted had been a few monkeys.[27]

By this time, half of the provisions were already gone. By Cherrie's estimate, the party had at best only twenty-five days' rations. The officials in the party tried to make each food can—originally planned as one day's rations for five men—last a day and a half and gave some of the contents to the camaradas. The boatmen gorged on palm hearts to keep their stomachs full. Every day, two men were assigned to cut down enough of the fibrous vegetable to supply all the paddlers. Pessimistic and hungry, Cherrie worried that "we may all be reduced to that ration!"[28]

Underway again, the canoes ran for a mile before the river began racing and churning around half-submerged boulders. Antonio Correa, the most skilled of the boatmen, shook his head when he heard the thunderous roaring ahead. Those were bad rapids, he told Rondon, worse than they had seen so far. He warned his commander not to try running the dugouts through, even if unloaded. "I was brought up in the water, and I know it like a fish, and all its sounds."[29]

After cutting a portage trail through the woods on the left side of the river, the camaradas carried the supplies and tents down below the last rapids to Camp 17. Kermit saw the fatigue in the men's faces and volunteered to shoulder some of the loads.[30]

While combing the riverbank for a passage through the rapids, Rondon was surprised to find another river, nearly 130 feet wide and with a greater volume of water than any previous tributary found, flooding into the Rio Roosevelt from the west.

Rondon called this "unquestionably the most remarkable and the most important of all the geographical discoveries which we had made since the 27th of February." The size of this new tributary reinforced Rondon's growing conviction that the Rio Roosevelt must be the principal drainage for the whole territory lying between the Madeira and the Tapajós. Since the expedition was still within the boundaries of Rondon's native Mato Grosso, he named the new stream the Rio Taunay, to honor that state's greatest hero, a nineteenth-century Brazilian explorer, soldier, writer, and statesman.[31] By coincidence, Kermit had two of Taunay's novels in Portuguese in his duffel bag, and the Colonel had read an English translation of Taunay's account of the bloody 1865 war with Paraguay.

Nothing would do but to celebrate the discovery of the Rio Taunay in grand style. Bursting with provincial pride, Rondon chose a tree "full of sap and life" and had one side of its bark stripped off. He grabbed a hammer and chisel and cut an inscription into the raw sticky wood:

> Rio Taunay. In front of the waterfall of the same name. Homage of the Roosevelt-Rondon Expedition at 156,280 meters from Passo da Linha Telegraphica, March 24th, 1914.[32]

These marks on a tree underscored once more how little progress the expedition had made. One more day would mark a full month since the party had departed the telegraph bridge, wrote T.R.:

> We had come only a trifle over 160 kilometers [100 miles], thanks to the character and number of the rapids. We believed we had three or four times the distance yet to go before coming to a part of the river where we might hope to meet assistance, either from rubber-gatherers, or from Pyrenius, if he were really coming up the river we were going down. If the rapids continued to be as they had been it could not be much more than three weeks before we were in straits for food . . . and . . . we would . . . still have several hundreds of kilometers of unknown river before us.[33]

March 25 . . . It took all morning to drag the canoes over a portage road of hastily cut log rollers down to Camp 17. "Hard work; men disanimated," was Kermit's terse summation.[34] He and Lyra pushed the boatmen hard. Somehow, by 1:00 P.M. they brought the last canoe down below the falls without incident. Two hours later, all six were reloaded and set in motion again downstream.

But after just fifteen minutes, the boatmen backed their paddles and pulled for shore when they heard roaring water ahead. Rondon, Lyra, and Kermit explored both sides of the river and reported finding a side channel safe enough for empty canoes. The loads would have to be carried nearly a mile around the rapids.

Finding a navigable side channel for much of the eleven-hundred-yard-long rapids was an unexpected blessing. It would save the killing work of having to cut another long road through the forest. With only a few hours of daylight left, Rondon decided to wait until the next day to run the dugouts.

"There is a feeling of great depression in our camp tonight," Cherrie noted sadly.[35] Even Lyra's surprise find of a few edible Brazil nuts—"the first good ones we have found"—failed to lift their spirits.[36] Since leaving Camp Duas Canôas four days before, the party had traveled only sixteen miles.

The physical strength of the company shrank daily. Weakened by hunger and endless labor, the camaradas were succumbing to sickness and depression. Two men were disabled by malaria; others limped about on feet grossly swollen from infected insect bites. Tested by adversity, most had proven to be "good men," in Roosevelt's judgment, and "some of them very good indeed." But those who did not pull their own weight earned his special scorn, like the notorious, overweight Julio, whom T. R. wrote off as "utterly worthless . . . an inborn, lazy shirk with the heart of a ferocious cur in the body of a bullock."[37]

Until the rapids began, Roosevelt's own health had remained good. But from that time on, as the doctor noted, his resistance began to fade from hunger, fatigue, and worry. His heart raced and he frequently gasped for breath during the long portages. Characteristically, he made light of his ailments, preferring to ignore them, on the theory that they would go away. Roosevelt's indestructible cheerfulness inspired his comrades. Cherrie, whose expeditions to South America would eventually span four decades, considered T. R. "the ideal camp mate."[38]

Roosevelt's apparently bottomless fund of hunting tales served as a tonic for the tired, hungry, and discouraged men, who did not want to think about the next day. Cherrie remembered one evening when one of T. R.'s spellbinders came to a rude halt:

> I lay in my hammock, listening and watching the Colonel's little group that gathered about one of the camp tables on which two or three candles sputtered. All were intent on his story, when a huge centipede crawled on the table top! Who saw it first I don't know because, apparently with one accord, all fell backward in their chairs, their feet overturning the table. Then what a scramble there was! That particular story of the Colonel's was never finished.[39]

March 26 . . . The entire day was devoted to moving men, gear, and canoes around the rapids encountered the previous day. Lyra and his best paddlers successfully jockeyed the dugouts down a channel on the left side of the river. On the opposite bank, the rest of the party carried the baggage and ration boxes to a new campsite. Between the two groups, the river raced and roared for a thousand yards, hurling against dark boulders and sending up bursts of spray.

It was during this portage that Cherrie stumbled onto a real archaeological mystery. Searching for birds halfway down the rapids, he came across some huge granite and quartzite boulders on which many strange figures had been carved. The markings of the sides facing the water were badly worn from erosion, but those on the landward side were deeply cut and well preserved. Near the top of the largest rock, someone had carved three sets of concentric rings, each with a dot in the center, and measuring about eighteen inches in diameter.

Below these, on a slanting, nearly vertical surface, Cherrie saw three sets of inverted Ws.[40]

He did not have a camera and afterward drew the figures from memory in his diary. No one in the party knew what the symbols meant or who had made them. Perhaps, Roosevelt speculated, "in a very remote past some Indian tribes of comparatively advanced culture had penetrated to this lovely river, just as we had now come to it." Rondon had never found such stone carvings in his explorations in Mato Grosso. It was all the more strange, then, wrote T. R., "to find them in this one place on the unknown river, never before visited by white men, which we were descending."[41]

Lyra and his paddlers had made a more practical discovery while floating the dugouts through the rapids. They found an abundance of Brazil nuts scattered on the ground and carried back a bushelful in their shirts. The brown, three-sided little nuts were roasted over the fire and divided equally among the camaradas. Cherrie sampled one and pronounced it "very much better than the old hard dry nuts that we get at home."[42] The cook chopped up dozens of palm hearts, and boiled them into a bland but hot stew that tasted like mushy celery. One of the boatmen caught two big piranha, so everyone had a few mouthfuls of fish. For dessert, each man cupped his hand to receive two tablespoons of honey scraped out of a tree nest of wild bees.[43]

March 27 . . . The euphoria of going to sleep on a full stomach was short-lived. By midmorning, it was clear to the explorers that they would make no better progress than in recent days. Steep hills, thickly mantled in green, tropical growth, rose on either side of the river. The current began to race. Less than two miles below the Camp of Indian Inscriptions, the paddlers in the lead canoe swerved to avoid turbulent water and signaled to the other boats to make for shore.

During the ensuing portage, the explorers almost lost two canoes. Cherrie had wandered away from the shore party to watch the paddlers bring the bigger of the double canoes around a sharp turn in the rapids. Rounding it, the boatmen misjudged the force of the current. The inside dugout caught on the rocks and jammed beneath a mass of fallen trees and bejuca vines. Within seconds, the racing water tore the outer canoe loose from its rope bonds and drove it under the bow of the inside boat, which was lying on its side. Both filled up and sank. By strange luck, the fierce pressure of the current kept the sunken hulls pinned beneath the debris, instead of hurling them into the rapids to be wrecked.

Cherrie heard the terrified screams of the men in the water and tried to help, but then realized that more strength was needed. Slogging ashore, he ran as fast as he could to the others at the baggage dump and yelled in his powerful baritone: "Two boats are capsized and held against the rocks by the current; if they wash loose they will be crushed among the boulders."[44]

Roosevelt waded into the water at once, followed by the other men. They chopped the ropes holding the twisted pair of dugouts together so that the hulls could be individually raised. Kermit and a handful of camaradas peeled off their clothes and swam out to a small rock outcrop a little distance upstream. From there, Kermit threw out a line that was tied to the bow of the outside hull. His father and the others fought to keep their footing in chest-deep water and lifted and pushed the sunken dugout. As they did so, Kermit and his helpers hauled on the rope and tied the slack to a half-sunken tree. Three exhausting hours later, both canoes had been hauled up to Kermit's rock, emptied out, and turned over to the paddlers.

While working in the water, the Colonel banged his right shin against a jagged rock, reopening the injury he had suffered in the 1902 carriage accident in which he had suffered bone damage. Dr. Cajazeira dressed the wound in antiseptic solution and gently wrapped cotton bandages around the Colonel's calf. In the damp, unsanitary conditions of the river camps, the gash in Roosevelt's leg never properly healed. He blamed his own clumsiness for getting hurt and dismissed the resulting inflammation as being merely "somewhat bothersome."[45] But Cherrie believed the injury marked a turning point for Roosevelt: "From that time on, he was a very sick man."[46]

The Colonel limped down to his dugout with the doctor's help, and at 4:00 P.M. the party made another start. But ten minutes later, this ended in bitter disappointment. As soon as they got out of one set of rapids, they faced another.

Kermit and Lyra climbed out to make an inspection. Drenching rain—the first in several days—obscured the view downstream, but there appeared to be mountains ahead flanking the river. The scouting team soon returned with nothing encouraging to say to those waiting in the canoes. Beyond the immediate rapids, the river disappeared into a gorge; this would have to be explored the following day.

There was no question that they were facing a formidable obstacle. Utterly discouraged, the explorers made camp in the rain. When it let up, small bees of many kinds swarmed around the men's heads and tried to crawl into their ears and noses. Somehow, the cook had managed to brew some hot coffee, but the wood was too wet to fuel a cooking fire. "We are unable to dry our clothing," Cherrie grumbled in his diary, "and will of course have to put on wet clothing in the morning."[47]

March 28 . . . The explorers crossed to the left side of the river and emptied the dugouts. They carried the baggage along the bank until their path was blocked by a small tributary too deep to ford. Rondon named it for Cherrie, so that now all three North Americans had a river to call their own. One of the burlier camaradas, Macario, was detailed to chop down a giant tree as a bridge across the Rio Cherrie. When it fell, the proud axman walked out onto the middle of the trunk to pose with arms akimbo for Cherrie's box camera.[48]

From a quickly established Camp Rio Cherrie, a scouting party composed of Rondon, Lyra, Kermit, and the keen-eyed Antonio Correa headed north along the base of the gorge to see if the canoes could be let down by ropes. The others remained in camp, waiting for what was certain to be bad news.

Meanwhile, in the United States, worried officials of the American Museum of Natural History tried to get information about the expedition they had sponsored. The last word Frank Chapman had from Roosevelt was three months old, a letter dated January 16, from Tapirapuan, in which the Colonel had informed him, "We are now about to go into the real wilderness..."[49] After that, there was no word. As weeks went by, rumors swept South America of a disaster—the loss of the entire expedition. These rumors were fed in part by erroneous reports about Fiala's canoe accident on the Rio Papagaio in mid-February. Communications within Brazil were so primitive that neither Fiala nor Miller, as he came down the Gy-Paraná after waiting weeks for dugouts to be built, had been able to find a cable office to send word out. With nothing better to go on than hearsay, the *New York Times* front page for March 23 announced:

ROOSEVELT PARTY LOSES EVERYTHING
IN RAPIDS OF A BRAZILIAN RIVER;
MEMBERS OF PARTY PROBABLY SAFE;
MAY BE ON AN UNKNOWN RIVER."[50]

Reading that morning headline spurred Chapman to cable the U.S. consul at Para, Brazil: "Can you obtain any information concerning the Roosevelt party? . . . Advise by telegram at earliest possibility. All expenses guaranteed."

Consul Pickering replied promptly: "Roosevelt all right. Arriving at Manáos by way of [P]apagaio River."[51]

Pickering was mistakenly referring to Fiala, who by this time was steaming up the Amazon for Manáos. Mourning the loss of his films, he was interested in getting back to his family and his job at Rogers Peet, but he wanted to be on hand when Roosevelt arrived at Manáos. As he was the first member of the expedition to emerge from the wilderness, he stopped off at Santarem, found a cable office, and sent the *New York Times* an optimistic report: "The Roosevelt Party is in good health, exploring the Dúvida River. It is expected to reach Manáos early in April."[52]

On the Rio Roosevelt, however, the reality was very different. By midafternoon on March 28, Rondon's exploring party returned, soaked in sweat and exhausted from climbing. What they had seen crushed any hope of reaching Manáos by early April—or later.

The river at this point cut its way through a low range of mountains not to be found on any map. The slopes appeared to be too steep and stony to drag dugouts over, let alone walk over with loads. Within the mile-and-a-half-long canyon, there were half a dozen waterfalls, one of them as high as a house, and it was extremely doubtful that the canoes could be brought through.

Rondon saw no way out of this predicament except to abandon the canoes and build new ones on the other side of the mountain.[53] But to do so would take many days of brutal labor and leave the party vulnerable to Indian attack. And while the boat building went on, their food supply would dwindle further.

Kermit alone among the explorers believed that he could get some of the canoes down the gorge. His skill at rope handling gave weight to his words, and Lyra was willing to help him. Rondon thought it was hopeless, but the Colonel backed his son's idea. What other choice did they have?[54]

"Every one is now obliged to cut down his baggage to practically what he has on his back," Cherrie noted after the decision was made. "We do not know what the morrow will bring forth."[55]

NOTES

1. T. R., *Brazilian Wild.*, p. 275. **2.** Rondon, *Lectures*, p. 88. **3.** T. R., *Brazilian Wild.*, p. 277. **4.** Roosevelt, Kermit, *Diary*, 3-17-14. **5.** T. R., *Brazilian Wild.*, p. 276. **6.** Cherrie, *Dark Trails*, p. 295. **7.** Rondon, *Lectures*, pp. 88–89. **8.** T. R., *Brazilian Wild.*, p. 279. **9.** Cherrie, *Diary*, 3-18-14. **10.** Rondon, *Lectures*, p. 91. **11.** Ibid., p. 87. **12.** Cherrie, *Diary*, 3-19-14. **13.** Roosevelt, Kermit, *Diary*, 3-20-14. **14.** Cherrie, *Diary*, 3-20-14. **15.** T. R., *Brazilian Wild.*, p. 303. **16.** Cherrie, *Diary*, 3-20-14. **17.** Ibid. **18.** Roosevelt, Kermit, *Diary*, 3-22-14. **19.** Cherrie, *Dark Trails*, p. 291. **20.** Viveiros, Esther, *Rondon*, pp. 400–401. **21.** T. R. to John Scott Keltie, 12-17-14, *PPS*. **22.** Rondon, *Lectures*, p. 92. **23.** T. R., *Brazilian Wild.*, pp. 285–86. **24.** Ibid. **25.** Roosevelt, Kermit, *Diary*, 3-23-14. **26.** Rondon, *Lectures*, p. 93. **27.** T. R., *Brazilian Wild.*, p. 287. **28.** Cherrie, *Diary*, 3-24-14. **29.** T. R., *Brazilian Wild.*, p. 288. **30.** Roosevelt, Kermit, *Diary*, 3-24-14. **31.** Rondon, *Lectures*, p. 94. **32.** Ibid., p. 95. **33.** T. R., *Brazilian Wild.*, p. 289. **34.** Roosevelt, Kermit, *Diary*, 3-25-14. **35.** Cherrie, *Dark Trails*, p. 300. **36.** Cherrie, *Diary*, 3-25-14. **37.** T. R., *Brazilian Wild.*, p. 290. **38.** Cherrie, speech, "Roosevelt in the Field," 5-26-27. **39.** Ibid. **40.** Cherrie, *Diary*, 3-26-14. **41.** T. R., *Brazilian Wild.*, pp. 292–93. **42.** Cherrie, *Diary*, 3-26-14. **43.** Ibid. **44.** Cherrie, *T. R., Memorial Meeting*, pp. 24–25. **45.** T. R., *Brazilian Wild.*, p. 309. **46.** Cherrie, *T. R., Memorial Meeting*, 3-1-19. **47.** Cherrie, *Diary*, 3-27-14. **48.** Ibid., 3-28-14. **49.** Frank M. Chapman to Robert Bridges, 3-17-14, *Scrib;* T. R. to Frank Chapman, 1-16-14, *Letters*, Vol. 7, #5880, p. 758. **50.** *New York Times*, 3-23-14. **51.** Ibid., 3-24-14. **52.** Ibid. **53.** Roosevelt, Kermit, *Diary*, 3-28-14. **54.** T. R., *Brazilian Wild.*, p. 294. **55.** Cherrie, *Diary*, 3-28-14.

XI
Some of Us Are Not Going
to Finish This Journey

March 28, continued . . . Except for the rations, every ounce of weight the explorers could do without had to be scrapped, and Camp Rio Cherrie became a dumping ground.[1] All six of the officials would sleep under a single tent. The camaradas were left, as always, to improvise their own shelters from branches and palm fronds. Roosevelt permitted himself—besides the clothes he wore—a suit of pajamas, an extra pair each of drawers and socks, some handkerchiefs, his spare eyeglasses, and two remaining volumes of Gibbon's Roman history. All this and his medical kit, insect repellent, and writing materials went into one duffel bag, which also bulged with his folded cot, army blanket, and mosquito netting. A smaller bag contained his cartridges, gloves, and head net. He laced on his spare pair of boots and gave his old ones to Kermit, whose own boots had disintegrated from constant soaking and scraping on the rocks.[2] Fortunately, they both wore a size seven.

Cherrie gave up hope of collecting any more birds, but he was determined to save the trunk of specimens he had accumulated. In some last-minute hunting, he shot "a pack of fine tanagers . . . with deep red bills," and then threw away the remainder of his bird-shot shells, which had been ruined by dampness. He glanced up at the brassy sky and noticed several black turkey vultures sailing high over the trees. They were not forest birds, and he took sudden heart that more open country would be found "once we have cut our way through this chain of mountains."[3]

The Colonel was much more pessimistic over whether everyone in the party would get through the gorge, including himself. By nightfall of March 28, twenty-four hours after stumbling against the sharp rock in the water, the throbbing pain in his leg was accompanied by a sharp attack of malaria. "This is not written very clearly," he jotted in the margin of his *Scribner's* manuscript. "My temperature is 105."[4]

He was depressed about his sudden incapacity at such a time. Kermit and Cherrie took turns watching over him that night—one of many nights they would do so. Toward dawn, Cherrie had crawled into his hammock to get some sleep, when he heard the Colonel ask his son, "Did Cherrie have a good dinner tonight?" Kermit, realizing his father had a high fever, lied swiftly, "Yes, we all had a fine dinner." "That is good," T. R. replied.

A few hours later, Cherrie's sleep was broken again when he heard Roosevelt calling out his name excitedly. The naturalist jumped out of his hammock and stood by T. R.'s cot with Kermit. They spoke about the hard portage facing them and the dangers involved. Finally Roosevelt said to them, "Boys, I realize that some of us are not going to finish this journey." He looked at Cherrie. "I want you and Kermit to go on. You can get out. I will stop here."[5]

Cherrie sensed immediately that Roosevelt was talking about taking his own life. "There wasn't a moment from that time forward," he recalled, "that either Kermit or myself didn't watch the Colonel, to prevent him from carrying out what he felt was a necessity . . . that he must relieve the party of what he considered a burden . . ."[6]

March 29, 30, 31 . . . The final three days of March were consumed in the transporting of twenty-one men, their food and belongings, and six dugouts a distance of just under two miles through the gorge to the first navigable place on the river. Kermit and Lyra, aided by a few of the best boatmen, began the ticklish job of trying to inch the canoes over the first of the six falls. Roosevelt, an unwilling invalid, remained at the previous camp with Dr. Cajazeira and Cherrie. He kept up his writing and fought a losing battle with the ants that swarmed into his tent. "I thought I had put my clothes out of reach," he wrote one morning, "[but] both the termites and the *carregadores* ants got at them, ate holes in one boot, ate one leg of my drawers, and riddled my handkerchief"—none of which he could spare.[7]

There was no safe footway along the base of the rock-walled canyon for the camaradas to carry the canoe loads, so Rondon's axmen cleared a trail over the mountain on the western side of the river. At the summit, Rondon had trees cleared from the rocky outcropping that overlooked the northern slope and the river beyond. Cherrie, who had made the steep climb behind the road builders, looked out over "a vast panorama of forest clad mountain tops and valleys with the [Rio] Roosevelt rushing like an arrow of light straight away toward the distant hills . . . there to be enveloped in the sea of forest."[8]

As magnificent as the view was, though, Cherrie felt his heart "sink with dread" as he watched the river disappear into more mountains far ahead. "We were so weak from the lack of food, the lack of proper food," he remembered afterward. "We had been eating a great deal of the tops of the palms . . . and eating it raw . . . We had nothing else a good many days." It did not seem possible that they would have the strength to make another long portage after this one.[9]

Three hundred feet below where Cherrie stood, at the bottom of the gorge, the most dangerous work of the end of March portage was in progress. Clinging like insects to narrow, foam-dashed rock ledges, Kermit and Lyra with their helpers guided each of the dugouts over the spilling falls with long ropes. They shouted instructions and encouragement to each other over the roar of the water and tried to forget the knifing ache in their arms and backs and the sting of blistered hands. "Lyra & I worked all day with the canoes," Kermit recorded in his terse way on the evening of March 29. "Got one down to below the 3rd falls, & one just to it. Nearly lost one. One of my feet is bad with sore."[10]

By the next day, working nonstop until dusk again, they passed three of the six dugouts all the way down to the head of the last falls, which was considered too steep to risk descending with ropes. But the fourth canoe—the smallest one—crashed on the rocks when its tow ropes slipped out of the boatmen's water-shriveled hands. The loss of a canoe depressed everyone. "Men very disheartened," wrote Kermit. "Hard work; wet all day; half ration." In this gloomy mood, he also recorded smoking the last pipeful of his "Injus Bill" tobacco.[11]

There was, however, the solace at day's end of a carefully rationed swig of scotch from the bottle Kermit shared with Cherrie, the only other member of the official party with a taste for hard liquor. The first two bottles had gone quickly; "We had quite generous drinks," Cherrie said later. But when they got down to the last bottle, they began marking the label with pencil lines, lines that grew increasingly closer together as the days passed. The Colonel found it amusing to watch his son and Cherrie stare longingly at the bottle. "I am sorry I can't enjoy that," he told them on one occasion, "but I wouldn't, if I could. It would take too much away from your pleasure."[12]

On the 31st, Kermit's work party passed the remaining pair of dugouts down the first five falls without damage. Also by this time, the other camaradas had carried all the baggage down to the northern end of the canyon, where a new camp, No. 22, had been established.

This same day, Roosevelt had rallied enough from his fever to be able to move to the new encampment with Cherrie and the doctor. Despite his bad leg, he insisted on walking, but his heart bothered him on the climb over the mountains. Three or four times, evidently in great pain, he threw himself down and begged Cherrie to go on. When he reached the new campsite, he lay on the damp ground for some time before recovering.[13]

The plight of the camaradas moved Roosevelt deeply. He felt bad about eating when he could not help them work and started giving them his food when Kermit and Cherrie were not looking. "We had to watch him constantly," Cherrie said later, "and [it] reached the point where if he didn't eat all of his share, either Kermit or I would take what was left and guard it until a later meal."[14]

April 1 . . . In an all-out effort, despite having to work with "a disheartened bunch of camaradas," Kermit and Lyra succeeded in dragging all five surviving canoes several hundred yards around the last falls.[15] After the dugouts had been eased back into the water and tied up, there was a round of handshakes for the two young men and their exhausted helpers. In four days they had accomplished what no one else had thought possible at the start, without loss of life, and at the cost of a single canoe, which could be replaced.

April 2 . . . Nobody had slept during the night. After several dry days, the rains had come again with a vengeance. The deluge collapsed the common tent on top of the six officials, who remained beneath the damp tarpaulin in sodden blankets, too weary to move. They crawled out at daybreak to find a drenched camp, but fortunately the dugouts still floated. Franca used his native genius to breathe fire into wet kindling. The smell of wood smoke and hot coffee gave the men a lift.

The camaradas bailed out the two smallest canoes and roped them together as a cargo raft. They loaded the other dugouts separately with what remained of the food cans and camping gear. Roosevelt, the paddlers, and the steersmen climbed in, while the rest of the party started walking along the riverbank. The question on everyone's mind was how soon they again would find rapids.

After an hour's march, they had their answer. Just as Cherrie had seen from the overlook, the river again converged into a narrow, boulder-strewn gorge where two mountains came together. In places, the width of the channel shrank to less than fifty feet, leaving little room to steer a dugout. The steep rock walls of the canyon were carpeted with green moss and small trees and bushes that grew in the crevices. There appeared to be no easy way around or through the chasm, the second one encountered by the explorers in less than a week. Rondon, Kermit, and Lyra went ahead and explored for more than a mile, finding rapids and falls as far as they went. All this meant a portage of at least two or three days, and risking lives and canoes yet again.

The discouraging news brought an end to the day's advance, which measured less than two miles. The single dugouts were emptied and run down a short distance to a new campsite just above the main rapids. To save labor, the paddlers took a chance and rode the loaded double canoe down without an accident. Carrying the remainder of the loads was slow and treacherous. With their arms laced around crates and duffel bags, the camaradas felt their way along a rocky shelving that seemed at times to merge with the perpendicular rock face and the surging river below. When it came the Colonel's turn, he found the trail "rather hard to follow,"[16] even though he carried only his rifle and cartridge bag. When he reached the other end, he was so breathless that Kermit thought his father's heart would give out.[17]

While exploring the canyon with Rondon, Kermit had caught a small turtle and picked a strange-looking fruit "which we none of us knew."[18] The cook quickly disemboweled the hapless turtle and boiled it for the next morning's breakfast soup. When the fruit was sliced open, it contained a sweet jelly around the seeds that Kermit shared with the men.

These small supplements to the communal larder did little for the hungry camaradas. Food was their overriding obsession. One of the men, the troublemaker Julio, tried to improve his own chances for survival by breaking into the rations boxes after dark. He was suspected of having stolen food before, but this time he was caught by Sergeant Paixão. The huge black soldier punched him in the mouth and warned him never to steal again. Bleeding freely from the nose and blubbering in Portuguese, Julio ran to Kermit and the Colonel to complain about being mistreated. On investigation, Roosevelt told the camarada that he "had gotten off uncommonly lightly," considering that a number of his fellow workers had rifles and would have been justified in shooting him dead on the spot.[19]

April 3 . . . The heartbreaking labor of the last days of March had to be repeated during the descent of the second chasm. "It was found that we [have] a very long and exceedingly difficult carry before us," Cherrie noted with resignation.[20] The plan was to run the emptied dugouts through the rapids to the halfway point, where Kermit and Lyra would let them down the steeper falls with ropes as far as possible, and then drag the canoes some distance to bypass the highest cataract. Earlier in the day, Rondon had climbed to the top of the mountain on the river's left flank, searching for an easier trail for his load bearers, but he had scrambled down the steep incline in disappointment. As it was, the camaradas were forced to shoulder the baggage along what Rondon termed "regular goat tracks" at the bottom of the shadowy gorge.[21]

Misfortune marred the portage from the start. Cherrie witnessed how, in bringing the smallest of the canoes down to where Kermit and Lyra were waiting, the paddlers realized they had forgotten to put a tie rope on board:

> They came in towards shore, caught at overhanging [boughs] and bejucas which broke with them. The canoe was being whirled on; both Juan and Antonio Correa leaped out to save themselves and try to save the canoe but without a tie rope it was useless. The canoe was whirled out of their hands to be crushed to splinters in the whirlpools and rapids below! A disaster, for we now have only four canoes![22]

But the loss of a dugout was not all. The never-ending rapids, the loss of energy from too little food, and the torment of being bitten repeatedly by wasps, flies, and poisonous ants had created a psychosis of fear among the camaradas. "Under such conditions whatever is evil in men's natures come to the front," wrote T. R. "On this day a strange and terrible tragedy occurred."[23]

By late morning, the working parties were spread out over the canyon. On the wooded heights at the north end, Rondon's axmen were steadily chopping a path for dragging the canoes. Lyra and a few helpers were stationed at the water's edge, cutting back brush and vines from the cliff base so that the rope handlers would have room to work. From the south end of the gorge, Sergeant Paixão and the other camaradas carried the food and baggage down to a staging point just above the first falls, where the canoes had been brought. At one point, Paixão rebuked Julio for lagging behind and not carrying his share of the loads. Earlier that day, Julio had been caught wolfing down some of the men's supply of cured meat by Pedrinho, the camp guard, who reported the incident to Paixão.

Near the falls, the Colonel, Kermit, and Cherrie sat on the rocks, each engrossed in a book, waiting for the baggage to catch up. They paid no attention to the comings and goings of the boatmen, until Roosevelt glanced up to see Paixão drop the crate he was carrying, lay his carbine against it, and walk back up the trail for another load.

Julio then appeared, moaning out loud, and threw his burden down. Cherrie joked that "one would know who that was by the groans," to which the Colonel and Kermit grunted laughing assent.[24] Julio, still talking to himself, turned to go, and in so doing, quietly picked up Paixão's rifle. "We thought nothing of it," Roosevelt recalled, "for he was always muttering," and, with the need to hunt for food, "it was never surprising to see a man with a carbine."[25]

A few minutes later, a gunshot cracked over the rumble of the falls. "I wonder what he has shot at?" Cherrie asked idly, hoping it might be a monkey or a tapir. With that, several camaradas came running up the path with crates in their arms, shouting that Julio had killed Paixão.[26]

The Colonel got to his feet at once, ignoring the pain in his leg, and sent two of the men ahead to alert Rondon and Lyra. He reached for his rifle and said to Kermit and Cherrie, "You boys guard the canoes and the food here. I'll go and warn the others."[27] At any moment, Roosevelt expected to hear more gunfire, and feared that Pedrinho, unarmed and alone at the camp, would be Julio's next victim.[28]

Reinforced by Dr. Cajazeira, who had a revolver, and a few of the boatmen, the Colonel limped back up the trail and found Paixão's body. He lay huddled in a pool of blood, shot through the heart. The doctor bent down next to the body. The murderer had fired at point-blank range, the bullet entering the right armpit when Paixão had raised his arm to defend himself.[29]

On reaching the camp, they found Pedrinho unharmed and no sign of Julio. The doctor noticed Roosevelt squinting hard at the surrounding woods while gasping for breath. "My eyes are better than yours, Colonel," he said. "If he is in sight, I'll point him out to you, as you have the rifle."[30]

Rondon soon arrived with Kermit and Lyra, after having placed guards at the baggage dump by the falls. A quick head count showed that there were no more victims, but Julio, who had fled into the forest after shooting Paixão, was still armed. Rondon and Lyra were enraged at the death of the well-liked Paixão; they wanted to immediately track down Julio and kill him.[31] As they argued with Roosevelt about stopping the portage to do this, Rondon ordered Antonio Correa, his best scout, to go back and try to pick up Julio's trail. The camarada had pushed only a few yards into the screen of trees before letting out a whoop of surprise. He came back holding Julio's weapon—a Winchester 44—over his head. In his rush to get away, the killer had lost it when it caught on a branch. Finding the gun brought an immense relief to the party and temporarily ended the debate about apprehending Julio.

In the sad silence of the camp, Franca quoted a melancholy Brazilian proverb: "No man knows the heart of any one." Then he made a strange prophecy: "Paixão is following Julio now, and will follow him until he dies; Paixão fell forward on his hands and knees, and when a murdered man falls like that his ghost will follow the slayer as long as the slayer lives."[32]

Using knives, axes, and fingers, the camaradas scraped out a shallow grave in a cleared space a few feet from where Paixão lay. Together, the three Brazilian officers and the three North Americans lifted the heavy body and placed it carefully in the hole, with the feet pointing toward the river. The dead man was wearing a pair of the Colonel's khaki trousers, which Roosevelt had lent him a few days before when he noticed the soldier wearing only the remnants of a pair of old drawers. Someone had decently placed a handkerchief over his strong, black face. The men gently mounded the spongy dirt over the body and pushed a simple cross of tied branches into the earth at the head. "We fired a volley for a brave and loyal soldier who had died doing his duty," T. R. wrote. "Then we left him forever, under the great trees beside the lonely river."[33]

The portage resumed. Rondon took no chances and detailed an armed escort for the men carrying loads up and down the steep trail. Men with rifles also stood at each end of the gorge, watching the cliff tops to prevent Julio from dislodging rocks onto the heads of the boat handlers working below.

By nightfall on this day of death and fear, two of the four dugouts and a portion of the baggage still sat at the head of the gorge, where half of the party spent the night. The other two canoes had been carried down to above the last falls. Here a second camp was made, shoehorned onto a narrow, slanting rock shelf between the cliff side and the rushing water. Kermit and Cherrie swung their hammocks between the few available trees and made room for the Colonel's sagging cot.[34] Roosevelt reached the bivouac at 5:30, his heart racing, and completely exhausted from the climb.[35]

April 4 . . . By means of "lots of work," lasting until 4:00 P.M., Kermit, Lyra, and Cherrie successfully brought the last two canoes down to the bivouac on the sloping stones. One of the dugouts was leaking badly from being battered against boulders in the rapids. Even after the splits in the hull were caulked, there was a question of how long it would stay afloat. This new uncertainty depressed Kermit, who described himself as being "in a blue funk, as I have been for some time to get Father out of the country."[36]

Kermit had reason to be gravely concerned for his father's health. The Colonel had awoken this day feeling feverish, despite having faithfully swallowed the twice-daily dose of quinine mixed with his coffee. His leg wound had become inflamed, swelling under the damp bandages and exquisitely painful. At about 2:30 P.M., as he was talking with the doctor while they waited for the dugouts to come down, his face suddenly turned pale under its tan and he began to shiver uncontrollably. Roosevelt's teeth were chattering too much for Cajazeira to risk putting a thermometer in his mouth, so he helped him remove his shirt and inserted the glass rod under his armpit. The Colonel's temperature was already 100.4 degrees. Cajazeira covered him with a blanket, then quickly diluted a half gram of quinine salts in a cup of water and made him drink it down.

An hour later, Roosevelt's fever had subsided, but it was essential that he be moved at once from what the doctor called a "disagreeable bivouac." Several of the camaradas carried the Colonel in their arms down to the biggest canoe. Rondon and the doctor climbed in with him.[37]

The four dugouts had hardly begun moving downstream before a combination thunderstorm and hailstorm erupted, soaking everyone. There was no means to set up an awning over Roosevelt, who lay shivering in his waterproof poncho on top of crates and duffel bags. The doctor held his own felt hat over Roosevelt's face to ward off the pelting hail. In half an hour they landed on the opposite, or right, side of the river, as a precaution against Julio's return. The Colonel was lifted out of the canoe and carried up the bank. There was a miserable, bone-chilling wait in the rain while the camaradas cut through the undergrowth to clear a space for the tent.

Finally under the canvas shelter, Roosevelt became agitated and delirious. The doctor began injecting him with quinine hypodermically through the stomach every six hours in an effort to bring down the fever.[38] Drifting in and out of delirium, the Colonel told Rondon that the expedition must proceed without further delay. "It must go on at once. Please give the order." Rondon realized that he was dealing with a very sick man and suggested soothingly that they talk the matter over later, saying that Roosevelt *was* the expedition, and "the rest of us must wait for you."[39]

Kermit took the first watch by his delirious father's side that night. "The scene is vivid before me," he wrote later:

> The black rushing river with the great trees towering high above along the bank; the sodden earth underfoot; for a few minutes the stars would be shining, and then the sky would cloud over and the rain would fall in torrents, shutting out sky and trees and river. Father first began with poetry; over and over again he repeated, "In Xanadu did Kublai Khan a stately pleasure dome decree," then he started talking at random, but gradually he centered down to the question of supplies, which was, of course, occupying every one's mind. Part of the time he knew that I was there, and he would then ask me if I thought Cherrie had had enough to eat to keep going. Then he would forget my presence, and keep saying to himself: "I can't work now, so I don't need much food, but he [Kermit] and Cherrie have worked all day with the canoes, they must have part of mine." Then he would again realize my presence and question me as to just how much Cherrie had had.

At midnight, Kermit felt a light touch on his shoulder, as "good, faithful Cajazeira" came to relieve him, and he crawled into his soggy hammock.[40]

April 5, Palm Sunday . . . By morning, the Colonel's fever had broken, and though weak, he was able to be moved. At Dr. Cajazeira's urging, Rondon chose a healthier campsite on higher ground, but it was still locked within the steaming, twilight confines of the river gorge. Noticing his famous patient's weakened condition, the doctor wanted him carried on his cot, but the Colonel objected strenuously to being handled like a corpse. "I do not wish to become a *burden* on our expedition," he said, and started walking, accompanied by Cherrie, Kermit, and the doctor. A few paces behind, two camaradas discreetly carried his canvas cot and folding chair.

Every few hundred feet, overcome by the heat and exhaustion, the Colonel had to stop and rest, alternately sitting on the cot or the chair, until he he had had strength to stand again.[41] Slowly, painfully, he made the half-mile march on his own, waving off help. Kermit remembered how cheerful his father remained, "every ready with a joke," sometimes a humorous reference to his mountaineering abilities. When he reached the new camp, he was content to sit with his back against a tree by the river, reading one of his volumes of Gibbon and keeping out of the way.[42]

When he glanced up from his book, Roosevelt could watch the dark-haired Correa brothers—Antonio and Louis—skillfully paddling each of the dugouts around half-submerged boulders in the rapids. So much for the notion that Brazilians were lazy, he said to Rondon. "A country that has men like these has assured a great future for itself, and will certainly carry out the biggest undertakings in the world."[43]

For his own part, the Colonel made himself useful by volunteering to do whatever camp chores he could manage. On one occasion, Cherrie was about to do some laundry when Kermit asked for his help in dragging the canoes. As the naturalist stashed his dirty clothes between some rocks, T. R. said to him, "Never mind those things. I'll take care of them." When Cherrie returned that evening, he found his underwear and socks neatly spread out on bushes to dry. It was, he recalled, "the only time I have ever had my clothes washed by an ex-president of the United States!"[44]

Two events on this Palm Sunday gave hope to the dejected explorers. Although shivering and glassy eyed himself from a renewed attack of fever, Kermit had insisted on joining Rondon and Lyra to explore the river for several miles. The young Roosevelt brought back to his father the wonderful news that "after these rapids we're out of the hills."[45]

Toward dusk, Antonio the Parecis heard rustling in the canopy of trees sheltering the campsite. He ran for his rifle and shouted in Portuguese that "monkeys . . . are in sight." Cherrie described how he, Kermit, and Lyra "each grabbed our gun and hurried after Antonio. There was a big troupe of Barigudos [howler monkeys] . . . they were very high up and moved with surprising speed through the tree tops. I however got two and Kermit got one. They will give us a taste of fresh meat that we all crave."[46]

A grin creased Cherrie's bearded face as he handed over his pair of dead monkeys to the cook. It was the only trace of vanity that Roosevelt could ever recall seeing in the otherwise exceedingly modest naturalist.[47]

"Our prospects look brighter this evening," Cherrie noted in his diary. "The mountains, that have so long hemmed us in, seem to be falling away from the river. The river seems to be broadening." After being in South America for six month with no mail, the ache of homesickness had become physical. "I cannot begin to tell how we Americans all long to get to Manáos and home. How I long for Rocky Dell and . . . Stella and the children."[48]

April 6 . . . Kermit's report of what lay ahead proved accurate. Only one more stretch of rapids had to be traversed, and the gorge, which Rondon named for Paixão, was left behind for good. The river reemerged as a wide, sky-reflecting stream flowing placidly northward. For the first time in weeks, the entire company—now numbering nineteen—was able to crowd into the four canoes and ride rather than walk. Rondon resumed charting the river, although he now used the less-accurate rapid survey method demanded by Roosevelt. From their canoe, Rondon and Lyra took compass bearings on significant shore features, then estimated the distance by noting how long it took the canoe to reach a given point.

Absorbed in their mapping, Rondon and Lyra had drifted considerably downstream from the others when they heard a man's voice call out from the shore, "Tenente!" ("Lieutenant!") At first Rondon did not recognize the voice, but then he was startled to see Julio's frightened face peering through tree branches onshore. He had assumed that Julio would try to work his way back south along the river toward the telegraph bridge and the settlement at José Bonifácio. Instead, the murderer had followed the dugouts for three days, keeping out of sight in the forest, and now he begged the Senhor Coronel to forgive him and take him along.[49]

"It isn't possible to stop the canoe now," Rondon answered, intent on his surveying work.[50] Those in the other dugouts showed no pity either and glided by without halting. The Colonel merely glared at the pleading figure. Afterward, Cherrie recorded the rough justice that had taken place: "Julio is left to his fate in the great forest."[51]

With every stroke of the paddles, the mountains that had formed the Paixão Canyon fell farther behind, but low hills rising beyond the forested banks caused the explorers to dread that at any moment they would come upon another mountain gorge.

By noon, though, the last of the hills were gone. The river sank into a level plain of tall, slender uauássú palms and lofty rubber trees. Only once did the explorers stop to disembark for a short portage. Later on, they chose to race over a string of minor rapids fully loaded rather than lose momentum. As the miles peeled away behind them, the party felt a surge of optimism. "We all feel more cheerful," Cherrie noted of this day's passage, "and that the greater part of our river troubles are behind us." The talk in the boats was now not *if* but *when* they would meet up with Pyreniuś's detachment on the lower Aripuanã. Birds reappeared, always a good sign. Cherrie pointed up at a brilliant South American cardinal carrying twigs and grass in its beak. Blue and yellow macaws, flying in pairs, screeched overhead.[52]

By late afternoon, the dugouts reached the mouth of a large stream gushing into the Rio Roosevelt from the right. This gave Rondon an excuse to halt what turned out to be a record run of twenty-four miles— the best advance since the expedition had begun descending the unknown river.

The men pitched a camp at the confluence of the two rivers, and Rondon set about measuring the lesser stream. Nearly three hundred feet across, it was the biggest of all tributaries yet encountered. Both the Colonel and Kermit suspected it was the Ananás, which had been their second choice to explore when the expedition had gotten under way. Rondon was less certain about this and marked it down for later exploration. For the time being, he named it Rio Capitão Cardoso, in memory of "an old and constant companion in my work in the wilderness," a fellow officer of the Telegraph Commission who had died of beriberi at one of the construction camps earlier in the year.[53]*

Joined by the powerful flood of the Cardoso, Rondon's once "doubtful" river swelled to truly noble proportions, measuring more than four hundred feet from bank to forested bank. Gazing out at the expanse of shining water that now bore his name, the Colonel considered it nothing short of extraordinary "that here about the eleventh degree [of latitude] we were on such a big river, utterly unknown to the cartographers and not indicated by even a hint on any map."[55]

Not for almost a month—since March 21—had Lyra been able to verify the party's latitude, an essential element in mapmaking.** The high walls of the mountain gorges had prevented Lyra from using his theodolite to measure the angle of the sun to the horizon at the noon hour. Since the junction of the Cardoso with the Rio Roosevelt was an important reference point, Rondon decided to stay at this camp an extra day. The only problem was how to disguise the delay from the North Americans.

There was a devious streak to Rondon. He now invented an urgent need to go back and arrest Julio and bring him to justice, claiming that

---

* The two Roosevelts were half right in their guess. In 1915, a year after the Rio Roosevelt was explored, Rondon sent one of his lieutenants, Marques de Souza, to explore the Ananás. De Souza's party was attacked by Indians, and he and one of his canoemen were killed, but the survivors of the expedition pressed on. They found that the Ananás was one of two feeders creating a larger river, the identity of which was known only after the explorers traced it to its mouth on the Rio Roosevelt and found Rondon's camp marker bearing the name Rio Cardoso.[54]

** The Rio Roosevelt's course—for all its tortuous twistings and turnings—flowed so nearly due north that determining longitude en route did not matter as much to Rondon as fixing the latitude of important tributaries.

he had intended to take him into custody earlier that day on the river, but he wanted to consult with Roosevelt first. Rondon spoke of seeing Julio tried before a court of law, which would mean guarding and feeding him for the rest of the voyage.

Roosevelt realized what Rondon was up to and refused to waste a day trying to apprehend a murderer whom he thought deserved to starve to death in the wilderness. "Rondon [deliberately] vacillated about Julio with 100 lies," Kermit noted angrily after listening to the exchange. "He wants to take the latitude but Father won't let him."[56]

April 7 . . . Rondon and Lyra continued to beg the Colonel to let them look for Julio, even though, in Kermit's words, "they were in a blind rage to kill him" three days before, after Paixão's murder.[57] Finally, too ill to keep on arguing, Roosevelt compromised. Rondon was responsible for upholding the laws in his country, and he "must act as his sense of duty bade him."[58] But at least he should use the time spent at this camp sensibly by having the camaradas carve some spare paddles (a laborious task, beginning with a log), and sending someone to investigate the rapids downstream, the roar of which could be plainly heard in the camp. Even this required what Kermit called "a fight" on his father's part, since Rondon seemed to have convinced himself that there was no need to explore ahead with the river at such a low altitude.[59]

"Antonio Correa has returned and reports serious rapids and falls!" Cherrie recorded a few hours later. "It may well be that we are 'up against it' again and good and hard!"[60]

Besides finding more cataracts, Antonio had shot a monster catfish in the shallows, which excited the naturalists in the party. Measuring over a yard long, the ugly, whiskered fish had enough succulent flesh to feed all nineteen men. When Franca slit the belly open with his carving knife, he pulled out the partially digested head and arm of some species of monkey, apparently swallowed alive while it perched on a branch drinking from the river. "We Americans were astounded at the idea of a catfish making prey of a monkey," wrote T. R., but Dr. Cajazeira told an even stranger story of a nine-foot-long catfish found on the Amazon, called by the four-syllable word *paraiba*, and which had lunged at two fishermen in their canoe before being killed with machetes. Rondon, joining in the conversation, told of how, in many villages on the lower Madeira, people built bathing stockades in the river to keep the *paraiba* from attacking them.[61]

Full of catfish stew and catfish tales, the explorers put aside their differences for a while and savored the simple gift of watching the sun go down, after so many days of being walled up in canyons. The Colonel found time to bring his *Scribner's* manuscript up-to-date.

> This evening at sunset the view across the broad river, from our camp, was very lovely . . . for the first time we had an open space in front of and above us, so that after nightfall the stars, and the great waxing moon, were glorious overhead, and against the rocks in midstream the broken water gleamed like tossing silver.[62]

It was after dark when the two scouts sent by Rondon to find Julio returned empty-handed. They had spent the day shouting his name in the woods and firing their rifles into the air and probably had frightened him away.

April 8 . . . Lyra had worked out the latitude of the Rio Cardoso camp as 10 degrees 59 minutes south and due north of the telegraph bridge. This meant that in forty-one days of canoeing, the expedition had come exactly 125 miles, not much more than 3 miles a day.[63] The advance on this day was no better, thanks to the rapids that Rondon had not thought important enough to investigate. "Our march a short one," Cherrie noted flatly, after the party had struggled through four stretches of rapids:

> Twice the boats were carried forward loaded, but with only the paddlers on board. Twice there were portages where the cargo had to be carried overland, 400 and 100 meters respectively, and the boats were run down empty.[64]

Walking with the Colonel on the longer of the two marches, Cherrie realized again how Roosevelt's stamina was ebbing. "He was completely tired out at its end, and yet it was over level ground. Kermit is more and more worried about his father." Cherrie blamed chronic malnutrition as "one potent reason why we are all physically below normal."

By late afternoon, the boatmen were drooping from fatigue when new rapids appeared. No one had the heart to make another portage, and Rondon ordered a landing on the left bank. In turning toward shore, Antonio the Parecis, bowsman in the Colonel's dugout, broke his paddle against a submerged rock. There was momentary panic until he found a spare one behind him. Before departing that morning, Cherrie had remarked on the absence of an extra paddle on board, and

Roosevelt had waited for Rondon to produce one before getting in. Without it, Cherrie explained afterward, "we would have been almost at the mercy of the waters for the canoe is too big and heavy to be managed and propelled by one small paddle in the hands of the steersman."

Roosevelt's reaction to nearly going down rapids without a paddle went unrecorded, but Cherrie let go in his diary what he, as a subordinate, could not say out loud:

> In many ways, in lack of foresight regarding special details, Col. Rondon had proved himself incompetent as the head of such an expedition![65]

On landing, there was an immediate search for food. Cherrie heard the chatter of howler monkeys nibbling on fruit up in the trees. Out of a troupe of a dozen, he killed three with his shotgun, but one of the dead monkeys remained coiled to a branch. Antonio the Parecis promptly shimmied up the tall trunk and shook the limb until the animal fell off. Meanwhile, Lyra had caught two fat piranha, using pieces of fresh monkey meat as bait. Supper that night consisted of one soda cracker, handfuls of fish, and a cup of coffee. "Not a very hearty meal for a full grown man!" Cherrie growled. "The monkeys will be for breakfast."[66]

When there was so little to eat, as on many days going down the river, Roosevelt and Cherrie swapped daydreams about food. "My favorite dish, when I got home, was going to be pancakes and maple syrup with cream," Cherrie recalled. "The Colonel said he was going to have mutton chops with the tail to them. Kermit would listen as long as he could, and finally would get up and go away where he couldn't hear us talking about things to eat."[67]

April 9 . . . Any hope of making a good start on this day was ended when Rondon went through his morning ritual of reading the Order of the Day to the assembled explorers. He had to raise his voice to be heard over the roar of falling water and announced that the rapids ahead were too dangerous for loaded canoes. The baggage would have to be carried around them for a distance of half a mile.

The ensuing portage dragged on until noon. Under way again, the canoes ran for only twenty minutes before the tired occupants were again forced to land and investigate another stretch of white water blocking their way. Fortunately, the boatmen found a side channel that was calm enough for the loaded dugouts to be run through. Twice more that afternoon there was the maddening repetition of a fifteen-minute passage followed by several hours portaging around rapids, while the paddlers took their chances again with the empty canoes. The sheer waste of time involved made the Colonel long for "a big Maine birch-bark"— the swift canoe he remembered as a young man on North Woods hunting trips. "It would have slipped down these rapids as a girl trips through a country dance. But our loaded dugouts would have shoved their noses under every curl."[68]

Late afternoon found the embattled voyagers no more than three miles farther downriver, camped once again at the head of rapids. Flanking the river were ranges of low hills, which on the side opposite the camp rose to a towering ridge. Such hills meant only one thing— still more rapids.

There was enough daylight for Rondon to make a reconnaissance and to report that the party faced another half-mile-long carry of the loads the next day. His voice carried no conviction, as if he was tired of the struggle. Cherrie described him as being discouraged and gloomy. "This long series of rapids . . . has knocked a little of the cock-suredness out of Rondon, who during the unnecessary delay at the Rio Cardoso insisted there were no rapids ahead!"[69]

Roosevelt's own account of the river journey makes no mention of Rondon's strange overconfidence at the Rio Cardoso or of his subsequent depression at finding more rapids. Unlike Cherrie, who was able to vent his frustration in the pages of a private journal, the Colonel kept no diary, nor did he write letters in which he could unburden his doubts and anger. Instead, in his *Scribner's* articles, he went out of his way to praise Rondon and ignored the disputes that peppered their relationship. Roosevelt was always aware that he was a guest of the Brazilian government.

His real opinion of Rondon was revealed, indirectly, in a letter to Kermit, written a year after the expedition disbanded, in which the Colonel agreed with his son that, of all the Brazilians, Dr. Cajazeira "was the best of the outfit."[70]

April 10 . . . Rondon had more cause to brood on this Good Friday, as did his companions. "The hills that came into view yesterday afternoon have caused all the trouble that could be expected of them," wrote Cherrie. "We did not get away from the foot of the carry, above which we camped last night, until noon."

There had been no time to let the camaradas cut down a supply of palm hearts, which was by now their principal diet. Intense hunger pains drove some of them to steal food at night as Julio had done.

Canned bacon was high on their list. Cherrie discovered that his canisters of heavy-gauge shotgun shells were missing, stolen by "some one of the camaradas, who doubtless thought the cans contained meat." The naturalist fired his last round at a spider monkey before departing but only wounded it, and watched the animal scamper away.[71]

Kermit succumbed to fever again. The evening before, he had collapsed with a 104-degree temperature. The doctor watched him through the night, as he had the Colonel, and injected quinine into his upper arm at six-hour intervals. Kermit diagnosed himself as "better this morning but with bad head & back aches, and too weak to help with the portage." In leaving camp, he crawled onto the double canoe and burrowed under the tarpaulin covering the food crates. Trigueiro followed him onto the raft but leaped back to shore when the paddlers pushed off. Kermit was too groggy to notice the dog's absence.[72]

Launched once again, the four canoes looked suddenly small and vulnerable on the wide, fast-moving river. The bowsman in the lead dugout never took his eyes from the front, maintaining his paddle stroke and watching for the telltale swirl of rapids ahead. At one point, the current carried Kermit's raft into the protruding tops of small trees and shrubs on a submerged island in midstream. There were some anxious moments, as the paddlers worked frantically to get clear of the snags before the tidal force of water tore the twin hulls apart and scattered the expedition's remaining food supply.

After forty minutes of riding the river's writhing back, the paddlers abruptly steered for the left bank when new rapids began forming ahead. The passengers got out and walked around these, and waited as the pilots guided the loaded dugouts down. It was then that Kermit realized Trigueiro was missing and had probably been left behind at the previous camp. There was no chance of sending a canoe back for the animal—the boatmen did not have the strength to fight upstream against the current. Besides, a more important problem faced the explorers. Within a few hundred yards from where they stood, the river once more divided into numerous channels, some relatively smooth and others full of boulders against which the water slammed with hurricane force. Cherrie described the thunder of these rapids as "ominous."[73] Rondon walked down to explore them and found that they extended almost a mile. From what he could see from the left bank, the water funneled so furiously that not even an empty canoe would have survived.

Rondon had the boatmen ferry the party across to the right shore, hoping to find a more navigable channel. It was a good move. He found that the empty canoes could be run down part of the way, then let down for some distance by ropes, and finally run empty down the last stretch to smooth water.

The camaradas cut a path along the shoreline and carried the baggage and food below the rapids. It was after dark and raining when they had erected the canvas fly for the officials. The Colonel, huddling in his dripping poncho, found the wait "a good exercise in patience for those of us who were still suffering somewhat from fever."[74]

April 11 . . . After another look, Rondon changed his mind about the severity of the rapids and decided to let the pilots run the empty canoes down the full mile-long distance. The loads were piled up on the riverbank below the falls. A departure as early as 9:00 A.M. might have been possible if the Colonel, acting on Kermit's urging, had not prevailed on Rondon to send some men back to look for Trigueiro. Rondon, a dog lover as much as the two Roosevelts, could hardly refuse.

It was nearly sundown when the dog searchers returned, preceded by a hungry, panting Trigueiro, who bounded into Kermit's open arms and eagerly licked the young man's face. The usually loyal Cherrie confided in his journal that stopping to save a dog was "a great mistake on Col. Roosevelt's and Kermit's part, when we are so anxious to get ahead . . . A precedent is established of which our companions will doubtless avail themselves when again they may wish to stop for a day or part of a day."[75]

There was, however, an unexpected benefit in staying a second night at this twenty-ninth camp. "We were all much excited by news that Louis Correa brought in [this] evening," Cherrie related. "He had gone across the river to fish and as he worked his way along the shore in the canoe, [he] found a place where a bejuca [vine] had been cut off with a knife or an axe! It was in a place where the work could only have been done from a canoe." The Indians in this region were not canoe users, so it must have been done by some enterprising *seringueiro*, a rubber tapper, making his way up the Rio Roosevelt.[76]

April 12 Easter Sunday . . . The prospect of meeting up with the rubber gatherers restored Kermit's faith that he would get his father out of the jungle and see his fiancée. He was still "very ragged" from fever, but "much more cheerful than on Xmas day for I have 3½ . . . [months] less of that dreary vista stretching between B[elle] & myself." To keep his mind distracted, the convalescing bridegroom-to-be had begun reading Sir Walter Scott's historical novel *Quentin Durward*.[77]

The river soon put a damper on any notions of a premature rendezvous with the rubbermen. "[This day] we spent in the fashion with which we were altogether too familiar," wrote the Colonel. "We only ran in a clear course for ten minutes all told, and spent eight hours in portaging the loads past rapids down which the canoes were run . . ."[78]

In negotiating these rapids, the boat handlers had to carefully let each of the dugouts down a three-foot drop with ropes. The stage was set for an accident, which Cherrie witnessed:

> In nearing the little falls, our oldest and poorest canoe got beyond control of the canoe men; and was hurled in among the rocks. Fortunately where she was thrown the water was not deep although very swift. After about three hours of heart-breaking toil directed by Lyra and Rondon, she was finally rescued. She had sustained some damage requiring caulking. But a great weight of uncertainty was lifted from us when we knew she was not lost.[79]

On this Easter night, Cherrie turned philosophical: "What lies before us tomorrow no man knoweth. However, there are hills in sight ahead—not a good augury."[80]

April 13 . . . As expected, those hills held rapids, which the party encountered within five minutes of departing from Camp 30. Everyone but the pilots lifted their legs out to begin walking. Rondon believed the paddlers could get the loaded canoes through the rapids safely.

All went well until the bowsmen in one of the double canoes broke their paddles against the rocks. There were no spare paddles on board, and they sat helpless, gripping the sides of the hulls. Only by good luck and the efforts of its steersman, Louis Correa, was another catastrophe averted.

Afterward, Roosevelt demanded that Rondon search all the baggage for more paddles, but there were none. There was no choice but to stop and make new ones from logs.

By noon, after three hours of industrious carving, the camaradas had five crudely shaped paddles, and a second start was made downriver. But within minutes, the hot, sweating, and angry travelers were forced to carry their baggage and food cans around a five-hundred-yard portage.[81]

They were on their way again by 2:30, but without much hope of making up for lost time. Every turn in the river set their nerves on edge, but for two blessed hours the canoes ran freely, making a solid gain of ten miles. They came to a point on the river beyond earshot of any sound of roaring water. "We're camped in silence [without] the noise of [rapids] for the first time in a month," Kermit wrote that evening. The unfamiliar quiet should have been cause for rejoicing, but Kermit had a more pressing personal concern: "Father not well; much worried."[82]

Besides fever and malnutrition, still another threat to the Colonel's life loomed. The gash on his right leg had not healed and was so painful he could not bear to put his weight on it. The doctor peeled off the dirty, sweat-stained bandages and found the middle third of Roosevelt's leg swollen with cellulitis, a deep-seated inflammation of the tissue. Alarmed at what he saw, Cajazeira wanted to immediately lance and drain the wound, but Roosevelt insisted on waiting a few more days, hoping for a natural cure. The doctor agreed to do so but made clear to Roosevelt that he did not expect such an outcome.[83]

April 14 . . . The Colonel traveled flat on his back, stretched out on a row of food cans in the bottom of his canoe and covered with a piece of stiff canvas to keep the rain off. Although his was the largest of the four dugouts, it was not wide enough for an awning to be erected over him. He shielded his face from the merciless sun with the remains of a wide-brimmed straw hat and nearly fainted from the heat—too sick and weak, he said later, to even splash water on his face. Worst of all were the halts for rapids, as happened twice on this day. The Colonel had to lift himself out of the canoe, with every movement an agony, and climb steep, gravelly ravines, half carried by Kermit and Cherrie.[84]

The men around Roosevelt became his devoted nurses, but the doctor regretted that in spite of "the care given him by all of us, we were unable to make Colonel Roosevelt more comfortable." Cherrie remembered how on this morning, as on many others, "I looked at [him] and said to myself, 'he won't be with us tonight'; and I would say the same thing in the evening, 'he can't possibly live until morning.'"[85]

Roosevelt also believed that he had come to the end of the line. "This looks like the last for me," he said to Dr. Cajazeira, as they rested during one of the portages. "If I'm to go, it's all right. You see that the others don't stop for me . . . I've the shortest span of life ahead of any in the party. If anyone is to die here, I must be the one. The others must look out for themselves. You are all strong and can make it."[86]

Unknown to anyone, including Kermit, the Colonel had made up his mind to keep going as long as he could, "if necessary on all fours,"[87] but when that was no longer possible, he planned to arrange for the expedition to go on without him.[88] Buried deep in his personal kit, the Colonel carried a small bottle of morphine—enough for a lethal dose. He had always taken it with him on hunting trips, to avoid being "caught by some accident where I should have to die a lingering death." He preferred to "have it over with at once" in such a case.[89] By April 14 Roosevelt's physical decline had brought him to the point of deciding to take his own life, not from being despondent, but out of a sense of moral duty to his companions.[90]

But the issue of suicide for the greater good was not all that clear-cut, as T. R. explained afterward to the newspaperman Oscar K. Davis:

> When I found myself so ill that I was a drag on the party, and it began to look as if we could not all get out alive, I began to think it might be better for me to take my morphine and end it. I could not stand the thought that my illness was likely to keep Kermit in that jungle too. His life was all before him. He was coming out to be married, and I could not endure the idea that because of my failure to keep up he might not make it, when without me he could. Then the other side of it came to me, and I saw that if I did end it, that would only make it more sure that Kermit would not get out. For I knew he would not abandon me, but would insist on bringing my body out. That, of course, would have been impossible. I knew his determination. So there was only one thing for me to do, and that was to come out myself.[91]

"We have had a fairly good day," Cherrie noted after arriving at the camp on April 14. His only disappointment was "that we did not have *all* clear sailing." Four hours had been lost in portaging around the rapids, but they had come twenty miles, a near record and six times the distance they had been averaging since leaving the junction with the Rio Cardoso a week before.[92]

At this camp, the doctor had his hands full treating an outbreak of food poisoning that threatened to put an end to the expedition. One of the camaradas, poking around in the forest away from the river, had used his shirt as a sling to bring back a pile of strange-looking nuts. He claimed that they were similar in taste to the Brazil nut, which had proven so nonexistent as a food source. "It was a truly tasty fruit," the doctor reported, so much so that many of the famished camaradas gorged themselves. Within a few hours, they were nursing monumental belly-aches, followed by vomiting, severe diarrhea, and dizziness. Some of the men's heart rates slowed down so much that Cajazeira had to inject them with cardiac stimulants. To his regret, not a single nut remained for later examination under microscope.[93]

There was more evidence that rubbermen had come this far upstream at some time in the recent past. Near the campsite, Kermit picked up a weathered walking staff, whittled from a long, straight branch. It looked to be a year old.[94]

April 15 . . . Some of the camaradas were still too dizzy to load the dugouts or ply a paddle. Kermit volunteered as bowsman on the kitchen raft. He paddled all day long, his arms hurting from the puncture marks of the doctor's quinine injections.[95] In the big dugout ahead of him, the Colonel lay wrapped in canvas, his face half screened by the rim of a straw hat, quietly enduring the pain in his swollen leg.

For a change, there were no rapids to overcome. The dugouts had glided steadily downstream for nearly three hours, when Rondon made a discovery that marked a turning point for the unlucky expedition. He had just asked Lyra to record the name Serra da Cigana (Gypsy Hills) on his survey chart, to denote a range of hills on the left bank. Then his eye fell on something on the same shore that made him excitedly wave the other canoes to turn landward after him. He leaped to the bank and knelt beside a wooden board nailed to a post. On the face, someone had burnt the letters "J. A." with a hot poker. The sign board was the type used by rubber gatherers to mark the boundaries of their claims. It appeared to be of recent origin.[96]

NOTES

1. Roosevelt, Kermit, *Diary*, 3-28-14. **2.** T. R., *Brazilian Wild.*, p. 295. **3.** Cherrie, *Diary*, 3-28-14. **4.** Robinson, *My Brother, T. R.*, p. 278. **5.** Cherrie, *Dark Trails*, pp. 308–9. **6.** Cherrie, *T. R., Memorial Meeting.*, p. 26. **7.** T. R., *Brazilian Wild.*, p. 298. **8.** Cherrie, *Diary*, 3-29-14. **9.** Cherrie, *T. R., Memorial Meeting.*, p. 27. **10.** Roosevelt, Kermit, *Diary*, 3-29-14. **11.** Ibid., 3-30-14. **12.** Cherrie, *T. R., Memorial Meeting.*, p. 28. **13.** Cherrie, *Diary*, 4-2-14; Cherrie, *Dark Trails*, p. 306. **14.** Cherrie, *T. R., Memorial Meeting.*, p. 25. **15.** Roosevelt, Kermit, *Diary*, 4-2-14. **16.** T. R., *Brazilian Wild.*, p. 300. **17.** Roosevelt, Kermit, *Diary*, 4-2-14. **18.** Ibid. **19.** T. R., *Brazilian Wild.*, p. 303. **20.** Cherrie, *Diary*, 4-3-14. **21.** Rondon, *Lectures*, p.104. **22.** Cherrie, *Diary*, 4-3-14. **23.** T. R., *Brazilian Wild.*, p. 302. **24.** Cherrie, *Diary*, 4-3-14. **25.** T. R., *Brazilian Wild.*, p. 304. **26.** Cherrie, *Diary*, 4-3-14. **27.** Cherrie, *Dark Trails*, p. 311. **28.** T. R., *Brazilian Wild.*, pp. 304–5. **29.** Cajazeira, *Relatorio Apresentado.* **30.** T. R., *Brazilian Wild.*, p. 305. **31.** Roosevelt, Kermit, *Diary*, 4-7-14. **32.** T. R., *Brazilian Wild.*, p. 305. **33.** Ibid., p. 308. **34.** Ibid. **35.** Cherrie, *Diary*, 4-3-14. **36.** Roosevelt, Kermit, *Diary*, 4-4-14. **37.** Cajazeira, *Relatorio Apresentado.* **38.** Ibid.

39. Rondon, "Col. Roosevelt as His Guide Remembers Him," *New York Times.* **40.** Roosevelt, Kermit, *The Long Trail,* pp. 161–62. **41.** Cajazeira, *Relatorio Apresentado.* **42.** Roosevelt, Kermit, *Happy Hunting Grounds,* p. 46. **43.** Rondon, *Lectures,* p. 109. **44.** Cherrie, *Dark Trails,* p. 301. **45.** Roosevelt, Kermit, *Diary,* 4-5-14. **46.** Cherrie, *Diary,* 4-5-14. **47.** Cherrie, "To South America for Bird Study," *American Museum Journal.* **48.** Cherrie, *Diary,* 4-5-14. **49.** Rondon, *Lectures,* p. 114. **50.** Viveiros, *Rondon,* p. 406. **51.** Cherrie, *Diary,* 4-6-14. **52.** Ibid. **53.** Rondon, *Lectures,* p. 111. **54.** Ibid., p. 113 (footnote). **55.** T. R., *Brazilian Wild.,* p. 310. **56.** Roosevelt, Kermit, *Diary,* 4-6-14. **57.** Ibid., 4-7-14. **58.** T. R., *Brazilian Wild.,* p. 307. **59.** Roosevelt, Kermit, *Diary,* 4-7-14. **60.** Cherrie, *Diary,* 4-7-14. **61.** T. R., *Brazilian Wild.,* pp. 311–12. **62.** Ibid. **63.** Rondon, *Lectures,* p. 110. **64.** Cherrie, *Diary,* 4-8-14. **65.** Ibid. **66.** Ibid. **67.** Cherrie, *T. R., Memorial Meeting.,* p. 27. **68.** T. R., *Brazilian Wild.,* p. 313. **69.** Cherrie, *Diary,* 4-9-14. **70.** T. R. to Kermit, 5-31-15, *PPS.* **71.** Cherrie, *Diary,* 4-10-14. **72.** Roosevelt, Kermit, *Diary,* 4-10-14. **73.** Cherrie, *Diary,* 4-10-14. **74.** T. R., *Brazilian Wild.,* p. 314. **75.** Cherrie, *Diary,* 4-11-14. **76.** Ibid. **77.** Roosevelt, Kermit, *Diary,* 4-12-14. **78.** T. R., *Brazilian Wild.,* p. 314. **79.** Cherrie, *Diary,* 4-12-14. **80.** Ibid. **81.** Ibid., 4-13-14. **82.** Roosevelt, Kermit, *Diary,* 4-13-14. **83.** Cajazeira, *Relatorio Apresentado.* **84.** Ibid. **85.** Ibid. **86.** *New York Times,* 1-7-19 (T. R. quoted). **87.** T. R., *Brazilian Wild.,* p. 319. **88.** Roosevelt, Kermit, *Happy Hunting Grounds,* p. 46. **89.** Davis, *Released for Publication,* p. 434. **90.** Abbott, Lawrence, *Impressions of T. R.,* p. 276. **91.** Davis, *Released for Publication,* p. 434. **92.** Cherrie, *Diary,* 4-14-14. **93.** Cajazeira, *Relatorio Apresentado.* **94.** Roosevelt, Kermit, *Diary,* 4-14-14. **95.** Ibid. **96.** Rondon, *Lectures,* pp. 117-18.

XII

It Seems like a Dream
to Be in a House Again

April 15, continued . . . Feverish excitement gripped the explorers as they found another sign board on the opposite bank, bearing the same initials. These were the first marks of civilization they had encountered since leaving the telegraph bridge on February 27, forty-eight days earlier. The settlements of the rubber gatherers could not be very far off now.

Half an hour later, everyone in the canoes broke into cheers when they saw a humble *baraca*, or reed house, standing in a planted clearing onshore. All at once, six weeks of uncertainty came to an end. Roosevelt's party was no longer descending an unknown river. Thus began what Cherrie called "a day of many agreeable surprises."[1]

The newly built house, its palm-thatched roof still green, was empty except for three dogs, which barked at first and then turned friendly, sniffing at the legs of the bearded, emaciated men shambling up to them. A small, smoky outbuilding contained a primitive rotisserie, fueled by nutshells, on which the sticky latex "milk" drawn from rubber trees was cured into large balls. The absent owner, the "J. A." of the claim stakes, apparently had just gone out on his daily rounds of tapping trees. Inside the main dwelling, the searchers found bags of rice, manioc, and piles of rusty-colored yams. There was no one to bargain with, and in a sudden fit of virtue, Rondon decided not to take anything, even though his camaradas were starving. He left a piece of paper on which he had written the names of the official members of the expedition and where they had come from.[2]

Several miles farther down, an elderly black man paddling a small canoe looked up in amazement at four dugouts descending on him. Only

Indians came from upriver, and he stabbed at the water in an effort to get to land. Rondon stood up, waved his helmet, and shouted at him to come alongside. As his panic faded, the old man identified himself as Raymundo José Marques, a native of the northeastern Brazilian state of Maranhão. Rondon introduced him to the Colonel, who was lying under a sheet of canvas in the adjoining canoe. When told he was shaking hands with an American ex-president, the *seringueiro*'s eyes widened, and he asked, "But is he really a president?" Rondon explained patiently that Roosevelt had been president of the United States at one time but was no longer. "Ah," Raymundo said with awe, "he who has once been king, has always the right of majesty." Roosevelt, touched by the graciousness of the translated remark, assured Rondon that no sharecropper in his own country could have responded with such wit and courtesy.[3]

From this man, the explorers got the first real information on their whereabouts. They learned that they were descending what was locally called the Rio Castanha—ironically, the Indian word for Brazil nut, which grew plentifully this far down. The Castanha was said to be one of the main tributaries of the Aripuanã, as Rondon had long suspected.[4]

Raymundo lived alone and had no food to share, but he told Rondon that there were many rubber gatherers living along the river. He gave him a bamboo horn and warned him to sound it and to fire three rifle shots in the air when approaching, so that the settlers would not think Indians were about to attack.[5]

Some time later, the famished party came upon another solitary palm hut, but no one answered their shouts, gunfire, and horn blowing. They drifted on, hoping to find an inhabited shelter by nightfall. It was midafternoon and raining when the paddlers pointed excitedly to smoke curling up from the chimney hole in a thatched roof. Someone was cooking a meal in that house. Rondon raised his rifle and let off three rounds, then blew lustily into the horn. The camaradas called out a ragged greeting. These peace signals, however, produced exactly the opposite of the intended effect. A woman stepped out of the house, holding a baby in her arms, and screamed at the sight of approaching canoes. She ran away from them, stumbling in the mud and calling to her husband for help.

Welcome or not, the explorers landed and took possession of what Cherrie called "a fair share of provisions" inside and a vegetable garden outside. Seeing some old hens scratching in the dust and clucking after their young broods made the Vermonter think immediately of his farm at Rocky Dell.[6] After Rondon decided to stop here for the night, Cherrie and Kermit lifted the Colonel out of his canoe and carried him up to the house. His ulcerated right leg was so swollen that he could no longer walk.

Franca had kindled a cooking fire in the yard when the frightened woman's husband and two neighboring tappers returned, brandishing rifles and expecting to find an Indian raid in progress. What they found instead were nineteen gaunt-eyed, fever-ridden men who appeared to have gone through some terrible ordeal. Some wore ragged military uniforms, and others shreds of cotton shirts and trousers. Their faces and hands were puffed and pockmarked with insect bites. Some hobbled like old men. When the rubber gatherers learned that they were looking at a government expedition that included a former American president and his son, they became friendly and talkative, chattering as they helped feed their unexpected guests. The sense of being saved was felt most deeply by the camaradas, who had suffered the most. Antonio Correa confided to Kermit: "It seems like a dream to be in a house again, and hear the voices of men and women, instead of being among those mountains and rapids."[7]

From their host, Senhor Honorata, Roosevelt's party learned that the Rio Castanha was actually the left, or western, fork of the Rio Aripuanã. About fifteen days' traveling distance downriver, it was joined by the eastern branch, which kept the name Aripuanã in its upper reaches. It was to the confluence of these two branches that Rondon had sent his assistant Pyrenius to wait for the expedition coming down one or the other fork.

Roosevelt felt immensely relieved to hear this news. "We had passed the period when there was a chance of peril, or disaster, to the whole expedition," he wrote afterward. Lives might still be lost in accidents, but they had conquered the River of Doubt. "We now no longer had to face continual anxiety, the need of constant economy with food, the duty of labor with no end in sight, and bitter uncertainty as to the future."[8]

After the nightmare of fighting so many rapids, Roosevelt took grim satisfaction in what his expedition had accomplished at so great a cost:

> We were putting on the map a river, running through between five and six degrees of latitude—[or] between seven and eight if . . . the lower Aripuanã is included as part of it—of which no geographer, in any map published in Europe, or the United States, or Brazil, had even admitted the possibility of the existence.[9]

He and Rondon were proving that all the existing maps of the region were wrong, full of imaginary rivers and mountain ranges that bore no relation to what was actually on the ground. They were tracing, for the first time, the greatest tributary of the Madeira, and thereby opening up the vast basin between the Tapajós and Gy-Paraná rivers for future scientific exploration. Roosevelt considered it "a great piece of good fortune to be able to take part in such a feat"—a feat made possible only by the work of Rondon's Telegraph Commission during the preceding seven years.[10]

For weeks Kermit and Cherrie had jealously guarded their last bottle of whiskey until, as Cherrie put it, "we should come to the first rubber signs." Swinging comfortably in adjoining hammocks outside Honorata's thatched house, the two thirstiest members of the expedition "found it necessary to draw the cork this evening." As they shared the bottle, Cherrie looked up into the black April night and picked out a brilliant cluster of stars, just above the northern horizon, that looked oddly familiar. It was the Big Dipper, "upside down to be sure," because he was viewing it from a southern latitude, "but how good it looks. Almost as if it had come as an old friend from home."[11]

The Colonel saw the Dipper too, and it made him think of homecomings that were not so far away now:

> The north was calling strongly to the three men of the north—Rocky Dell Farm to Cherrie, Sagamore Hill to me; and to Kermit the call was stronger still . . . In our home country spring had now come, the wonderful northern spring of long, glorious days, of brooding twilights, of cool delightful nights. Robin and bluebird, meadow-lark and song sparrow, were singing in the mornings at home; the maple-buds were red; windflowers and bloodroot were blooming while the last patches of snow still lingered; the rapture of the hermit-thrush in Vermont, the serene golden melody of the wood-thrush on Long Island, would be heard before we were there to listen. Each man to his home, and to his true love! Each was longing for the homely things that were so dear to him, for the home people who were dearer still, and for the one who was dearest of all.[12]

April 16 . . . The pain of his swollen right leg had become so severe that Roosevelt could no longer put off surgery. The operation took place outdoors, without anesthetics, while the dugouts were loaded. Wasting no time, Dr. Cajazeira pressed his scalpel blade deep into the mound of inflamed tissue, releasing a thick stream of yellowish white pus. The smell of blood drew swarms of flies, which the doctor had to wave away in order to insert a drainage tube into the incision. Roosevelt refused to flinch or cry out when the knife sank in. Kermit remembered how "Father's courage was an inspiration never to be forgotten by any of us."[13]

Kermit and Cherrie helped the Colonel down to his canoe, and the party set off for what was to be a record eight-hour passage without once having to stop for rapids. Less spectacular, though, was the actual distance gained this day. With no falls to impel the current, the river grew sluggish, and the canoes drifted only twenty-five miles. The camaradas were too weak from hunger and food poisoning to do more than poke at the water with their paddles. But at least, as Cherrie noted, "there were no surprises and we did not strain to see and dread to learn what might be around each bend of the river."[14]

April 17 . . . A gain of only eighteen miles was made on this day, much of it in torrential rain that by midafternoon forced the explorers to take refuge in an abandoned hut on the left bank. "Hammocks & everything wet," Kermit recorded after arriving. But he could also add, with relief, "Father better." Lancing the abscess had brought the Colonel's fever down, much to the doctor's satisfaction. From a rubber gatherer living across the river, Kermit bought a chicken, some lemons and bananas, and a sweet pineapple, to be divided up among men who had forgotten the taste of such luxuries.[15]

April 18 . . . This was a day of real hope, during which the canoes ran nearly thirty miles without meeting rapids, the best single day's passage since the expedition had started out. Midmorning brought another cause for celebration when the bowman in the leading canoe sighted a wide tributary pouring into the Rio Roosevelt from the left. Rondon named it for the Baron Rio Branco, the brilliant foreign minister who had guided Brazil's development into a major power until his death in 1912. As noon approached, Lyra took advantage of clear skies to work out the latitude of the Rio Branco—9 degrees 38 minutes south, or about 230 miles north of the February 27 starting point.[16]

While Rondon and Lyra bent over their chart, Kermit borrowed a canoe and with Cherrie paddled across to a rubberman's hut on the side opposite the Rio Branco. They found the poor *seringueiro* inside not much better off than themselves. He could spare only half a bag of rice, but he told Kermit to look for "a certain Barbosa" near the Chuvisco Rapids—

about six hours' paddling time downstream. This Senhor Barbosa was a prosperous settler who could offer them food, shelter, and new canoes.[17]

Through the long, hot afternoon, the four crowded dugouts ran unhindered by rapids, borne on a current quickened by the added waters of the Rio Branco. Cherrie counted a variety of birds overhead—turkey vultures, cormorants, and snake birds. Once he saw a great white egret gliding majestically above the trees.[18] No amount of hard paddling could outrun the clouds of ravenous sand flies, nor was there any shade to be found on the wide river. The rainy season was drawing to a close. Kermit would later recall how the sun "hung above us all the day like a molten ball and broiled us as if the river were a grid on which we were made fast." He thought that for a sick man like his father, lying in a narrow dugout with only a rimless straw hat to shield his face, "it must have been intolerable."[19]

Nightfall brought relief from the torturous sun, but there was still no sign of Barbosa's establishment. The parched travelers took over a deserted hut to sleep in. The Colonel, on his cot, shared the hard-packed dirt floor with half a dozen camaradas, who mumbled and cursed in various stages of fever delirium.[20]

April 19 . . . A short canoe ride this morning led the explorers to Senhor Barbosa's sprawling house. "He was a most kind and hospitable man," Roosevelt said of the good Samaritan who did much to save his life. "[He] gave us a duck and a chicken and some mandioc and six pounds of rice, and would take no payment."[21] Barbosa's dark-skinned, cigar-smoking wife brewed pots of strong Brazilian coffee, while her younger children took turns peeking out at the collection of strange-looking men littering their front yard. Most important, Barbosa lent the expedition a large, flat-bottomed boat, wide enough that Kermit could rig a tent over his father to protect him from the sun and rain. In return, Barbosa got one of the party's small canoes.[22]

Soon after leaving Barbosa, the explorers reached the Chuvisco Rapids, which caused only a temporary delay as the loaded canoes were run through. It was a different matter farther down, at the boulder-filled Panella Rapids, the first serious obstacle to navigation encountered in a week. Fortunately, rubbermen living at the head of these rapids volunteered to help pass the canoes and carry the baggage over a well-used trail. The Colonel hired one of these *seringueiros* to act as guide until the party got down to the lower Aripuanã and found Pyrenius's camp. Rondon was obliged to take a back seat to a native who knew the river firsthand. From this point, apprehension about what lay ahead evaporated, but so did the excitement. "We knew exactly what channels were passable when we came to the rapids . . . and where the carry-trails were," wrote T. R. It was all child's play compared to what we had gone through."[23]

The same could not be said of Roosevelt's own struggle to survive the final weeks on the River of Doubt. During this time he suffered a plague of ailments that ultimately shortened his life. Rondon recalled that T. R. "never was himself again" following the fever attack at the Paixão Gorge.[24] Malaria hung around him like an assassin waiting for a second chance. The wound in his leg had begun to heal, but the cellulitis infection had spread through his body. He complained to the doctor of severe pain in the right buttock, so bad that he could not sit down. Cajazeira found an abscess there but was unable to treat it without surgical instruments.[25]

Roosevelt also had stopped eating. After too many days of living on half-cooked monkey meat and palm hearts, his stomach had finally rebelled with a gastrointestinal disorder that killed his appetite and left him apathetic and depressed. "He eats very little," Cherrie recorded somberly. "He is so thin that his clothes hang like bags on him."[26] In six weeks, Roosevelt had lost one fourth of his 220-pound body weight.

April 20 . . . The canoes were reloaded and launched again by 8:00 A.M. for what proved to be the longest run yet on the river—thirty-two miles. Forced to lie on his stomach because of the abscess, Roosevelt endured the long hours by feeding bits of fruit to a tamed trumpeter bird, "very friendly and confiding," which Dr. Cajazeira had bought as a companion for him from a settler at the Panella Rapids.[27]

Near noon, they came upon a store run by the rubber traders. The bare shelves inside spoke of the year-long absence of the big supply boats, which had not yet worked their way this far upstream. Rondon was able to buy, at hugely inflated prices, enough rice, sugar, and tobacco for his men. What they really craved, however, were cans of condensed milk; a 10-cent can was being sold for $4, at 1914 prices.[28] Roosevelt, unable to tolerate any food, watched in "amused horror" as the camaradas "solemnly proceeded each to eat a canful of the sweet and sticky luxury."[29] Afterward, many of them doubled up with cramps from having eaten too much and were no good for paddling.

April 21 . . . The dangerous Infernão Rapids, at 8 degrees 19 minutes south latitude, held the day's run down to just over thirty miles. Without the guide Roosevelt had hired earlier, it would have taken several days to find a way through them. But portages had been made here many times, and the guide knew the safe channels. Before descending these rapids, the explorers traded two more of their dugouts to rubbermen for another wide, plank-built boat.

The owner of a trading store below the falls offered the party shelter for the night. Kermit and Cherrie celebrated the completion of the river journey a little early by chipping in to buy a dusty, flyblown bottle of Italian vermouth. "It cost 10,000 Reis," Cherrie allowed, "but was worth the price!"[30] They sat outside on the rickety steps, divided the contents "with meticulous accuracy" into tin cups, and toasted their success as explorers.[31]

April 22 . . . It took all morning to pass the two boats and the dugout through the Infernão Rapids and reload. Nine miles farther down, the explorers struck the formidable Gloria Rapids and feared they would lose more time in portaging. But to their surprised delight, the guide ferried the boats around the rocks without accident.[32] As so many times before, the Colonel made the agonizing trek down the carry trail supported on the arms of his son and Cherrie.

April 23 . . . Before departing, Dr. Cajazeira took a long time dressing the Colonel's leg, in an effort to make him more comfortable. The late start did not detract from another impressive thirty-mile advance made by dusk. Only once did they encounter rapids. The boats ran these fully loaded, with the camaradas bailing furiously as the waves crashed over the sides. On the quieter stretches of the river, the explorers met half a dozen slow-moving *batelãos* bringing provisions up from the rubber ports. The crews of these broad-beamed boats pulled themselves along the banks by hooking long poles tied with forked branches into the tree limbs over their heads. They shouted greetings to Rondon and gave him news of Pyrenius, whose camp was only four days' paddling away. This gladdened every member of the expedition, most of all Kermit, who was preoccupied with getting his father to Manáos and a hospital.

Evening brought a landing at an open-sided shed packed with people and animals. Cherrie was quick to record his disgust: "Our stopping place filth[y], wet and dark. [P]igs, chickens and dogs contend for a place." In this pigsty of a shelter, the Colonel was able to buy some eggs, which he swallowed raw—the only food his stomach would hold.[33]

April 24 . . . The river still offered one more obstacle. After running until late afternoon for a gain of thirty-four miles, the boats were brought up short against the Carapanã Rapids—the last of the dangerous falls on the Rio Roosevelt. Had the explorers still been on their own, it would have taken them several weeks to get through these seven miles of rapids. The Colonel probably would have died from starvation in the meantime. But the descent took only a day and a half, thanks to the help provided by José Caripe, self-styled king of the rubbermen, who happened to be visiting one of his company stores at the Carapanã Rapids when the explorers arrived.

Caripe, described by T. R. as "cool, fearless, and brawny as a bull," owned a fleet of rubber steamers and several islands on the lower Aripuanã.[34] Most of the rubber gatherers on the Rio Castanha worked for him. A generous, impulsive character, Caripe took pity on Roosevelt and volunteered to guide his party through the rapids. He gave them one of his wooden boats in exchange for the last of the dugouts.

April 25 . . . In a whirlwind of portaging, led by the energetic Caripe, the boats were unloaded three times in succession and run through as many rapids. Caripe pointed out places where boatmen had drowned in the past and recalled his own adventures as a rubber tapper, including the time he was stalked by a pair of jaguar as he returned to camp after having been lost in the forest for eight days. While one of the boats was being emptied, Trigueiro wandered off into the bush. Kermit searched for him as long as he could, but then had to give up. He hoped the dog would find its way to one of the rubber camps and be sent to him.[35]

April 26 . . . There was one final portage to be made, at the Gallinha Rapids, during which Kermit and Cherrie's craft took on water and would have sunk without some frantic bailing by all on board.[36] After that, the three boats, packed with men and equipment, glided down the broad, sunlit river without further incident. The width of the river here reminded the Colonel of the Paraguay River at Corumbá, where the expedition had begun its journey into the unknown five months before.[37]

At 1:00 P.M., the tired but excited explorers reached the junction where the Castanha (Rio Roosevelt) met the unexplored upper Aripuanã branch coming in from the east. The merging waters created what the rubber gatherers called the lower Aripuanã, which emptied into the Madeira.

At the confluence of the two rivers stood the trim-looking tents of Lieutenant Pyrenius's detachment. As the boats drew up to shore, the North Americans cheered at the sight of the Stars and Stripes flying next to the green-and-gold Brazilian flag. Pyrenius, a scholarly young officer, greeted his commander Rondon enthusiastically and helped carry Roosevelt up to the camp. To celebrate the occasion, Pyrenius opened a bottle of champagne and proposed a toast in Portuguese and English on the success of the expedition.[38] He had been waiting for them for six weeks, not knowing whether they would come down the Castanha, or the upper Aripuanã, or not come at all. In the meantime, he had completed mapping the lower Aripuanã from its mouth all the way up to this camp, which was located at latitude 7 degrees 34 minutes south. Pyrenius had come up from Manáos on a steamer, leaving it below a final stretch of rapids at Sehnor Caripe's little port town of Sao João, about four hours downriver.

From Pyrenius, Roosevelt learned that the other two exploring teams of the original expedition—Fiala's and Miller's—had already made it safely to Manáos. Anthony Fiala had reached the rubber capital as early as March 26, after losing all his film and equipment in the canoe accident on the Papagaio. He had waited around for several weeks, run out of money, and then gone home. Leo Miller and Amilcar had reached Manáos on April 10. Miller was reported to be hard at work collecting specimens for the museum while waiting for Roosevelt.

April 27 . . . This day marked two months exactly since the expedition had left the telegraph bridge to begin the voyage down the River of Doubt. During those sixty days, the explorers had traveled an estimated 426 miles by dugout and in the process traced a major new river.

To commemorate this achievement, Rondon supervised the erection of a monument and summoned the members of the expedition to hear a reading of his final Order of the Day. The camaradas lined up on either side of the post. They looked subdued, holding their calloused hands in front of them or behind their backs, while Rondon nailed up a gleaming oval plaque bearing the words "Rio Roosevelt." From this time forward, he announced, the rivers that the rubbermen and the Indians had long known as the Castanha and the Aripuanã were to be considered as one river and would carry the name Roosevelt for its entire length. When Rondon finished speaking, Cherrie took a photograph of the group gathered around the marker, and one of the somber-faced camaradas broke into a grin.

The Colonel stood during the ceremony, which Kermit feared "tired [him] a lot."[39] Gaunt and weak from living on nothing but raw eggs, he allowed himself to be photographed, but forbade the picture to be published. He did show a spark of humor, however, when he suggested to Rondon that the name Rio Téodoro might sound easier on Brazilian ears than his harsh Dutch surname.[40]

With the river properly christened, Roosevelt was helped into Caripe's boat for a final ride with Kermit, Cherrie, and the doctor. Four hours later, after racing through the last of the rapids on the river, they reached Caripe's plantation at Sao João. There they found the white-hulled government steamer *Cidade de Manáos* lying at anchor.

The startled officers on the steamer at first stared open-mouthed, then broke into cheers as the boatload of shabbily dressed explorers bumped alongside. Using T. R.'s cot as a stretcher, Kermit and the others lifted the Colonel up onto the deck. After months of living in a tent, T. R. found the private cabin reserved for his use unbelievably comfortable.[41] But he had arrived without a change of clothes. His khaki trousers and silk dress shirt were torn and rank with dirt and sweat. Senhor Caripe remedied this by going home and bringing back one of his own suits, several sizes too big for Roosevelt's shrunken waistline. Caripe insisted on photographing him in it, despite T. R.'s protests.[42]

That evening, Cherrie sat up late recording his delight to finally be "in quarters where we care little if it rains or is dry!" He could still taste the fresh beefsteak and fried potatoes Pyrenius's cook had served up as a surprise breakfast. In forty-eight hours they would be in Manáos and starting for home. Behind the wooden partition, in the adjoining cabin, the Colonel was asleep. "He seems really better tonight," Cherrie wrote, and shuddered at how close to death Roosevelt had come: delirious with fever . . . enduring the hideous pain in his leg and hip . . . and even now, with help at hand, unable to eat anything solid. How close to death they all had been . . . seeing their food dwindle . . . the canoes wrecked one after another in the rapids. A sense of deliverance swept over him. "It seems very strange to be writing under a bright electric light and not with a sputtering candle for light."[43]

At noon on April 28, Rondon and Lyra turned up at Sao João, accompanied by the thirteen camaradas, already filling out from eating double portions. The work of the expedition was done. With the exception of its headwaters in the Parecis Mountains, the survey of the Rio Roosevelt had been completed. Rondon estimated the length of the new river at between nine hundred and a thousand miles.

At 1:40 P.M., wood smoke belching from its stack, the *Cidade de Manáos* began pulling away from the riverbank for the thirty-six-hour run to Manáos. Senhor Caripe had decided to come along, bringing a pot-bellied barrigudo monkey in a cage, a gift from his wife for the expedition's animal collection.[44]

Rain and wind squalls pursued the steamer through the afternoon. The throbbing of its engines sounded good to Cherrie as he worked at his skinning table, preparing the last specimen caught on the former River of Doubt—a parrot new to the collection. The naturalist felt disappointed at not finding more river birds—terns, gulls, and ducks—this far down the river but consoled himself with the thought that "the disagreeable troubles and discomforts of our long trip are about over."[45]

For Kermit, it could not be fast enough. His thoughts were on Belle and their forthcoming marriage. Not until the steamer reached Manáos would he learn whether the wedding was to take place at her home in Virginia or in Spain. In January, en route to Tapirapuan, he had written her: "I have your picture & your letters always in my pocket day & night."[46] They were still in his shirt pocket, worn from dampness and refolding. Going down the Dúvida, he had been unable to write her but had told himself over and over again that "this time has to end & we'll be together." Now he was counting the weeks rather than months.[47]

To take his mind off the thousands of miles still separating him from Belle, Kermit tried reading "a crazy novel" that Caripe had given him, titled *The War of the Vampires*.[48] When that palled, he looked in on his father. The Colonel lay on his side in the stuffy cabin, unable to sit up because of the abscess.[49] Dr. Cajazeira hoped to operate on it when they reached Manáos, but until then, T. R. was a prisoner in his bed. He was not gaining strength as rapidly as Kermit had hoped, nor could he shake off the gastric disorder that kept him from eating anything more nourishing or appetizing than raw eggs. Kermit had been fortunate in finding some fresh milk for him that morning. The Colonel spoke to his son about coming home and how he "looked forward with dread" to what he would be called on to do in the 1914 election.[50] The Progressive Party probably would pressure him to run for governor of New York on his return.

"We entered the Madeira River about 3 A.M.," Cherrie recorded after breakfast on April 29. He noted that its slow-moving waters were stained yellow by the tropical forest mud it carried away to the Amazon, rather than being clear like the granite-bedded Rio Roosevelt.[51] Twelve hours later, they entered the Amazon and turned upstream toward the Rio Negro and the city of Manáos. Miles wide at this point, the greatest river on earth seemed to Kermit to consist mainly of "lots of floating logs & islands. Picturesque houses . . . Fat cattle & green meadows."[52]

At the town of Amaraty, where the Amazon Telegraph Company maintained a station, Rondon went ashore to wire ahead to the governor of Amazonas. Out of consideration for Roosevelt, Rondon requested that their arrival time be kept secret—he would arrange to have the steamer arrive after midnight, to avoid the huge crowds that inevitably would gather to see the Colonel. In his message, Rondon also asked the authorities to have an ambulance and stretcher ready.[53]

At 2:30 A.M. on April 30, the *Cidade de Manáos* eased up against the wooden pilings of the municipal wharf of Manáos. Despite Rondon's request for secrecy, a fair-sized crowd of government officials and newspaper reporters were waiting under the cold glare of arc lights on the dock. A number of automobiles, including a French-built Chenard-Walcker fitted with beds, stood behind them with motors running.

A delegation composed of Governor Pedrosa, the inspector general of the Military Region, and other army officers came on board with a tray of iced champagne and crowded into Roosevelt's small cabin. Champagne was the last thing T. R. wanted at this hour of the morning, but he sipped politely and responded in French, telling his visitors that he was "enchanted with the wealth of the Amazon" and affirming his friendship with the Brazilian people.[54]

The stretcher bearers came in, and under Dr. Cajazeira's supervision, Roosevelt was carried out to the waiting ambulance. Rondon described him as "lying helpless" as he was transferred inside.[55] Arrangements had been made to take the party to the Palacette, the official residence of the governor. Kermit and Cherrie piled into one of the other automobiles, and the entourage sped through the empty streets of Manáos. At the palace, Cherrie found, to his surprise, letters from his wife, Stella—the most recent one more than four months old, dated December 13, 1913. Kermit was handed a packet of letters from Belle, postmarked London and Madrid. He stayed up all night reading them and feeling "very very happy." The wedding, he learned, was to take place in Spain in June.[56]

Manáos, the capital of Amazonas, had been built on the vast fortunes created during the late nineteenth and early twentieth centuries, when Brazil controlled the world's supply of rubber. In its heyday, it was the richest city in South America. Manáos millionaires built extravagant mansions and thought nothing of sending their laundry to Paris—confident that the stream of "black gold" produced by the lowly rubber tappers would flow forever. It did until 1910, when the market price for rubber collapsed as a result of overproduction and foreign competition, mainly from British Malaya.

By 1914 Manáos was already in decline; this may explain the extreme sensitivity of one of its daily newspapers, which attacked Roosevelt's son and Cherrie for their personal appearance. Cherrie noted that "the burden of their complaint was that we had dared to appear on their streets in the clothes in which we had arrived from the expedition, and the fact that we had not shaved and had our shoes polished before showing ourselves!"[57]

Roosevelt saw little of this fabled city in the jungle. He arrived in a haze of pain and fatigue and said afterward that he had no clear recollection of events during the day-and-a-half stopover.[58] While Kermit sweated over getting their luggage collected and checking steamship schedules, T. R. remained in bed at the governor's palace, attended by Dr. Cajazeira. He suffered through a courtesy call by state and municipal officials, which had to be conducted in French—a considerable mental effort for a sick man. Cherrie, who was present, reported that Roosevelt was "completely exhausted after the interview."[59]

Roosevelt's cable to his wife gave no hint of how seriously ill he was. "Successful trip," he wired Edith after two months of silence, and asked her to notify Henry Cabot Lodge and other close friends of his arrival. He was franker with his cousin, Emlen Roosevelt: "Have had hard trip. Have been pretty sick, but am better now. Kermit all right."[60]

The Colonel summoned his strength to write out a detailed report in pencil to Lauro Müller at Rio on what the expedition had accomplished. T. R. mistakenly dated the telegram May 1, but it was actually sent on April 30 by telegrapher James G. Gulliver:

> We have had a hard and somewhat dangerous but very successful trip. No less than six weeks were spent in slowly and with peril and exhausting labor forcing our way down through what seemed a literally endless succession of rapids and cataracts. For forty-eight days we saw no human being. In passing these rapids we lost five of the seven canoes with which we started and had to build others. One of our best men [Simplicio] lost his life in the rapids. Under the strain one of the men [Julio] went completely bad, shirked all his work, stole his comrades' food and when punished by the sergeant [Paixão] he with cold-blooded deliberation murdered the sergeant and fled into the wilderness. Col. Rondon's dog, running ahead of him while hunting, was shot by two Indians; by his death he in all probability saved the life of his master. We have put on the map a river about 1500 kilometers in length running from just south of the 13th degree to north of the 5th degree and the biggest affluent of the Madeira. Until now its upper course has been utterly unknown to everyone, and its lower course altho known for years to the rubber-men utterly unknown to all cartographers . . .

> My dear Sir, I thank you from my heart for the chance
> to take part in this great work of exploration.[61]

Leo Miller rejoined the expedition at this time. He had spent nearly a month collecting specimens along the Rio Solimões southwest of Manáos while awaiting Roosevelt's party. The young naturalist had gotten "some nice things in the mammal line" for the museum, including a rarely seen three-toed sloth.[62] The Colonel was fascinated by Miller's account of collecting the intact nest, eggs, and young of the hoatzin, the strange lizard bird that swims and crawls as much as it flies. Miller, who had not seen Roosevelt since February 27, was appalled at his chief's shrunken appearance: "He had wasted to a mere shadow of his former self; but his unbounded enthusiasm remained undiminished."[63]

On May 1 Roosevelt departed for Belém, the port city near the mouth of the Amazon where the expedition would disband. From Belém, Kermit planned to sail directly to Spain to join Belle. The Colonel was to return briefly to the United States, then cross the Atlantic in June to attend his son's wedding.

Before leaving Manáos, Roosevelt underwent an operation to open the abscess that had caused him such excruciating pain for weeks. A few hours later, in better spirits, he was carried on board the Booth Line freighter *Dunstan*, whose captain vacated his cabin for the former president. Kermit, Cherrie, and Miller were left to find places on deck to swing their hammocks. Rain and the rattle of the ship's winches hoisting tons of Brazil nuts into the hold drove the three into the dining saloon, where they slept on the floor.[64]

En route to Belém, the Colonel stayed in his cabin, taking his meals in bed and only picking at the food on the plate. By the fourth day out, he was able to stand up and walk with a cane.[65] As his strength slowly returned, Roosevelt made plans to capitalize on the success of the expedition. Using the stub of his last remaining pencil, he wrote his British friend Arthur Lee to contact the head of the Royal Geographical Society in London for an invitation to lecture "on a genuine bit of South American exploration." He and his party had traced "an absolutely unknown river" extending through seven degrees of latitude to the Madeira. "No map has a hint of it, yet it is the biggest affluent of the biggest affluent of the mightiest river in the world."[66]

At Belém, where he arrived on May 5, the Colonel was able to walk down the ship's accommodation ladder and get into the launch for the short ride to the Booth liner *Aidan*, which had been held for him. There was a final, wearying round of official sight-seeing in the port city, during which Roosevelt held his first press interview since coming out of the wilderness. The most important achievement of his expedition was geographical, he told the Associated Press. "We have put on the map a river nearly one thousand miles long," he said, and compared its volume to that of the Rhône in southeastern France and the Hudson River in New York State.[67]

No less significant were the thirty-two crates of specimens hoisted on board the *Aidan*. In six months of work, Cherrie had collected more than 1,500 birds—many new to the museum's collection, and some new to science. Miller had accumulated 450 mammals, including jaguar, tapir, anteaters, peccaries, deer, and mice. Taken together, the specimens represented one of the most important acquisitions of South American wildlife ever made by the American Museum of Natural History.[68]

Two days later, on May 7, the expedition Father Zahm had conceived in such secrecy years earlier officially broke up. Rondon and the Brazilian Commission came on board the *Aidan* to say good-bye. Roosevelt asked the camaradas, now grown fat from overeating, to form a line. "You are all heroes," he told them in a short speech translated by Kermit. He shook hands with each man and handed each two gold sovereigns as mementos of their shared experiences. Simplicio, the drowned boy, was not forgotten on this sentimental occasion. T. R. asked that the coins be sent to his mother, along with his back pay.[69]

Dr. Cajazeira advised Roosevelt to continue taking quinine on the voyage home and for some time after, to prevent a relapse of fever. For Rondon, the end of one journey meant the start of another; he would be returning to the wilderness to complete construction of the telegraph line. Roosevelt invited him to visit Sagamore Hill some day. "I shall be there," Rondon answered, "when you are once again elected president of the United States."[70]

NOTES

1. Cherrie, *Diary*, 4-15-14. **2.** Rondon, *Lectures*, p. 118. **3.** Ibid., pp. 119–20. **4.** Cherrie, *Diary*, 4-15-14. **5.** Rondon, *Lectures*, p. 119. **6.** Cherrie, *Diary*, 4-15-14. **7.** T. R., *Brazilian Wild.*, p. 316. **8.** Ibid., p. 319. **9.** Ibid., p. 317. **10.** Ibid., p. 318. **11.** Cherrie, *Diary*, 4-15-14. **12.** T. R., *Brazilian Wild.*, p. 320. **13.** Roosevelt, Kermit, *Happy Hunting Grounds*, p. 48. **14.** Cherrie, *Diary*, 4-16-14. **15.** Roosevelt, Kermit, *Diary*, 4-17-14; Cherrie, *Diary*, 4-17-14. **16.** Rondon, *Lectures*, p. 123. **17.** Roosevelt, Kermit, *Diary*, 4-18-14. **18.** Cherrie, *Diary*, 4-18-14. **19.** Roosevelt, Kermit, *Happy Hunting Grounds*, p. 48. **20.** Roosevelt, Kermit, *Diary*, 4-18-14. **21.** T. R., *Brazilian Wild.*, pp. 321–22. **22.** Roosevelt, Kermit, *Diary*, 4-19-14. **23.** T. R., *Brazilian Wild.*, p. 321. **24.** Rondon, *Lectures*, p. 128. **25.** Cajazeira, *Relatorio*

Apresentado. **26.** Cherrie, *Diary,* 4-21-14. **27.** T. R., *Brazilian Wild.,* p. 322. **28.** Cherrie, *Dark Trails,* p. vii. **29.** T. R., *Book-Lover's Holiday,* p. 163. **30.** Cherrie, *Diary,* 4-21-14. **31.** Cherrie, *Dark Trails,* p. vii. **32.** Cherrie, *Diary,* 4-22-14. **33.** Cherrie, *Diary,* 4-23-14; Roosevelt, Kermit, *Diary,* 4-28-14. **34.** T. R., *Brazilian Wild.,* p. 328. **35.** Roosevelt, Kermit, *Diary,* 4-25-14. **36.** Ibid., 4-26-14. **37.** T. R., *Brazilian Wild.,* p. 327. **38.** Cherrie, *Diary,* 4-26-14. **39.** Rondon, *Lectures,* p. 137; Roosevelt, Kermit, *Diary,* 4-27-14. **40.** Viveiros, *Rondon,* p. 409. **41.** T. R., *Brazilian Wild.,* p. 332. **42.** *New York Times,* 7-10-27. **43.** Cherrie, *Diary,* 4-17-14. **44.** Ibid. **45.** Ibid. **46.** Kermit Roosevelt to Belle Willard, 1-2-14, *KRP.* **47.** Kermit Roosevelt to Belle Willard, 1-17-14 *KRP.* **48.** Roosevelt, Kermit, *Diary,* 4-28-14. **49.** Viveiros, *Rondon,* p. 410. **50.** T. R. to Kermit Roosevelt, 11-11-14, *PPS.* **51.** Cherrie, *Diary,* 4-29-14. **52.** Roosevelt, Kermit, *Diary,* 4-29-14. **53.** Viveiros, *Rondon,* p. 410. **54.** *Jornal do Commercio,* 5-1-14. **55.** Rondon, "Col. Roosevelt as His Guide Remembers Him," *New York Times.* **56.** Cherrie, *Diary,* 4-30-14; Roosevelt, Kermit, *Diary,* 4-30-14. **57.** Cherrie, *Diary,* 5-1-14. **58.** T. R. to J. A. Zahm, 7-18-14, *JAZP.* **59.** Cherrie, *Diary,* 5-1-14. **60.** *New York Times,* 5-1-14. **61.** T. R. to Lauro Severiano Müller, 4-30-14, *Letters,* Vol. 7, #5881, pp. 759–60. **62.** Leo E. Miller to Frank M. Chapman, 4-24-14, *AMNH.* **63.** Miller, *In the Wilds,* p. 264. **64.** Cherrie, *Diary,* 5-4-14. **65.** *New York Times,* 5-19-14. **66.** T. R. to Arthur Hamilton Lee, 5-4-14, *Letters,* Vol. 7, #5882, p. 761. **67.** *New York World,* 5-6-14. **68.** *New York Times,* 5-20-14. **69.** Viveiros, *Rondon,* p. 411; T. R., *Brazilian Wild.,* p. 335. **70.** Viveiros, *Rondon,* p. 411.

XIII
The River Is Still There

The passengers on the *Aidan* were shocked by Roosevelt's thin and haggard appearance when he came aboard. During the first days out, the ship's surgeon found him despondent and subject to frequent attacks of fever. But the combination of rest and sea air managed to perk him up and he soon put back twenty of the fifty-five pounds he had lost in the jungle. When the liner stopped at Bridgetown, Barbados, on May 12, he went ashore, purchased fifty books, and read them all during the remainder of the voyage to New York, sitting on deck in the sun.[1]

While at Bridgetown, Roosevelt had been angered by press accounts of prominent European and American geographers questioning his claim to have found the biggest tributary of the Madeira. No less an authority than Sir Clements Markham, former head of the Royal Geographical Society, confessed to feeling "somewhat incredulous" at reports that the Colonel had explored an unknown thousand-mile-long river between the Madeira and the Tapajós. It did not "seem to fit in with the known aspects of the country," Markham was quoted as saying. He doubted the Rio Roosevelt could be a very big river, because existing maps indicated larger rivers too close to its supposed location. It was much more likely, he thought, that T. R. had descended one of the known tributaries of the Madeira—the Canuma, for example, which was three hundred miles long, not one thousand.[2]

Similar questions had been raised by the American-born Hamilton Rice, a Harvard man like Roosevelt and a veteran explorer of the Amazon Valley. In London to accept the 1914 Gold Medal of the Royal Geographical Society, Rice dismissed T. R.'s claim out of hand. It was "perfectly ridiculous" to suppose that the principal tributary of a river as big and as well traveled as the Madeira could have gone undetected until now. He questioned Roosevelt's credentials as an explorer and saw an ulterior motive in his South American trip. "He is doing it for effect, as an asset on his next political campaign, whereas true explorers travel for love of exploring."[3]

News dispatches coming out of Brazil in the early days of May created more confusion by mixing up the Colonel's exploring team with Miller's and Fiala's. With stunning confidence, the *New York Evening Journal* declared on May 1: "The River Dúvida or the 'River of Doubt' was found to be unquestionably the River Gy-Paraná." Anyone familiar with South America was sought out for an opinion. A British geographer quoted by the *New York Times* was certain that Roosevelt had gone down a tributary of the Tapajós and thought he was descending an unknown river. If not, then he must have drifted across a flooded forest at the height of the rainy season from one river to another and not realized it.[4]

The Colonel's initial reaction to such doubters was typically forthright: "One might as well doubt the existence of the Hudson River or the Rhine. . ."[5] But until he reached New York and gave a full account of his explorations, mapmakers on both sides of the Atlantic remained skeptical. To many of them, it did not seem probable that a new river over a thousand miles long should suddenly be discovered in a region of South America that had been explored for a century and a half.[6]

Roosevelt's arrival in New York on May 19 was an even quieter affair than was his departure the previous October. His cousin Emlen Roosevelt hired a tugboat to meet the ship and take him directly to Oyster Bay, thereby avoiding what Edith feared would be "committees on the dock."[7] Shortly before 4:00 P.M., the *Aidan* dropped anchor off Quarantine for the routine health inspection required of all vessels entering the harbor. Edith waved up to her husband and then retired to the tug's cabin to wait for him. The first person to greet Roosevelt was Dudley Field Malone, the collector of the port, who had come to personally clear the former president's luggage through customs. Close behind him came Ted, Jr., and other family members, Anthony Fiala, and a group of reporters who had hired their own boat.

Like everyone else, the newspapermen were startled at the change in Roosevelt's appearance since seeing him off for South America eight months before. His eyes looked bright and keen, and he spoke with the same old vigorous snap of the jaws, but his dark suit coat hung unaccustomedly loose on his shoulders. Lines of fatigue creased his sun-burned face. At times he leaned on a malacca cane for support but acted as if he would soon be throwing it away. When his son offered an arm to help him back to his stateroom, T. R. pulled away, remarking, "I am all right. I can take care of myself."[8] He refused to talk about politics, saying only that he had no interest in running for president in 1916. In two weeks he would be leaving again, this time to attend his son's wedding in Spain. In the meantime, he had been invited to speak before the National Geo-graphic Society in Washington, where he would talk about the river he had explored and "answer any question on geography from any reputable man." This would be the only speech he would give before going abroad.[9]

Collector Malone congratulated the Colonel on his safe return and asked what he had to declare. T. R. showed him some pieces of lace he had brought back for Mrs. Roosevelt, several jaguar skins, and two silver christening mugs. Malone asked with a smile if he had brought back the River of Doubt for customs appraisal. "Well, replied Roosevelt, "it is rather an extraordinary thing to do to place a river as large as the Rhine upon the map."[10]

As the ship's stewards began collecting the trunks for transfer to the tug, Roosevelt saw one of them reach for a black leather bag containing the final chapters of his *Scribner's* manuscript. "Please do not touch that," he told the man. After carrying it around countless rapids, he was not about to part with it now.[11]

The Colonel shook hands with the *Aidan*'s captain and officers and said good-bye to Cherrie and Miller, who were staying on board until the ship docked. He was seen limping as he went down the ladder, before disappearing into the tugboat's cabin for a long-awaited re-union with Edith. A short time later, as the tug swung away from the side of the bigger ship, T. R. reappeared on deck and waved his hat in response to cheers.

It was after 8:00 and nearly dark when the tug reached Oyster Bay and stopped at a floating dock five hundred feet from shore. The Colonel's party transferred to a large rowboat and were rowed to the Emlen Roosevelt property, where a small crowd was waiting for them. Edith was the first to step out when the boat scraped against the pier, followed by T. R., who moved as quickly as he could with his cane. On seeing her father, Ethel cried out and ran down the walkway into his open arms. "Oh, my darling," he said, kissing her and gently patting her on the shoulder, while she told him that during his absence he had become a grandfather.[12]

The family walked up the pier to be greeted by a line of servants and hired hands from Sagamore Hill. The Colonel called out to each of them by name, saying how glad he was to be home again. As he spoke, a group of photographers snapped away, the popping of their flashpowder charges sounding like a series of pistol shots in the dark. The Colonel recognized some of the newspapermen present from earlier political campaigns and told them, "By George, this seems like old times." He repeated his earlier statement that he didn't have a word to say on politics. He would have said more had Emlen Roosevelt not pushed him into the backseat of a waiting car. "I'll see you at the house, Pop," Archie called out when the door slammed. "All right," responded T. R., and the car started up the road.[13]

The Colonel rose early on his first day back to confer with Progressive leaders and tackle the mountain of letters and telegrams that had accumulated for months. In the interludes, he found time to see the reporters who had made Sagamore Hill a daily beat. To those present, he "looked as fit as he said he was," even if the belt buckle on his old tan riding suit was drawn in four inches closer than before.[14] He spoke and gestured "with his old-time vigor," especially when it came to those geographers who questioned the existence of the River of Doubt. They could go down to Brazil themselves, he suggested with a laugh. "The river is still there."[15]

"We really performed quite a feat," T. R. wrote Arthur Lee that same day. The worth of the achievement was proved by the reaction of Sir Clements Markham "and the other men who doubt my having done what I say I have done." If he had climbed a mountain or gone to the North Pole, he would have only his word and that of his companions to offer as proof. But it was a different matter with an unexplored river. His expedition could not have made the journey from the telegraph bridge to Manáos in sixty days except by the river, and they had the diaries, photographs, and astronomical observations to prove it.[16]

A week later, on May 26, the Colonel traveled to Washington, D.C., to give the first official account of his exploration before the National Geographic Society. Cherrie and Miller came down on the train with him, along with Fiala, who was to operate a film projector. Father Zahm had been invited to join them at the lecture hall. At Philadelphia and at Wilmington, delegations of Progressives came on board and filled the cars with talk of the coming fall congressional campaign. When Roosevelt grew bored with their conversations, he was seen making discreet dives into Booth Tarkington's new novel, *Penrod*.

An enthusiastic crowd greeted Roosevelt's train when it pulled into Washington's Union Station just before 3:30 P.M. T. R. was escorted across the packed station concourse and into the privacy of the President's Room, to be welcomed by friends—including Frank Chapman—and thirty policemen and detectives assigned to guard him during his nine-hour visit to the capital. The entourage then rushed into waiting automobiles and taxis and sped across town to the National Museum of the Smithsonian Institution, where Roosevelt inspected the trophies from his African expedition. In the company of museum officials, he moved from one display to another, admiring the taxidermist's skill and the lifelike poses of the animals. He stopped before the rhinoceros exhibit and recalled a hunting incident. "Do you know," he exclaimed, "I tried to photograph that big fellow there, but he was too ugly and I had to shoot him."[17]

Roosevelt next paid a call on President Wilson at the White House. It was only his second visit since leaving office. The two rivals temporarily put aside their differences and spent a cordial half hour on the breezy South Portico, sipping lemonade and swapping what Wilson's secretary, Joe Tumulty, called "jokes of a literary character." When T. R. rose to leave, he excused himself by saying, "I must hurry along, for I have an engagement to talk with some friends about *that* river!" Both men laughed and the President saw him off at the door.[18]

A reception followed at Senator Lodge's home on Massachusetts Avenue, where the diplomatic corps had assembled. Lodge, T. R.'s closest friend, was waiting for him on the steps. They threw their arms around each other before going in. Afterward, Roosevelt attended a private dinner in his honor, and by 8:30 P.M. he arrived at the Convention Hall for his speech to the National Geographic Society.[19]

An usher stationed at the foot of the stage waved a white handkerchief when the doors at the rear of the hall swung open. The audience, four thousand strong, broke into cheers and applause as Roosevelt, dressed in evening clothes, marched down the aisle. Perspiring in the intense heat—Washington was undergoing a heat wave—he looked tired but determined. One reporter detected a forced quality to his smile, as if he was depending on willpower alone to carry on. His voice, when he began to speak, sounded husky; at times the reporters taking down his words could barely hear him.[20]

The Colonel warned his listeners to expect a dull lecture: "I wish to put before this audience the exact descriptions of what we have done." He first paid homage to previous explorers, including the work of Rondon and the Telegraph Commission. "All that we did was to put the cap on the pyramid of which they had laid deep and broad the foundations." It was impossible for him to show on a standard map of Brazil what his expedition had achieved, because the maps were "so preposterously wrong." To demonstrate this, he walked over to a blackboard on which had been chalked in a sketch map of the Madeira-Tapajós region. He drew a dotted line running north and south. "Here's the River of Doubt," he said, and recounted the hardships involved in descending it. As further evidence, he offered "Exhibits A, B, C, and D," as he called his four fellow explorers present on stage. Together they had put on the map a river as long as the Rhine. He was grateful to the Brazilian government for such an opportunity, "a chance that from now on, in the present state of the world's geography, can come to only a limited number of men."[21]

The speech turned the tide in Roosevelt's favor. The National Geographic Society announced that it no longer doubted the authenticity of his report. While reserving final judgment until it could see a map, the American Geographical Society credited the Roosevelt-Rondon expedition with having apparently traced a previously unknown tributary of the Madeira from source to mouth.[22] From London came an invitation Roosevelt had been waiting for: The Royal Geographical Society—the final authority on exploration disputes—invited him to speak about his river.

On May 30, joined by his eldest daughter, Alice Roosevelt Longworth, and Philip Roosevelt, Emlen's son, the Colonel sailed for Europe to attend Kermit's wedding in Spain. Edith remained at home, not feeling emotionally strong enough to face foreign travel after the strain of the South American tour and Margaret Roosevelt's death.[23]

"I never saw two people more in love with each other," T. R. wrote Edith on June 11, after witnessing Kermit and Belle's wedding at a civil ceremony in Madrid.[24] The next day, he left for Paris, then crossed the Channel to London for his speech before the Royal Geographical Society.

When the boat train arrived at London's Charing Cross Station on the morning of June 13, the two dozen reporters waiting for him saw a different Roosevelt from the man they remembered from his 1910 European tour. One correspondent noted that "the old snap and bustle were not apparent" in T. R.'s manner, and he was reluctant to answer questions until he had his breakfast. The subsequent press interview took place at the townhouse of his friend and host, Sir Arthur Lee. Roosevelt described his visit as "purely a social and scientific one"; he was there to renew old friendships and lecture on his Brazilian travels—nothing more. He refused to talk about politics, "either American, British or French," and would not comment on English geographers' reactions to his exploration claims. "That is for them to say, not for me." An official map of the new river, he added, was being prepared in Brazil.[25]

A reception at the American ambassador's residence in Grosvenor Square followed, after which the Colonel motored out to Lee's country estate in Buckinghamshire, Chequers Court, for the weekend. Back in London on the fifteenth, he spent the next two days touring Westminster Abbey and other sights, lunching with naturalists and big-game hunters, and preparing his lecture.

Not since 1872, when Henry Morton Stanley announced that he had found Dr. Livingstone alive in deepest Africa, had an explorer's return generated such excitement within the venerable Royal Geographical Society.[26] On the evening of June 16, 1914, motorcars, cabs, and limousines filled narrow Bond Street in London's fashionable West End, creating a monstrous traffic jam around the Civil Service Commission Theater, where Theodore Roosevelt was to speak at 8:30 P.M. The doors had opened an hour earlier but were closed after thirty minutes when several thousand Society members attempted to squeeze into a hall built to hold only eight hundred. Policemen at the entrance linked arms to hold back the surging crowds of gentlemen and ladies in evening clothes who waved their cards and shouted their titles to get inside. Among those besieging the theater was the British foreign secretary, Sir Edward Grey, who had been invited to sit on the stage when T. R. spoke. The leanly built Grey neatly solved the problem of admission by scaling a stone wall "of moderate altitude" and sneaking in through a side door.[27]

Inside the small hall, every seat on the main floor and in the galleries was taken; people sat cross-legged in the aisles, perched on the edge of the stage, and crowded around doorways.[28] From the sustained applause that greeted the Colonel's entrance, it was clear that the audience was prepared to believe every word he said; his speech in Washington had removed the doubts in the minds of most of his critics, with the possible exception of Hamilton Rice, who remained unconvinced about the length of the river T. R. said he had explored. Rice was one of the lucky ones to get into the theater, but he made the mistake of sitting next to Philip Roosevelt and directly behind the outspoken Alice Roosevelt

Longworth, both of whom loudly expressed their annoyance at his presence.[29]

The proceedings got under way with a gracious introduction of the guest of honor by Douglas Freshfield, president of the Society. In what was undoubtedly a sublime moment for Roosevelt, Freshfield read a message from the ailing Sir Clements Markham, acknowledging that T. R. had made "a very important addition to our geographical knowledge by discovering this longitudinal valley between the Tapajós and the Madeira" and recognizing that "he must have overcome great difficulties in making this discovery."[30]

Roosevelt went on to describe those difficulties in detail, giving his account of traveling more than four hundred miles in a canoe down an unknown river. He again praised the achievements of the Rondon Commission, calling it "a very extraordinary work" and one that had not received proper recognition outside of South America. There was still much exploring to be done in Brazil, he told his English listeners. Except for a distance of one degree of latitude at the start of their trip, his expedition had not been able to take the time to accurately survey the upper half of the Rio Roosevelt. The Ananás River also remained to be explored. If the Royal Society would sponsor an expedition to go up or down either river, T. R. offered to provide letters of introduction to the rubber traders who could supply the necessary guides and provisions. There would be risk to life and limb, he warned, "but nothing like what we encountered," precisely because the river was no longer unknown. He advised any would-be explorer to take a number of big Canadian or American canvas-hulled canoes. "They are infinitely better than the dugouts."[31]

"It was a very good lecture," Hamilton Rice conceded to the press afterward. He was glad the Colonel had clarified the actual distance of the unknown portion of the river. Rice had been primed to ask Roosevelt questions, but T. R.'s voice had gone hoarse near the end and he declined to take questions from the audience. Before leaving London, Roosevelt consulted a throat specialist, who told him his larynx was in bad shape, the result of straining it in the 1912 campaign and from malarial infection. The doctor counseled him against making any outdoor speeches for some time.[32]

Fever struck the Colonel again on June 18, just after boarding the German liner *Imperator* to sail for America. The chills and sweats dragged on for several days. T. R. recuperated in the luxury of the ship's royal suite, catching up on his reading and dictating letters in a hoarse voice to a stenographer. There was no way for him to avoid being treated like a celebrity—each time he entered the first-class dining room, the diners stood and applauded him.[33]

Also traveling on the *Imperator* was Harry Houdini, the American magician and spiritualist. On the second day out, Houdini was asked by fellow passengers to conduct a demonstration of his clairvoyant powers. Among the audience would be Theodore Roosevelt. While still in London, Houdini had learned that T. R. had given one of the major newspapers a hand-drawn map illustrating the course of the River of Doubt, on the condition that it not be published until after his steamer had sailed. Through a friend on the paper, Houdini had managed to see the map and memorize its details. At the shipboard séance, Roosevelt asked Houdini to call upon his "spirit medium" to trace the route taken by the expedition. The magician went into a momentary trance, then reached for a slate and drew an accurate representation of the river. T. R. was astonished at the performance and afterward rushed up to Houdini to tell him that it was "the most amazing thing he had ever seen."

Roosevelt came home in late June 1914 to face a cloudy future. His family physician, Dr. Lambert, confirmed the London specialist's diagnosis of a damaged larynx and also found that Roosevelt's spleen was enlarged, the result of serious malarial infection. He ordered his patient to rest his voice and body for at least four months, a call seconded by Edith.[34] The Colonel followed this prescription for exactly one week before traveling to Pittsburgh to speak at a Progressive Party banquet. His reception there reportedly "surpassed anything in the 1912 campaign." Drawing strength from the crowds, he came out swinging against both the Republicans and Democrats, declaring that the Bull Moose Party still had life in it yet.[35]

Questions of his health ended any talk of Roosevelt running for the governorship of New York state—an office he had held in 1899 and that he did not want a second time. He campaigned for other Progressives, but never again could he wage a battle such as he had in 1912. Whether T. R. realized it or not, he was living on borrowed time. He had taxed his body too heavily in South America to ever fully recover. "His immense vitality kept him going for another four years," Nicholas Roosevelt recalled later, ". . . but the machine was running down and thereafter needed constant attention and repairs."[36]

Just how costly the South American adventure had been became evident shortly after Roosevelt got back from Brazil. Riding home on the train from New York City one day, he learned that a group of his Oyster Bay neighbors were on board and wanted to shake his hand. Although tired and weak, T. R. insisted on making a tour of the cars, greeting everyone he knew. He ended up in the baggage car, worn out by the effort. Sitting down to rest on a trunk, he asked a companion to bring him a glass of water. As he was about to drink it, Roosevelt noticed a dog chained to the wall, whimpering and panting in thirst. He walked over to the animal, drank half the water in the glass, and then tilted it down so the dog could drink the rest.[37]

For a time, the River of Doubt remained a great national preoccupation—the delight of cartoonists, Sunday supplement writers, and amateur poets like William F. Kirk, who penned the following:

> Oh, a wonderful stream is the River of Doubt
> That the wonderful Colonel has told us about
> It flows uphill with a swirl and a swish
> That bothers the gills of the Maneating Fish[38]

But events overseas soon overshadowed the Colonel's South American exploits. Roosevelt, like the rest of America, reacted in dumbstruck horror as Europe plunged into war in the early days of August 1914. One by one, the Great Powers—Germany, France, Russia, Austria-Hungary, and then England—were drawn into a conflict that would eventually involve the world. Out of office and without any real power, Roosevelt could only sit and watch the crisis unfold. If he had been president at the time, T. R. wrote his friend, the British ambassador Cecil Spring Rice, he would have used the United States' diplomatic influence to keep the war from starting, and "the American people would have followed me."[39]

The disruptions brought on by the war caused a delay in getting the long-awaited map of the Rio Roosevelt from Lyra in Brazil. Charles Scribner's Sons agreed to hold up publication of the Colonel's book, *Through the Brazilian Wilderness*, as long as possible so that the map could be included. Even before the war broke out, in a letter to Father Zahm on July 18, Roosevelt complained about the difficulty of trying to get "anything done from this distance in connection with Brazil." Fiala was still waiting for duplicate copies of motion picture film taken by a Brazilian photographer on the trip. Also missing were two crates of valuable animal skins left behind at the Rio Burity when the mule train collapsed, and which Rondon had promised to send back to New York.[40]

To expedite the completion of the map, Roosevelt used his contacts at the State Department. Secretary of State William Jennings Bryan asked the United States embassy at Rio de Janeiro to "cable immediately whether maps of unknown river had been forwarded." On September 12, Ambassador Morgan notified Roosevelt that the Brazilian Foreign Office, under instructions from Lauro Müller, had taken "considerable pains to hasten the preparation of the map." But by then, Scribner's had had to go to press using Roosevelt's hand-drawn map. When Lyra's map finally did arrive, in mid-October, T. R. was exasperated to find that it was twelve feet long, labeled in Portuguese, and lacking any references to latitude or longitude. The two boxes of specimens reached the American Museum of Natural History a month later.[41]

The publication of Roosevelt's *Through the Brazilian Wilderness* brought the story of the River of Doubt to a close. In November 1914, T. R. sent copies to the American and Brazilian members of the expedition. "You will be amused to know," he wrote Rondon, "that . . . various . . . gentlemen made a furious attack upon what we had done." But that was all over now.[42]

A foot of snow had fallen at Newfane, Vermont, and the temperature was down to six degrees below zero, when George Cherrie wrote to thank T. R. for his copy. It was two days after Thanksgiving, and Cherrie had recently come home from a month of campaigning for local Progressive Party candidates.

> About the first thing I heard from the boys was "Colonel Roosevelt has sent you his book and we've been reading it!" I have been going over it today and find it fine, in fact. I think it will be prized by me even more than the boys.[43]

Roosevelt remained on good terms with Father Zahm after the South American trip. Zahm resumed his practice of sending T. R. clippings from Catholic newspapers, but the old intimacy was gone. In the spring of 1916, Zahm sent his friend a proof copy of *Through South America's Southland*—his own account of the expedition—and asked Roosevelt to inspect it. Zahm indicated that he was contemplating a return to South America to complete the journey he had originally planned down the Tapajós and up the Rio Negro into Venezuela. "The idea becomes more dominant from day to day."[44]

Although he suffered from intermittent attacks of fever, Roosevelt was also thinking of mounting another expedition in the interest of the natural sciences, this time to another little-known part of the world. In December 1916, he asked Henry Fairfield Osborn at the American Museum of Natural History to sponsor a six-month voyage to the South Pacific. Roosevelt planned to sail there on the United States Fish Commission's steamer *Albatross*. He would pay for the coal and other expenses by once again writing a series of articles for *Scribner's Magazine*. "I believe I could make a trip that would be worth while, and that would do credit to the Museum."[45]

Plans were made to sail at the start of 1918 for what would have been a fabulous journey into Polynesia, but the United States' entrance into the World War, in April 1917, ended any possibility of T. R.'s going. He threw himself into war work, saw his four sons go off to fight, and tried to organize a division with himself at the head for service on the western front. The appearance of a former American president leading his troops into battle would have rejuvenated the sagging morale of the Allied armies, but Woodrow Wilson looked ahead to the next election, saw Roosevelt's heroics in political terms, and turned him down. "I had hoped that we might round out Africa and South America by a 'greater adventure' together," a bitterly disappointed T. R. wrote Kermit afterward; "as it is, I am not to serve at all . . . Well, we have to abide by the fall of the dice!"[46]

That same spring of 1917, the American Geographical Society awarded Roosevelt the David Livingstone Centenary Gold Medal for his exploration of the River of Doubt. The award, established in 1913 to mark the hundredth anniversary of the great African explorer, had been awarded only once before, to the English explorer Sir Douglas Mawson. In accepting it, T. R. told his audience that it should have gone instead to Colonel Rondon. He considered Rondon's work as head of the Brazilian Telegraph Commission second only in geographical importance to the discovery of the North and South poles. A year later, in August 1918, at a ceremony in New York's Carnegie Hall attended by Roosevelt, the Brazilian ambassador accepted this same gold medal for Rondon.

For Roosevelt, 1918 was marked by painful operations and long hospital stays. On February 6, he went under the knife for fever-induced abscesses in both ears and on his thigh—his old Brazilian trouble. He spent a month in bed and permanently lost the hearing in his left ear. While convalescing, the Colonel kept up with a flood tide of correspondence and a parade of visitors—"many more than you could ever see," as his secretary, Josephine Stricker, remarked to him one day.[47] By the end of March, he had rallied sufficiently to resume speaking around the country on behalf of war-bond drives. He also began making plans for a possible presidential run in 1920—this time as the Republican candidate, after the demise of the Progressives in 1916.

In July, as T. R. and Edith feared with four sons at the front, their youngest, twenty-year-old Quentin, a flyer in the American Army Air Corps, was shot down over German lines. "It is a very sad thing to see the young die," T. R. wrote the French premier, Georges Clemenceau, "when the old who are doing nothing, as I am doing nothing, are left alive."[48] It was said that the boy went out of Roosevelt's spirit when Quentin died.

As autumn came, the Colonel grew increasingly somber about his declining health. A friend, the novelist Owen Wister, recalled how at the table sometimes, Roosevelt would suddenly drop from vigorous talk into silence. Once, coming out of his silence, he said, "When I went to South America, I had one Captain's job left in me; now I am only good for a Major's." On October 27, he turned sixty years old.[49]

On November 18, the day the war ended, inflammatory rheumatism put Roosevelt back in the hospital, this time until Christmas. The doctors warned that he might have to spend the rest of his days in a wheelchair and live with pain. He reflected on that for a moment. "All right!" he said. "I can work that way too."[50] His only regret was that he had not been able to die for his country as Quentin had.

On Christmas Day, Roosevelt was driven back to Sagamore Hill to spend the holidays and expected to return to the hospital afterwards. The family physician, Dr. Faller, made two calls a day to check on him and was reassured by T. R.'s ruddy complexion and sturdy appearance. Faller recalled later how T. R. had refused to talk about his illness. "He talked about almost everything except himself and his condition of health."[51]

A change for the worse took place on Friday, January 3, when Roosevelt admitted to not feeling well. The next morning, Edith telephoned her husband's former manservant, James Amos, and asked him to come to Sagamore Hill and be prepared to stay. "Mr. Roosevelt wouldn't have anybody else," she told him.

Amos arrived at Sagamore Hill that evening and was saddened by Roosevelt's appearance. "His face bore a tired expression. There was a look of weariness in his eyes. It was perfectly plain that he had suffered deeply." The Colonel asked him to prepare a bath and change his pajamas. He was in great pain, and Amos worried that he had made it worse. After being put into bed, T. R. told him, "You never hurt me a little bit."[52]

On Sunday, January 5, for the first time, T. R. did not dress or come downstairs for breakfast. He stayed in Ethel's old bedroom, the room all the children had slept in when they were young. Its three windows faced south, making it the warmest room in the house. Edith kept him company during the day; the two of them took turns reading aloud. As it grew dark, the Colonel watched the flames in the fireplace and talked about the pleasures of being home. When Edith rose to go, he set aside the book he was reading and said to her, "I wonder if you will ever know how much I love Sagamore Hill."[53]

Dr. Faller came at 8:00 P.M., stayed briefly, and left James Amos sitting beside Roosevelt's bed. Three hours later, the doctor was called back, when T. R. complained about feeling short of breath. Faller gave him some medication, which seemed to relax him, and then went home. Edith came in for a final time and kissed her husband good night. As she walked out of the dimly lit room, Roosevelt said to his valet, "James, will you please put out the light?"[54]

In the morning he was dead.

As for the other members of the Roosevelt-Rondon Expedition, Lieutenant Lyra preceded all his companions to the grave when he drowned while surveying a section of the Rio Sepotuba in April 1917.

Father Zahm never made it back to South America. In the last years of his life, he turned his interest to the Near East and the Holy Land. The First World War delayed travel, but on October 4, 1921—eight years to the day that he and Theodore Roosevelt had set out for Brazil—the seventy-year-old Zahm, white haired and trim, sailed for Europe on the SS *George Washington*. He got as far as Munich, where a cold developed into bronchial pneumonia. He lingered in a hospital for several weeks, certain he would recover, and told a friend that he needed to live ten more years in order to write a life of Dante. He died on November 10, and his body was shipped back to Indiana for burial in the Community Graveyard at Notre Dame University.[55]

"... the bottom has dropped out for me," Kermit wrote Edith Roosevelt on learning of his father's death. It was an accurate self-diagnosis. Without T. R.'s steady guidance and companionship, Kermit became a lost soul, dissatisfied by married life, bored with business, and seeking satisfaction in frequent hunting expeditions and often from the bottle.

Like his father, he suffered recurrent attacks of the fever brought back from the River of Doubt. At the outbreak of the Second World War, Kermit volunteered for the British Army and served in Egypt until he was sent home with malaria. When America entered the war, he wangled a major's commission and was posted to the desolate Aleutians, the least active of the war fronts and a spiritual dead end for Kermit. On June 4, 1943, racked by alcoholism and depression, Kermit placed a .45 revolver under his chin and pulled the trigger.[56]

A year later, in far-off Paraguay, Jacob Sigg died at sixty-five in the tiny hamlet of Patino. Father Zahm's Swiss-born valet left a widow and no children; his occupation was listed as farmer.[57]

George Cherrie continued making frequent trips to South America to collect birds on behalf of the American Museum of Natural History, eventually working in every country on the southern continent except Chile. By the time he retired as a field naturalist in the late 1920s, he had made nearly forty expeditions and collected 120,000 birds. He always regarded the River of Doubt trip with Roosevelt as the most dangerous of his assignments and the most memorable. He was at the American consulate in La Guayra, Venezuela, on January 6, 1919, when a State Department cable came over the wire. The consul read it and silently handed it to Cherrie, whose eyes flooded with tears. Cherrie ended up keeping bees and tending his maple sugar trees on his farm in Newfane, Vermont, where he died, at age eighty-three, in 1948—the same year that Edith Roosevelt passed away at Sagamore Hill.[58]

On January 6, 1919, Leo Miller had just landed a training plane at an Army Air Corps field in Georgia when he heard a newsboy shouting about T. R.'s death. "For a long time," he recalled, "it seemed that it could not be possible that a man like that could ever die."[59] In that same year, Miller resigned from the American Museum of Natural History and turned to a more lucrative career in business. As a sideline, he lectured throughout New England on his South American experiences, including one popular talk titled "The Truth about the River of Doubt," which was illustrated with colored slides. He lived on until 1952.[60]

Anthony Fiala lived into his early eighties, dying two years before Miller. Fiala earned fame in the 1920s and 1930s as an outfitter to explorers, including Kermit Roosevelt on his expeditions to India and Turkestan. Fiala had the honor of receiving one of the last letters Theodore Roosevelt wrote—dated January 3, 1919, in which T. R. praised him for his work during the war as head of the small-arms proving ground in Springfield, Massachusetts.[61]

Rondon's association with Theodore Roosevelt brought him international recognition for his accomplishments. The American Geographical Society placed his name on a plaque with the other great twentieth-century explorers—Byrd, Amundsen, and Peary. For his work in pacifying and protecting the Indians of Mato Grosso, his government named him Civilizer of the Wilderness and created a new Brazilian state—Rondônia—out of what had been far-western Mato Grosso. At ninety, loaded down with honors, Rondon was named a marshal of Brazil. He died two years later, in 1958, nearly half a century after the journey down the River of Doubt.

The last survivor of the Roosevelt-Rondon Scientific Expedition was Frank Harper, T. R.'s former secretary, who died in 1971 at a Santa Monica, California, nursing home.

Since 1914, few explorers have been willing to risk their lives descending the Rio Roosevelt. Two early attempts by the Brazilian government to retrace the route taken by T. R. and Rondon ended in disaster—one party disappeared, presumably massacred by Indians, and the other turned back for fear of being attacked.

The first successful effort took place in 1927. The Roosevelt Memorial Association (now the Theodore Roosevelt Association) asked a British explorer, Comdr. George M. Dyott, to make a motion-picture record of the journey as part of a series of short films devoted to T. R.'s life.

Dyott and three companions used folding canvas canoes to shoot the rapids and kept in touch with civilization by means of shortwave radio. They found heaps of empty tin cans and square-faced mileage posts marking the camps of the first explorers. Lower down on the river, Dyott met José Caripe, the rubber king, who showed him the snapshot of a haggard, thin-cheeked Roosevelt wearing one of Caripe's oversized suits.

Decades passed before others tried to follow. When Kermit Roosevelt's son told his father he planned to go to Brazil's Mato Grosso to hunt jaguar and do some exploring, his father warned him that he "must on no account proceed north into the fever country."[62]

In 1992, the New Century Conservation Trust, headed by Charles T. Haskell and Elizabeth C. McKnight, led a new expedition down the former River of Doubt. Several organizations, including the Theodore Roosevelt Association, helped sponsor this successful reenactment of the 1914 descent. Among the explorers was Tweed Roosevelt, great-great grandson of T. R. The team was equipped with the latest technology, including rubber rafts and a Global Positioning System capable of computing longitude, latitude and even altitude to within a few yards by locking on to a satellite, something not even dreamed of in Theodore Roosevelt's day.

The river that Roosevelt and Rondon saw for the first time in 1914 has been called by many names. The rubber gatherers knew its lower course as the Rio Aripuanã and spoke of its upper reaches as the Castanha, the Indian name for the lowly Brazil nut. Rondon called it the Rio da Dúvida—the River of Doubt—a name T. R. and Kermit always thought best expressed its character. For a time, the entire 950-mile-long river was officially designated as the Rio Roosevelt. But the Brazilians soon changed this to the softer, more pronounceable Rio Téodoro. On most modern maps, the lower course has reverted back to being named Aripuanã. Only the wild upper stream, with its roaring cataracts and silent woods, still carries the name of the American ex-president who first explored it.

NOTES

1. *New York Sun*, 5-20-14. **2.** *New York Evening Journal*, 5-7-14. **3.** *New York World*, 5-9-14. **4.** *New York Evening Journal*, 5-1-14; *New York Times*, 5-7-14. **5.** *New York World*, 5-13-14; *New York Times*, 5-7-14. **6.** *New York Sun*, 5-8-14. **7.** Edith Kermit Roosevelt to Anna Sheffield Cowles, 5-18-14, *TRC*. **8.** *New York Sun*, 5-20-14. **9.** Ibid. **10.** *New York Times*, 5-20-14. **11.** Ibid. **12.** Ibid. **13.** *New York Tribune*, 5-21-14. **14.** *New York Sun*, 5-21-14. **15.** *New York Tribune*, 5-21-14. **16.** T. R. to Arthur Hamilton Lee, 5-20-14, *Letters*, Vol. 7, #5883, p. 762. **17.** *New York World*, 5-27-14. **18.** Ibid. **19.** *New York Tribune*, 5-27-14. **20.** *New York World, New York Times, New York Sun*, 5-27-14. **21.** *New York Times, New York Tribune*, 5-27-14. **22.** Joerg, W. L. G., "Col. Roosevelt's Exploration of a Tributary of the Madeira," *American Geographical Society Bulletin*, July 1914. **23.** Morris, *Edith Kermit Roosevelt*, p. 403. **24.** T. R. to Edith Kermit Roosevelt, 6-11-14, *KRP*. **25.** *New York World*, 6-14-14. **26.** *New York Times*, 6-17-14. **27.** Ibid. **28.** London *Times*, 6-17-14. **29.** *New York Sun*, 6-11-14. **30.** T. R., "A Journey in Central Brazil," *Geographical Journal*, p. 108. **31.** Ibid., pp. 97, 107. **32.** London *Times*, 6-18-14. **33.** *New York Times*, 6-24-14. **34.** Gardner, *Departing Glory*, p. 314. **35.** Ibid. **36.** Roosevelt, Nicholas, *T. R., The Man*, p. 125. **37.** Gilman, *Happy Warrior*, p. 332. **38.** Kirk, Wm. F., "The River of Doubt" (poem), *New York Evening Journal*, 6-9-14. **39.** T. R. to Cecil Spring Rice, 10-2-14, *Letters*, Vol. 8, #5921, p. 821. **40.** T. R. to J. A. Zahm, 7-8-14, *JAZP*. **41.** Cable, Wm. J. Bryan to U.S. Embassy at Rio, 8-28-14, Misc. State Dept. Communications. **42.** T. R. to Candido M. da Silva Rondon, 11-5-14, *PPS*. **43.** George K. Cherrie to T. R., 11-28-14, *PPS*. **44.** J. A. Zahm to T. R., 3-25-16, *PPS*. **45.** T. R. to Henry Fairfield Osborn, 12-5-16, *Letters*, Vol. 8, #6162, p. 1133. **46.** T. R. to Kermit Roosevelt, 6-8-17, *KRP*. **47.** T. R. to Kermit Roosevelt, 2-18-18, *Letters*, Vol. 8, #6296, p. 1285. **48.** Gardner, *Departing Glory*, p. 391. **49.** Morris, *Edith Kermit Roosevelt*, p. 427. **50.** Hagedorn, *Roosevelt Family*, p. 423. **51.** Gardner, *Departing Glory*, p. 797. **52.** Amos, James, "The Beloved Boss," *Collier's Weekly*, 8-7-26. **53.** Hagedorn, *Roosevelt Family*, p. 424. **54.** Gardner, *Departing Glory*, p. 399. **55.** Weber, *Notre Dame's John Zahm*, p. 196. **56.** Morris, *Edith Kermit Roosevelt*, pp. 435, 507. **57.** Sigg's obituary, letter to author from U.S. Consul (Asunción) William F. Finnegan, 7-19-76. **58.** Article on

Cherrie, Des Moines (Iowa) *Sunday Register Magazine,* 1-16-27; Cherrie, speech, *"T. R., Memorial Meeting."* **59.** Cutright, *T. R., The Naturalist,* p. 270. **60.** Data on Leo Miller from his son, Dr. Leo E. Miller, Jr., 1976. **61.** T. R. to Anthony Fiala, 1-3-19, *PPS.* **61.** Roosevelt, Kermit (Jr.) *Sentimental Safari,* pp. xv, xvi.

Afterword

Seventy-five years after his death, Theodore Roosevelt remains one of the most written about of American historical figures. Strangely enough, most biographers have tended to ignore his South American expedition, treating it like a kind of adolescent aberration. I believe that the journey down the River of Doubt represented the most dramatic episode of T. R.'s crowded life and deserves a full-length, objective treatment; hence this book.

My research took two years (1975–76) and was conducted during the course of a full-time career. For business and other reasons, I didn't start writing the book until 1987. I would never have gotten started on it if Peg Raasch, an old friend now enjoying early retirement in Arkansas, had not urged me on. My one regret for taking nearly twenty years to finish is that some of the people who helped me in my research may no longer be living.

Six years later, in 1993, my manuscript was accepted by Stackpole Books. Since that time I have had the good fortune to work with a truly gifted editor, Judith Schnell. Her sympathy and enthusiasm have never failed. I count her a friend as much as an editor. I also want to thank David Uhler, assistant editor at Stackpole, who has been supportive and encouraging as well.

From the start, my intention was to tell as factual a story as possible, using letters and diaries and firsthand accounts. There are no invented conversations in the book. I have tried to keep my opinions to a minimum, believing that the characters in the story will reveal themselves far better than I can.

I was able to locate the descendants of the men who had accompanied Roosevelt. Dr. Leo E. Miller, Jr., patiently answered my lengthy questionnaire about his naturalist father. Troman Harper, Frank Harper's oldest son, shared reminiscences about his father and permitted me to publish for the first time a photograph of his father and T. R. in South America. Two of Anthony Fiala's children, Rear Adm., Ret., Reid Fiala and Princess Lazarovich-Hrebelianovich (née Mary Maury Fiala), answered questions about their father. Thomas P. Zahm, great-great nephew of Father John Augustine Zahm, was attending Notre Dame University (and residing in Zahm Hall) in 1976; he pointed out to me Patrick J. Carroll's interesting, but now practically forgotten, biography of Father Zahm, which was published serially from January to July, 1946, in *The Ave Maria*.

Hubert and Ann Cherrie of Fleetwood, Pennsylvania, opened their home and their memories of George K. Cherrie to me during a research trip east in the spring of 1976. To know Hubert Cherrie, bright-eyed, genial, and young at heart, is to catch a glimpse of the kind of man his father was.

Two other people who knew George Cherrie personally shared their recollections with me. The late Paul G. Howes, a naturalist and photographer who accompanied Cherrie and Chapman on the spring 1913 expedition to the Colombian Andes, provided me with several anecdotes about Cherrie. J. H. Pierce of Fairmount, Minnesota, who had traveled with Cherrie on a "China boat" from New York to Hong King in 1932, recalled Cherrie's stories about the Roosevelt expedition. According to Mr. Pierce, Cherrie's trembling right hand made it difficult for him to hold a hand of cards steady, but it didn't keep him from typing up his diary entries each night.

Descendants of Theodore Roosevelt were helpful to me as I gathered information about the expedition. Thanks to Kermit Roosevelt II and the late Archibald B. Roosevelt for suggestions as to sources. Tweed Roosevelt, great-grandson of T. R. and one of the participants in the 1992 River of Doubt expedition, took time out of a busy schedule to carefully read my manuscript. His suggestions and corrections have made this a better book.

Over the years, Dr. John A. Gable, executive director of the Theodore Roosevelt Association, has provided me with both useful research tips and encouragement. He also took time out to read portions of my manuscript. I take my hat off to him.

A place in heaven is reserved for Wallace Finley Dailey, curator of the mammoth Theodore Roosevelt Collection at the Houghton Library of Harvard University. Every Roosevelt scholar is indebted to him. For eighteen or more years, he has answered my questions and pointed out potential sources. I was pleased to learn recently that he considers me his "oldest customer."

Special thanks are due to Dr. Dean Amadon, who in 1976 was curator of the department of ornithology of the American Museum of Natural History. Dr. Amadon found Cherrie's long-lost River of Doubt diary and allowed me to prepare a transcript. It is hard to describe my feelings of excitement as I turned the pages of Cherrie's diary—no more than a schoolboy's exercise book—and tried to decipher his spidery scrawl. Dr. Amadon also unearthed correspondence between Frank Chapman, Cherrie, and Miller pertaining to the expedition. These documents provided a real insider's view to the business of natural history, circa 1913.

I would also like to thank Paul Sweet, scientific assistant in the museum's ornithology department, for helping nail down some last-minute details. Likewise, thanks are due to Joel D. Sweimler of the museum's library services department for obtaining many of the photographs that grace my book.

The Explorers Club of New York allowed me the use of their library in 1976. I thank Stanford Brent, in 1976 the head of the library committee, for his courtesy. I also thank Janet Baldwin, curator of collections, for going over portions of my manuscript in 1994.

A number of research "assistants" helped me gather the information to put this book together. I drafted my two sisters, Sandy Schow and Pamela Clarke, very early on. Sandy spent many hot afternoons in the microfilm section of the old Chicago Public Library, poring over *New York Times* articles about Roosevelt's expedition. Pam kept me company during my 1976 research trip to Boston and New York. Larry Hallock traveled to the Library of Congress and diligently copied Kermit Roosevelt's many letters to Belle Willard. My able translator, Armand Petrecca of the Cosmopolitan Translation Bureau of Chicago, translated a number of lengthy Brazilian documents, including portions of a biography of Rondon, the official report of Dr. Cajazeira, and the recollections of Ruiz Moreno, the Argentine official who accompanied T. R. across the Patagonian desert in December 1913.

For information on Father Zahm, thanks are due the Province Archives at Indiana Province of the Congregation of Holy Cross. In 1976, Father Thomas F. Elliot let me go over Zahm's correspondence with Roosevelt and other members of the expedition. More recently, Jaqueline Dougherty helped me secure permission to quote from those records. Dr. William Kevin Cawley of the archives of Notre Dame University

double-checked my excerpts from Zahm's letters to his brother Albert
and provided help in securing photographs of Zahm and T. R. Ralph E.
Weber, professor of history at Marquette University and Zahm's official
biographer *(Notre Dame's John Zahm)*, gave me the benefit of his extensive knowledge of Zahm.

Other institutions that opened their doors and their files include
the National Geographic Society, Washington, D.C.; the reference
libraries of Northwestern University and the University of Chicago;
Margaret M. Sherry, reference librarian, Archives of Princeton University
Libraries; the Manuscript Division and the Photo Duplication Service
of the Library of Congress; the Defense Mapping Agency, Department
of Defense, for aerial maps of Mato Grosso and Amazonas; the Clifton
Waller Barrett Collection of T. R.'s correspondence at the Alderman
Library of the University of Virginia; the Civil Archives Division of the
General Services Administration for State Department files concerning
Roosevelt's tour of the capitals; Fundação Instituto Brasileiro de
Geografia e Estatistica, Rio de Janeiro; and the Royal Geographical
Society, London.

In 1976, Charles Scribner kindly checked his files for letters concerning the Roosevelt expedition, for which I again thank him. John P.
Kneuer of Rogers Peet Company of New York lent me a collector's
copy of their 1914 *RoPeCo* magazine, which contained Fiala's account
of his trip down the Rio Papagaio. Austin, Nichols and Co. of New York
put me in touch with Thomas F. McCarthy, a retired employee who
remembered "very well" the preparation of Fiala's ninety food cans
during the summer of 1913.

Soon after starting to write the book in 1987, I joined Eloise Bradley
Fink's creative-writing course in Winnetka, Illinois. Her constant encouragement and the feedback from my classmates were invaluable in the
final shaping of the book. In this connection, I have to single out one
particular fellow student, Margaret "Peg" Leonard, who persuaded me
to keep attending classes for the sake of the book. I'm glad I did.

It was through Eloise Fink's writing workshop that I met Lawrence E.
Jarchow, an editor and a history buff who took a personal interest in my
book. He suggested the opening chapter and taught me valuable
lessons in pacing and idea development. I am indebted to him.

Four special friends formed my support group during the final year
of rewriting. Euclides Agosto, lawyer and novelist-in-embryo, helped
me keep my focus and break through numerous writer's blocks. Keith
Sanderson's literary judgment is reflected in many of my pages. Geof-

frey P. Cooper-Stanton served as an uncomplaining "look-up man" when questions of geography and natural history arose. Kristin Lambrecht kept my faith from sinking on more than one occasion.

My typists deserve awards for deciphering my handwriting and putting up with endless rewrites. They are Robert F. Jones, Alma Stevens, and my secretary for many years (and friend as well), June P. Mauser.

My most heartfelt thanks go to my mother, Donna Ornig, who never gave up on this project, and to whom the book is dedicated.

Joseph R. Ornig

Bibliography

PRIMARY SOURCES

TRC   Theodore Roosevelt Collection, the Houghton Library, Harvard University, Cambridge, Massachusetts. Few letters survive from T. R.'s time in South America. I found only one of his letters to Edith Roosevelt, which made it difficult to assess his personal reactions to events. For a few weeks in December 1913, T. R. kept a diary, but it consists only of records of hunting kills and dates of arrival at different places along the upper Paraguay. Edith Roosevelt's 1913 diary and her letters to Kermit and other family members between 1913 and 1914 were useful in my research. An interesting find was Maj. James Ancil Shipton's typewritten account of Roosevelt's Argentine tour. Shipton was military attaché to the American legation at Buenos Aires between 1912 and 1914.

PPS   Theodore Roosevelt Letters, Presidential Papers Series, Library of Congress, Washington, D.C. On microfilm at the Regenstein Library, University of Chicago. Includes a number of unpublished letters from and to T. R. concerning the South American period.

KRP   Kermit Roosevelt Papers, Library of Congress, Washington, D.C. Documents consulted include Kermit's unpublished diary of the expedition, his letters to Belle Willard, and memorabilia of the tour. Also in this collection is a letter from T. R. to Edith Roosevelt, dated September 24, 1913, but actually written on Christmas Eve 1913, as the *Nyoac* steamed back to Corumbá.

JAZP   John A. Zahm, C.S.C., Papers, Indiana Province Archives
Center, Congregation of Holy Cross, Notre Dame, Indiana. Includes
letters between Zahm and Theodore Roosevelt, as well as documents
relating to the organization of the expedition.

CAZA   Albert Francis Zahm Papers, Box 4, Folder 9, University of
Notre Dame Archives, Notre Dame, Indiana. Contains John A. Zahm's
letters to his brother, Albert Zahm, between 1913 and 1914, concerning
the South American trip.

AMNH   American Museum of Natural History, New York, New York,
Department of Ornithology Archives. Resources consulted include
George K. Cherrie's unpublished diary of the River of Doubt expedition and his correspondence with Frank M. Chapman; correspondence
between Leo E. Miller and Frank Chapman; and miscellaneous letters
between Frank M. Chapman, Henry Fairfield Osborn, and H. Lucas.

SCRIB   Scribner's Archives, Manuscripts Division, Department of
Rare Books and Special Collections, Princeton University Libraries, Princeton, New Jersey. Documents consulted are found in Folder 8, Box 124
(for 1913); and Folder 10, Box 125 ("Brazilian Wilderness"), which
includes letters between Frank M. Chapman and Robert Bridges concerning Roosevelt's expedition.

CWBL   Theodore Roosevelt Collection (#5844), Clifton Waller Barrett
Library, Special Collections Department, University of Virginia Library,
Charlottesville, Virginia. Includes several unpublished letters from and
to T. R. concerning the South America trip.

AUTHOR'S QUESTIONNAIRES,
INTERVIEWS, AND LETTERS
Answered by descendants of participants in the expedition.
Adm. Reid Fiala, USN, Ret. (son of Anthony Fiala).
Princess Lazarovich-Hrebelianovich (née Mary Maury Fiala).
Hubert B. Cherrie (son of George K. Cherrie).
Dr. Leo E. Miller, Jr. (son of Leo E. Miller).
Troman F. Harper (son of Frank Harper).
Thomas P. Zahm (great-great nephew of Father Zahm).

NEWSPAPERS

Buenos Aires Herald, 1913–1914.
Des Moines Sunday Register, 1927.
El Tiempo, Montevideo, Uruguay, 1913–1914.
Jornal do Commercio, Rio de Janeiro, Brazil, 1913–1914.
London Times, 1914.
Montevideo Herald, 1913.
New York Evening Journal, 1913–1914.
New York Evening Post, 1914.
New York Sun, 1913–1914.
New York Times, 1913–1914.
New York Tribune, 1913–1914.
New York World, 1913–1914.

MAGAZINES

Carroll, Patrick J. "Mind in Action" (Life of John Augustine Zahm), published serially from January 5 through July 20, 1946, *Ave Maria*, Notre Dame, Indiana.

Cherrie, George K. "To South America for Bird Study." *American Museum Journal* (April 1917): 268–73.

"The Colonel in Chile." *North American Review* (1914).

de Lima, José Custodio Alves. "Reminiscences of Roosevelt in Brazil," *Bulletin of the American Chamber of Commerce of São Paulo*, as published in the *Brazilian American*, 1-29-27.

Elliot, C. Elwyn. "The Rondon Mission: The Lifework of a Great Empire Builder." *Pan American Magazine* (undated).

Fiala, Anthony. *The RoPeCo Magazine* (House organ for Rogers Peet Co.) (April–September 1914).

———"With Roosevelt in the Jungle" (press interviews). *Literary Digest*, 5-16-14, 1190–93.

Howes, Paul G. "Field Days with Chapman, Cherrie and Fuertes." *Explorers Journal* (June 1961).

Ibáñez, Eduardo Galvarino B. "Roosevelt Recuerdos" ("Roosevelt Memories"). *Y Sur* (Chile) (1930).

Moreno, Isidoro Ruiz. "At Lake Nahuel Huapi, in the year 1913, with Theodore Roosevelt, former president of the United States of America." *Annales del Museo Nahuel Huapi* (Buenos Aires) (1953).

Naumburg, Elsie M. B. "The Birds of Matto Grosso." *Bulletin of the American Museum of Natural History* LX (1930): 3.

Osborn, Henry Fairfield. "Theodore Roosevelt, Naturalist." *Natural History Magazine* 19, no. 9 (September 1919).

"The Progressing Colonel." *North American Review* (November 1913): 597–99.

Rondon, Candido Mariano da Silva. "Col. Roosevelt as his Guide Remembers Him." *New York Times Sunday Magazine*, 1-6-29.

Roosevelt, Theodore. "From Ox Cart to Motor Car in the Andes." *The Outlook* 107, 5-23-14.

——— "In the Argentine." *The Outlook* 106, 2-4-14, 803.

———"In Southernmost Brazil." *The Outlook* 106, 2-14-14.

——— "A Journey through Central Brazil." *The Geographical Journal* (London) XLV, no. 2 (February 1915).

———"São Paulo: An Old City That Is Carving New Ways." *The Outlook* 106, 1-31-14.

———"The Unknown River: A Preliminary Statement of Its Discovery and Exploration." *Scribner's Magazine* VI, no. 1 (July 1914).

"Theodore Roosevelt, Patron of the American Museum's Field Work in South America." *American Museum Journal* XIV, no. 4 (April 1914).

"T. R. at Buenos Aires." *Literary Digest*, 5-2-14.

Waldon, Webb. "Making Exploring Safe for Explorers." *Saturday Evening Post*, 1-30-32.

Well, Travis, B. "What the South Americans Think of Theodore Roosevelt." *Harper's Weekly*, 2-7-14.

Zahm, J. A. "Roosevelt's Visit to South America." *Review of Reviews* (July 1914).

————"Theodore Roosevelt as a Hunter-Naturalist." *The Outlook* (July 1914).

OFFICIAL REPORTS AND SPEECHES

Cajazeira, José Antonio. "Relatorio Apresentado Ao Candido Mariano da Silva Rondon," Commisão de Matto Grosso ão Amazonas, Publ. no. 55, Annex 6, 1916.

Chapman, Frank, Speech before Theodore Roosevelt Memorial Association, March 1928.

Cherrie, G. K. Copy of speech found in his River of Doubt diary, dated May 26, 1927.

Cherrie, G. K., Anthony Fiala, et al. *Theodore Roosevelt, Memorial Meeting at the Explorers' Club, March 1, 1919.*

Forty-Fifth Annual Report of Trustees for 1913, American Museum of Natural History.

Magalhães, Amilcar Botelho de. "Relatorio Apresentado Ao Candido Mariano da Silva Rondon," Commisão de Matto Grosso ão Amazonas, Publ. no. 54, Annex 5, 1916.

Oliveira, Euzebio Paulo de. "Expedicão Scientifica Roosevelt-Rondon" (Geologia), Commisão de Matto Grosso ão Amazonas, Publ. no. 50, Annex 1, 1915.

State Department Communications, 1913–1914. Decimal File 032.R 671, Record Group 69, Civil Archives Division, General Services Administration, Washington, D.C.

BOOKS

Abbott, Lawrence F. *Impressions of Theodore Roosevelt.* Doubleday, Page & Company, 1920.

Amos, James E. *Theodore Roosevelt, Hero to His Valet.* The John Day Company, 1927.

Bodard, Lucien. *Green Hell: Massacre of the Brazilian Indians.* Translated by Jennifer Monaghan. Outerbridge & Dienstfry, 1971.

Bryce, Sir James. *South America, Observations and Impressions.* The MacMillan Company, 1912.

Chapman, Frank M. *Autobiography of a Bird Lover.* D. Appleton Century Company, 1935.

———— Introduction to *Through the Brazilian Wilderness*, vol. 5, by Theodore Roosevelt. Scribner's National Edition, 1926.

Cherrie, George K. *Dark Trails: Adventures of a Naturalist.* G. P. Putnam's Sons, 1930.

Clemenceau, Georges. *South America To-day.* T. Fisher Unwin, 1911.

Cutright, Paul Russell. *Theodore Roosevelt the Naturalist.* Harper & Brothers, 1956.

Davis, Oscar King. *Released for Publication.* Houghton Mifflin Company, 1925.

Dyott, G. M. *Man-Hunting in the Jungle, Being the Story of a Search for Three Explorers Lost in the Brazilian Wilds.* Bobbs Merrill Co., 1931.

Fiala, Anthony. *Fighting the Polar Ice.* Doubleday, Page & Company, 1906.

Freyre, Gilberto. *Order and Progress: Brazil from Monarchy to Republic.* Alfred A. Knopf Co., 1970.

Gable, John Allen. *The Bull Moose Years.* Kennikat Press, 1978.

Gardner, Joseph L. *Departing Glory: Theodore Roosevelt as ex-President.* Charles Scribner's Sons, 1973.

Goodman, Edward J. *The Explorers of South America.* The MacMillan Company, 1972.

Hagedorn, Hermann. *The Roosevelt Family of Sagamore Hill.* The Mac-Millan Company, 1954.

Hellman, Geoffrey. *Bankers, Bones and Beetles.* The Natural History Press, 1968.

Howes, Paul Griswold. *Photographer in the Rain-Forests.* Adams Press, 1970.

Keller, Morton, ed. *Theodore Roosevelt: A Profile.* Hill and Wang, 1967.

Lewis, William Draper. *The Life of Theodore Roosevelt.* The United Publishers, 1919.

Lodge, Henry Cabot. *Selections from the Correspondence of Theodore Roosevelt and Henry Cabot Lodge, 1884–1918.* 2 vols. Charles Scribner's Sons, 1925.

Magalhães, Amilcar A. Botelhos de. *Impressões da Commisão Rondon.* Companhia Editoria Nacional, Vol. 211, Series 5-A. Biblioteca Pedagogica Brasileira, 1942.

Manners, William. *TR & Will: A Friendship That Split the Republican Party.* Harcourt Brace & World, 1969.

Miller, Leo E. *In the Wilds of South America.* Charles Scribner's Sons, 1918.

Morris, Sylvia Jukes. *Edith Kermit Roosevelt: Portrait of a First Lady.* Coward, McCann & Geoghegan, 1980.

Mozans, H. J. [John Augustine Zahm]. *Along the Andes and down the Amazon.* D. Appleton & Co., 1911.

————. *Up the Orinoco and down the Magdalena.* D. Appleton & Co., 1910.

Nash, Roy. *The Conquest of Brazil.* Brace & Co., 1926.

Osborn, Henry Fairfield. *Impressions of Great Naturalists.* Charles Scribner's Sons, 1924.

Pendle, George. *Uruguay.* Oxford University Press, 1957.

Pringle, Henry F. *Theodore Roosevelt: A Biography.* Harcourt, Brace & Company, 1931.

Robinson, Corinne Roosevelt. *My Brother, Theodore Roosevelt.* Charles Scribner's Sons, 1921.

Rondon, Candido Mariano da Silva. *Lectures Delivered on the 5th, 7th, and 9th of October, 1915.* Translated by R. G. Reidy and Ed. Murray. Rio de Janeiro: Leuzinger, 1916.

Roosevelt, Kermit. *The Happy Hunting Grounds.* Charles Scribner's Sons, 1920.

Roosevelt, Kermit, Jr. *A Sentimental Safari.* Alfred A. Knopf, 1963.

Roosevelt, Nicholas. *Theodore Roosevelt: The Man as I Knew Him.* Dodd, Mead Company, 1967.

Roosevelt, Theodore. *A Book-Lover's Holiday in the Open.* Charles Scribner's Sons, 1916.

————. Introduction to *Along the Andes and down the Amazon,* by Dr. H. J. Mozans (Zahm). D. Appleton & Co., 1911.

————. *Letters.* Edited by Elting E. Morison and John Blum. 8 vols. Harvard University Press, 1951–54.

————. *Ranch Life and the Hunting Trail.* Collected Works, National Ed., vol. 1. Charles Scribner's Sons, 1925.

————. *Through the Brazilian Wilderness*. Charles Scribner's Sons, 1914 edition.

Thayer, William Roscoe. *Theodore Roosevelt: An Intimate Biography*. Houghton Mifflin Company, 1919.

Viveiros, Esther de. *Rondon, Conta Sua Vida*. Rio de Janeiro: Cooperativa Cultural dos Esperantistas, 1969.

Wagenknecht, Edward. *The Seven Worlds of Theodore Roosevelt*. Longmans, Green Company, 1958.

Weber, Ralph E. *Notre Dame's John Zahm: American Catholic Apologist and Educator*. University of Notre Dame Press, 1961.

Weyer, Edward, Jr. *Jungle Quest*. Harper & Brothers, 1955.

White, William Allen. *The Autobiography of William Allen White*. The Mac-Millan Company, 1946.

Whitney, Caspar. *The Flowing Road: Adventures of the Great Rivers of South America*. J. B. Lippincott, 1912.

Wiley, Farida A. *Theodore Roosevelt's America: Selections from the Writings of the Oyster Bay Naturalist*. Devin Adair Co., 1955.

Wilson, R. L., and G. C. Wilson. *Theodore Roosevelt, Outdoorsman*. Winchester Press, 1971.

Worcester, Donald E. *Makers of Latin America*. E. P. Dutton & Co., 1966.

Zahm, John Augustine. *Through South America's Southland*. D. Appleton & Co., 1916.

Sources of Photographs

1. Theodore Roosevelt Collection, Harvard College Library. Quote: Manners, *TR & Will*, p. 237.

2. Neg. No. 326109. Photographer: Unknown. Courtesy, Department of Library Services, American Museum of Natural History. Quote: Zahm, *Through South America's Southland*, p. 17.

3. Inset of Neg. No. 104910. Photographer: Unknown. Courtesy, Department of Library Services, American Museum of Natural History.

4. (Portrait) Source unknown—image originally appeared as a newspaper illustration. Quote: *Letters*, T. R. to Arthur Hamilton Lee, 8-4-12, #5756, p. 596. (Photo) Theodore Roosevelt Collection, Harvard College Library.

5. Viveiros, Esther. *Rondon, Conta Sua Vida*.

6. Neg. No. 310857. Photographer: Kirschner. Courtesy, Department of Library Services, American Museum of Natural History.

7. Neg. No. 2A-5209. Photographer: Unknown. Courtesy, Department of Library Services, American Museum of Natural History.

8. Neg. No. 32896. Photographer: Unknown. Courtesy, Department of Library Services, American Museum of Natural History.

9. Inset of Neg. No. 104910. Photographer: Unknown. Courtesy,

Department of Library Services, American Museum of Natural History.

10. Courtesy, Troman Harper.

11. The Archives of the University of Notre Dame (Albert Francis Zahm Papers).

12. Neg. No. 104910. Photographer: Unknown. Courtesy, Department of Library Services, American Museum of Natural History.

13. Copyrighted 1912, Chicago Tribune Company. All rights reserved; used with permission.

14. Theodore Roosevelt Collection, Harvard College Library.

15. Theodore Roosevelt Collection, Harvard College Library.

16. Theodore Roosevelt Collection, Harvard College Library.

17. Theodore Roosevelt Collection, Harvard College Library.

18. Theodore Roosevelt Collection, Harvard College Library. Quote: *TRC*, T. R. to Anna Roosevelt Cowles, 11-11-13.

19. Theodore Roosevelt Collection, Harvard College Library.

20. Theodore Roosevelt Collection, Harvard College Library.

21. Theodore Roosevelt Collection, Harvard College Library.

22. Theodore Roosevelt Collection, Harvard College Library.

23. Courtesy, Troman Harper.

24. Theodore Roosevelt Collection, Harvard College Library.

25. Zahm, J. A. *Through South America's Southland*. Courtesy, Penguin USA.

26. Theodore Roosevelt Collection, Harvard College Library. Quote: T. R., *Through the Brazilian Wilderness*, pp. 49-50.

27. Zahm, J. A. *Through South America's Southland*. Courtesy, Penguin USA.

28. Zahm, J. A. *Through South America's Southland*. Courtesy, Penguin USA.

29. Theodore Roosevelt Collection, Harvard College Library. Quote: T. R., *Through the Brazilian Wilderness*, p. 141.

30. Theodore Roosevelt Collection, Harvard College Library.

31. Theodore Roosevelt Collection, Harvard College Library.

32. The Archives of the University of Notre Dame (Albert Francis Zahm Papers).

33. Cherrie, George K. *Dark Trails: Adventures of a Naturalist*. Courtesy, The Putnam Publishing Group.

34. Neg. No. 128457. Photographer: George K. Cherrie. Courtesy, Department of Library Services, American Museum of Natural History.

35. Neg. No. 128443. Photographer: Unknown. Courtesy, Department of Library Services, American Museum of Natural History.

36. Theodore Roosevelt Collection, Harvard College Library. Quote: T. R., *Through the Brazilian Wilderness*, p. 184.

37. Neg. No. 325971. Photographer: Unknown. Courtesy, Department of Library Services, American Museum of Natural History.

38. Theodore Roosevelt Collection, Harvard College Library.

39. Cherrie, George K. *Dark Trails: Adventures of a Naturalist*. Courtesy, The Putnam Publishing Group.

40. Courtesy, Hubert B. Cherrie.

41. Neg. No. 128470. Photographer: George K. Cherrie. Courtesy, Department of Library Services, American Museum of Natural History.

42. Theodore Roosevelt Collection, Harvard College Library. Quote: Chapman, Frank M. Introduction to *Through the Brazilian Wilderness*, p. xviii.

43. Theodore Roosevelt Collection, Harvard College Library.

44. Theodore Roosevelt Collection, Harvard College Library.

45. Neg. No. 18828. Photographer: Leo E. Miller. Courtesy, Department of Library Services, American Museum of Natural History. Quote: T. R., *Through the Brazilian Wilderness*, p. 250.

46. Theodore Roosevelt Collection, Harvard College Library.

47. Theodore Roosevelt Collection, Harvard College Library.

48. Neg. No. 326432. Photographer: Unknown. Courtesy, Department of Library Services, American Museum of Natural History. Quote: T. R., *Through the Brazilian Wilderness*, p. 252.

49. Theodore Roosevelt Collection, Harvard College Library. Quote: T. R., *Through the Brazilian Wilderness*, p. 258.

50. *The Geographical Journal*, February 1915. Courtesy, Royal Geographical Society.

51. *The Geographical Journal*, February 1915. Courtesy, Royal Geographical Society.

52. Theodore Roosevelt Collection, Harvard College Library.

53. Theodore Roosevelt Collection, Harvard College Library.

54. Neg. No. 128442. Photographer: George K. Cherrie. Courtesy, Department of Library Services, American Museum of Natural History.

55. Theodore Roosevelt Collection, Harvard College Library.

56. *The Geographical Journal*, February 1915. Courtesy, Royal Geographical Society.

57. *The Geographical Journal,* February 1915. Courtesy, Royal Geographical Society. Quote: Cherrie, George K. *T. R., Memorial Meeting,* 1919, p.27, and Cherrie, George K. *Diary,* 3-29-14.

58. Cherrie, George K. *Dark Trails: Adventures of a Naturalist.* Courtesy, The Putnam Publishing Group.

59. Cherrie, George K. *Dark Trails: Adventures of a Naturalist.* Courtesy, The Putnam Publishing Group.

60. Neg. No. 128444. Photographer: George K. Cherrie. Courtesy, Department of Library Services, American Museum of Natural History.

61. Theodore Roosevelt Collection, Harvard College Library.

62. Theodore Roosevelt Collection, Harvard College Library.

63. Theodore Roosevelt Collection, Harvard College Library. Quote: *New York Times,* 5-20-14.

64. *New York Sun,* 5-27-14.

65. Courtesy, National Geographic Society and Stock Montage, Inc.

66. Courtesy, Hubert B. Cherrie.

67. Theodore Roosevelt Collection, Harvard College Library.

68. Theodore Roosevelt Collection, Harvard College Library.

Index

ABC Powers (Argentina, Brazil & Chile), 59
Adolfo Riquelmo: flagship of Paraguayan Navy, 75, 77
African Expedition (1909–1910): results of, 8–9; T. R.'s preparations for, 7
African Game Trails, 11
Aidan: Booth Steamship Company liner 205, 206; passengers shocked at T. R.'s appearance, 208; voyage to New York, 209, 210
Akeley, Carl, 7
Along the Andes and Down the Amazon, 13
Amazon River: as possible outlet for Dúvida, 79
Amazonas (Brazilian State), 106
Amazonas State Boundary Commission, 107
American Geographical Society: awards T. R. and Rondon the David Livingstone Centenary Gold Medal, 219; credits Roosevelt-Rondon expedition with finding unknown tributary of Madeira, 213; honors Rondon as great 20th century explorer, 222–223
"American Ideals": T. R.'s final speech at Buenos Aires, 65
"American Internationalism": T. R.'s address at Rio de Janeiro, 54
American Museum of Natural History: financial problems in 1913, 27; publishes T. R.'s essay on concealing and revealing coloration, 12; Roosevelt family's close association with, 26; seeks information on Roosevelt expedition's whereabouts, 165; sends T. R. books on Africa, 7; South American mammal specimens desired by, 83; T. R.'s South American map furnished by, 107
Amos, James: T. R.'s manservant, 1, 220, 221
Ananás, Rio, (Pineapple River): later proves

to be tributary of Rio Cardosa, 179; Rondon discovers, 79; supply of food left at Bonifacio for possible descent, 127; T. R. offers help to would-be explorers of, 215; T. R.'s second choice for exploration, 107
Angel of Fortune: name of launch expedition used to ascend upper Paraguay River, 95, 96
Angel Falls: Cherrie's mule on overland march, 102
Anglo-Brazilian Iron Company: Kermit goes to work for, 19; Kermit's near-fatal accident, 47
Argentina: T. R. tours provincial capitals, 65–73
Araputanga: Species of softwood tree used to build two new small dugouts at Camp Duas Canôas, 154
Arinos, Rio: headwater of the Rio Tapajós, 46
Aripuanã: new dugout built at Broken Canoe Rapids, 145, 149
Aripuanã, Rio: previous exploration of, 156; Rondon believes Dúvida is upper course of, 107
Arizona: T. R.'s 1913 cougar hunt in, 24, 29
Asunción, Paraguay: Cherrie and Miller begin collecting at, 60; T. R. departs from, 75
Austin, Nichols & Co (New York): provides food for expedition, 33

baraca: dwellings of the rubber-gatherers, 191
Barbosa, Senhor: prosperous settler gives food and wide boat to explorers, 195–196
Bariloche, Argentina: T. R.'s party arrives at, 71
Barrett, John A: director-general of Pan American Union, 6